Download Forms on Nolo.com

You can download the forms in this book at:

www.nolo.com/back-of-book/IEP.html

We'll also post updates whenever there's an important change to the law affecting this book—as well as articles and other related materials.

More Resources
from Nolo.com

Legal Forms, Books, & Software
Hundreds of do-it-yourself products—all written in plain English, approved, and updated by our in-house legal editors.

Legal Articles
Get informed with thousands of free articles on everyday legal topics. Our articles are accurate, up to date, and reader friendly.

Find a Lawyer
Want to talk to a lawyer? Use Nolo to find a lawyer who can help you with your case.

NOLO
LAW for ALL

10th Edition

The Complete IEP Guide

How to Advocate for Your Special Ed Child

Attorney Lawrence M. Siegel

Tenth Edition	JULY 2020
Editor	BETH LAURENCE
Production	SUSAN PUTNEY
Proofreading	IRENE BARNARD
Index	SONGBIRD INDEXING SERVICES
Printing	BANG PRINTING

Names: Siegel, Lawrence M., 1946- author. | Nolo (Firm)
Title: The complete IEP guide : how to advocate for your special ed child /
   Attorney Lawrence M. Siegel.
Other titles: Complete Individualized Education Program guide
Description: Tenth Edition. | Berkeley : NOLO, 2020. | Ninth edition
   published 2017.
Identifiers: LCCN 2020002127 (print) | LCCN 2020002128 (ebook) | ISBN
   9781413327427 (Paperback) | ISBN 9781413327434 (eBook)
Subjects: LCSH: Individualized education programs--Law and
   legislation--United States--Popular works. | Dispute resolution
   (Law)--United States--Popular works. | Special education--Parent
   participation--United States--Popular works.
Classification: LCC KF4209.3 .S57 2020 (print) | LCC KF4209.3 (ebook) |
   DDC 371.90973--dc23
LC record available at https://lccn.loc.gov/2020002127
LC ebook record available at https://lccn.loc.gov/2020002128

This book covers only United States law, unless it specifically states otherwise.

Please note

We believe accurate, plain-English legal information should help you solve many of
your own legal problems. But this text is not a substitute for personalized advice from a
knowledgeable lawyer. If you want the help of a trained professional—and we'll always
point out situations in which we think that's a good idea—consult an attorney licensed to
practice in your state.

Dedication

To the memory of my sweet daughter Catie; I see your beautiful smile and remember your wonderful and kind heart, every day of my life.

To my parents.

To my wife Gail, for that first day on the Wheeler steps, and ever since, her joyous smile, and

To my daughter Elisabeth, she inspires me with her energy and talent.

Acknowledgments

My appreciation to the entire Nolo staff, which, to a person, has always been professional and friendly and never seemed to feel those two concepts were incompatible.

Special thanks to Marcia Stewart for her superb editing, her patience as we worked through and wrote about the complexities of the IEP process, and her clear goal of making the IEP process friendly and useful for families of children with disabilities.

Thanks to Beth Laurence for her insight, patience, and devotion to children in special education.

Thanks also to my colleagues and friends on the California Advisory Commission on Special Education.

About the Author

Lawrence Siegel has been a special education attorney and advocate since 1979, and has represented children with disabilities extensively in IEPs, due process, complaints, legal action, and before legislative and policy bodies. Mr. Siegel has consulted with parent groups throughout the U.S. and has worked directly with special education experts in Japan. As a Fulbright specialist, he worked in Sweden at the University of Stockholm. He has taught special education law at Hastings College of the Law, was on the California Advisory Commission on Special Education for eight years, and has written and helped enact special education law in a number of states. He continues to travel the country giving workshops to families with children with disabilities. Mr. Siegel was given an endowed chair at Gallaudet University (2004–2005) in recognition of his work for children with disabilities and is also the author of *Least Restrictive Environment: The Paradox of Inclusion* (LRP Publications, 1994), *The Human Right to Language* (Gallaudet Press, 2008), and *Nolo's IEP Guide: Learning Disabilities*.

Table of Contents

Your Legal Companion for IEPs

Parents want the best for their children, and they're instinctive advocates. When your child is a student in special education, however, that advocacy can be quite challenging. The individualized education program (IEP) process is like a maze, involving a good deal of technical information, intimidating professionals, and confusing choices. For some families, it goes smoothly, with no disagreements. For others, it is a stressful encounter in which you and the school district cannot agree on anything. For most people, the experience is somewhere in between.

Whether you face a disagreement with your district or just want to be more informed about your rights, this book will assist you. It will explain the IEP process in great detail, including each step involved and the rights you and your child have in that process. It will teach you how to be an effective advocate for your child. This book provides you with all of the information you need, including:

- what the Individuals with Disabilities Education Act (or IDEA) guarantees for your child's educational needs
- details about the individualized education program (or IEP) process established by the IDEA
- eligibility rules and the role of evaluations in determining whether your child qualifies for special education
- how to gather the information and develop the material you need to determine your child's specific goals and educational needs
- how to develop a blueprint for your child's education that includes the placement, services, and teaching strategies your child needs, and
- how to deal with disagreements that arise between you and your school district in developing and implementing your child's IEP.

This book will explain that, first and foremost, the IEP process is meant to ensure that an appropriate educational program fits your child's needs, not the other way around. The book will help you proceed on your own through the IEP process, whether it's your first time or your fifth time. The suggestions and forms in the book will help you get—and stay—organized throughout the IEP process.

Detailed online appendixes provide invaluable information, including:

- key special education laws and regulations
- twenty forms, letters, and checklists to help you through every stage of the IEP process
- addresses and websites of national and state advocacy, parent, and disability organizations, and
- a bibliography of other helpful books.

After working through this book, you will be prepared to advocate for your child to receive the free appropriate public education that is guaranteed to all children who need special education services.

Get Forms, Resources, Updates, and More Online

You'll find forms, resources, and other valuable information on this book's Companion Page on Nolo's website (free for readers of this book) at

www.nolo.com/back-of-book/IEP.html

See Chapter 16 for more information.

Introduction to Special Education

What Is Special Education?

The details and reach of the Individuals with Disabilities Education Act are remarkable—no other law in this nation provides such clear and unique legal protection for children. Congress first enacted the IDEA in 1975 because public schools were frequently ignoring children with disabilities or shunting them off to inferior or distant programs. The IDEA set forth a number of legal mandates for children receiving special education. The most important ones are:

- Your child is entitled to a "free appropriate public education" in the "least restrictive environment."
- Your child is entitled to a comprehensive evaluation of his or her needs and the district cannot evaluate your child without your approval unless they take you to a due process hearing and prevail.
- Your child is entitled to have a written individualized education program (IEP) that is developed by an entire team, including you and school representatives, on at least an annual basis.
- Your child's IEP must include measurable annual goals.
- Your child is entitled to "related services" that will help your child benefit from his or her special education.
- Your child is entitled to placement in a private school at public expense if the school district cannot provide an appropriate placement.
- Your child is entitled to be educated as close to home as possible and in the school your child would attend if not disabled.
- You can ask for a mediation and hearing before an impartial third party if you do not agree with the district about any component of the IEP, including even whether your child is eligible for special education.
- Your child's IEP cannot be unilaterally changed by your school district. First, you must agree to that change.

What Is an IEP?

The acronym IEP can refer to several different things:

- the initial meeting that determines whether your child is eligible for special education (the IEP eligibility meeting)
- the annual meeting at which you and school representatives develop your child's educational program for the following school year (called the IEP program meeting), or
- the actual detailed, written description of your child's educational program.

The written IEP should include:

- the specific program or class for your child (called "placement")
- the specific services (called "related services") your child will receive, and
- other educational components, such as curricula and teaching methods.

There is one major caveat, however, in the rights that the IDEA grants to your child. The IDEA does not require that the school district provide the best possible program. The program that is individualized for your child only has to provide an appropriate educational experience. An appropriate educational experience is one that is reasonable, given your child's particular needs. For instance, you may feel that the private school across town would be the best for your child in terms of accelerating his or her growth. But if the district's program can provide a reasonable chance at growth, the law does not require the district to pay for private school placement. Or, you may feel that although three hours of speech therapy a week will work, six hours would be great. The IDEA does not require "great."

The key to preparing to advocate for your child is to focus on showing that the program and services you seek are appropriate. This book will explain the crucial steps in doing so, including:

- how to state your child's needs as specifically and narrowly as possible, and how to make sure those needs are reflected in program components. For example, it is one thing to say "my child needs help with his expressive language"; it is quite another to say "he needs three hours a week of one-on-one speech help to work on his articulation and verbal pragmatics." The first statement is much too broad; the second is specific and clearly states what assistance your child needs.

- how to provide specific proof of your child's needs, by using an evaluation, a report, or a testimony from an educator or professional who can specify what your child needs, why, and for how long.

- how to provide the evidence that backs up your position. It is always best if someone inside your school district—whether the classroom teacher, service provider, assessor, or administrator—agrees with you about what your child needs. But because you may not always have that support, you may need an expert outside of the district to describe your child's needs and recommend placement and services that will address those needs.

- how to use the proof you gather in the IEP process and, if the IEP team fails to agree with you, how to present it in a due process mediation or hearing.

- what to do when the district fails to follow the legal requirements set forth by the IDEA.

IDEA Statutes and Regulations

The laws that govern special education under the IDEA are primarily found in two places:

- statutes enacted by Congress and codified in the United States Code beginning at 20 U.S.C. § 1400, and

- regulations issued by the U.S. Department of Education and published in the Code of Federal Regulations beginning at 34 C.F.R. § 300.1.

The regulations clarify and explain the statutes. The statutes and regulations you need are on this book's Companion Page; see Chapter 16 for the link.

Being Your Child's Advocate

This book also highlights the practical aspects of being an advocate for your special education child. While these may seem obvious, it is always helpful to be reminded. The tips below can make the difference in whether or not you obtain an appropriate education for your child.

Organization, Organization, Organization

The path to success begins with meticulous organization, starting with knowing when there should be an IEP meeting and keeping track of your child's progress. File copies of all letters you write to the school district, as well as notes you make of what people say and when. For example, suppose your child's teacher tells you on Wednesday afternoon that your child needs speech therapy. You ask why and he explains. When you get home, you sit down and record the details (the date, time, place, and content of your conversation). This information may be vital at the next IEP meeting, when the issue of speech therapy comes up.

Always Ask Why

If you don't know, ask. And if an answer is provided and you don't feel it explained things fully, ask again. You are not an expert in IDEA law, but you will know enough of it to recognize the key components. If something does not make sense to you, or if an administrator says, "Well, we just don't do it that way," ask why. If he or she refers to a law (a statute or regulation) or a policy, ask to see a copy of it. If that does not work, write a letter asking for the information. You might phrase it like this: "You said last week [date] that the district could not provide my child with a one-on-one aide, that it was district policy [or because of budget cuts, or because you didn't think my child needed an aide]. I would appreciate it if you would provide me with the basis for that position. Is it part of the district's written policy, is it your opinion, or is it part of the law? If so, please send me a copy of that law. Thank you."

Style

It is likely that sometime during your child's years in special education, you will go to an IEP meeting or have a conversation during which someone from the school district says something that offends you or makes you angry. Please keep in mind that you are more likely to persuade the district of your position if you act reasonably rather than in anger. Of course, though you have to be true to your own style and there is nothing wrong with being emotional, blowing a gasket does not usually work and only signals that the discussion has come to a close. If possible, in these situations it is best to be clear, precise, and determined. Give your reaction but be as measured and calm as you can, as in "I know you would not want to deny students what they need, but I believe that the reports we have submitted are clear and there is no doubt that my daughter needs a one-on-one aide, two hours a day. Her teacher said as much. I think your position is not based on evidence and I do not appreciate your tone of voice or the manner in which you are treating us. I hope we can resolve this positively through the IEP, but if not I can assure you we will proceed as we must."

Your Child's Teacher

Your child's teacher is your best potential ally. My personal view is that teachers are as important as any working group in our nation. They teach, counsel, police, nurse, and often work all day, most nights, and many weekends to help children develop. And they do it for lousy pay, while shouldering a ton of paperwork (especially if they teach special education students), along with pressures from their own administration.

Your child's teacher knows your child better than anyone else in the school system. If you can work directly and positively with the teacher, you will have a strong ally at the IEP meeting. That does not mean that the teacher will always agree with you; in the areas that she does, however, her input is vitally important. Respect your teacher's intelligence, motives, and time. Be reasonable in your demands.

Setting Realistic Goals

One of the hardest things a lawyer sometimes has to say to a family is that their IEP goals are not supported by evidence. As a parent, I understand how difficult this is to hear. But there's no way around it: By looking at the evidence as objectively as possible, and recognizing when there is insufficient support for some or all of your goals, you will more effectively represent your child and eliminate wasted time and resources.

Remember as well that neither party to the IEP—not the parents nor the school district—has to agree to anything, no matter how powerful the support is or how effectively one side makes its point. Parents are often frustrated when the school administrator simply says "No, we don't agree about that." But you want to yell, "My child needs it, the support is there for it, how can you possibly say that!?" Each party to the IEP has the absolute right to make a decision and stick with it. Parents who remain dissatisfied with the school's position do, however, have a next step: They can challenge the school's factual conclusions (such as whether your child is eligible) through mediation (see Chapter 13); and they can challenge the school's interpretation of the law by filing a complaint (see Chapter 14).

It is imperative that you represent your child with a solid understanding of the law and its plusses and limitations. Otherwise, the process will be one of continual frustration. Think of it as going into a process where you will be a better advocate by knowing where the challenges are.

The IDEA's mandates—goals, placement, and related services as close to home as possible—are not absolute but determined through the IEP process and, therefore, whether your child is entitled to a specific goal, placement, or service will depend on your showing the need. For example, if you feel your child needs a related service or you want your child in her neighborhood school, it's possible your school district will disagree. You will have to prove your child's need and then the specifics of the related service—how often, provided by whom, and so on. That the law says your child is entitled to a related service is a broad mandate that's dependent on an agreement by you and the school district. You will need to specifically tie her special needs to the placement, goals, and services that you believe she needs to address her disability. As they say, the devil is in the details.

RESOURCE

If your child has learning disabilities. Nolo publishes a specialized version of this book just for parents of children with learning disabilities. *Nolo's IEP Guide: Learning Disabilities,* by Lawrence M. Siegel, addresses issues of particular concern for children with learning disabilities, including commonly used evaluations, special eligibility requirements, teaching methodologies, and more. If your child has learning disabilities, you'll want to use this more specific resource. Nolo will be happy to exchange this book for a copy of *Nolo's IEP Guide: Learning Disabilities.* Simply call 800-728-3555 Monday through Friday, 9 a.m. to 5 p.m. PST, and one of our customer service representatives will be happy to help.

Getting Help From Others

Other parents, local groups, and regional or national organizations can be of great help as you wend your way through special education. The amount of information these folks have is amazing. Other parents and parent groups can be your best resource. Parents who have been through the process before can help you avoid making mistakes or undertaking unnecessary tasks. Most important, they can be a source of real encouragement. Chapter 15 provides further thoughts on making use of your local special education community.

Note: Reference is made throughout this book to parents, but the term is used to include foster parents and legal guardians.

What This Book Doesn't Cover

This book focuses on the rights and procedures for children between the ages of three and 22. Other important issues fall beyond the scope of this book. These include:

- procedures for children under three
- transition services that help children prepare for a job or college, including independent living skills, and
- discipline issues including suspension and expulsion.

Use the resources in Appendix B to get more information and support on these issues. (See Chapter 16 for the link.) If you need help, especially for the complex issue of discipline, you should contact a special education attorney. (See Chapter 14.)

Overview of Special Education Law and the IEP

The Individuals with Disabilities Education Act (IDEA), a federal law, establishes a formal process for evaluating children with disabilities and providing specialized programs and services to help them succeed in school. Parents play a central role in determining their child's educational program. Under the IDEA, the program and services your child needs will be determined through the individualized education program, or IEP, process. The term IEP refers to both a meeting that is held and a plan that is written about your child's program. Your ability to understand and master the IEP process will shape your child's educational experience. Indeed, the IEP is the centerpiece of the IDEA.

This chapter discusses the specific requirements of the IDEA and how they apply to your child. It provides an overview of your child's legal rights, so you can effectively advocate for your child.

As you read this chapter, keep in mind the following:

- Don't let the word "law" throw you. The actual language of the IDEA and, more importantly, its underlying purpose, can easily be mastered. The legal concepts in the IDEA are logical and sensible.
- Developing a broad understanding of the law will help you when you review later chapters on eligibility, evaluations, IEPs, and other key matters.
- While we provide plain English descriptions of special education law in the body of the book, you can find key provisions of the actual law as passed by Congress in Appendix A on this book's Companion Page on Nolo.com (see Chapter 16 for the link). The IDEA is in the United States Code starting at 20 U.S.C. § 1400.
- The IDEA regulations found at 34 C.F.R. § 300.1 generally parallel the IDEA statutes but in some cases provide more detail. We refer to the regulations when that additional information is relevant. You can find key regulations in Appendix A. (See Chapter 16 for the link.)

The IDEA and State Special Education Laws

The IDEA is a federal law, binding on all states. The federal government provides financial assistance to the states to implement the IDEA; in exchange, states must adopt laws that implement the IDEA.

State laws generally parallel the IDEA and often use identical language. State laws can provide children with more, but not fewer, protections than the IDEA does. The IDEA is always your starting point, but you should check to see what your state law says about special education—it may provide more rights.

Each state's educational agency is responsible for making sure local school districts comply with the federal law. The federal government allocates billions of dollars a year to the states for special education. This amounts to only 8% to 13% of the costs of the IDEA, however, even though Congress initially promised the states that it would provide approximately 40% of the cost of the IDEA. The significant shortfall in federal funding puts great pressure on states and local school districts, particularly given competing interests for education dollars. The funding process varies from state to state, and is often complex. No matter how your state funds special education, remember this general rule: Money (and how it gets from Washington to your state to your district to your child) should not determine what is in your child's IEP—but in reality, financial constraints affect every school district.

What the IDEA Requires

The IDEA was enacted in 1975 and reauthorized and revamped in 2004. The purpose of the law is to ensure that children with disabilities receive an appropriate education. To achieve this goal, the IDEA imposes a number of requirements on school districts—the most important ones are discussed below.

As you'll see, significant changes brought about by the 2004 revamp are called out, which may help you in case you find yourself dealing with someone who, despite the passage of the years, is unaware of the updates.

When Congress enacted the IDEA, it chose not to tell school districts what they must specifically do for each specific child; for example, it did not establish what a child with a learning disability or a deaf child or a physically disabled child required. Congress left the specific decision making up to the family and the school district. Congress certainly set up parameters and created requirements (for instance, when an IEP meeting must be held, what topics are to be covered in an IEP, how one defines eligibility categories), but the specifics of a child's program are not established in the law.

By placing the emphasis on the process rather than specifics, Congress intended that school districts have strict processes they must follow, including rules for:

- establishing eligibility for special education
- evaluating a child
- holding an IEP meeting
- what must be covered in an IEP meeting and put on the IEP document
- what related services might be necessary for a child
- when an IEP must be in place and what must be done if an IEP is to be changed, and
- what to do when the family and the school district disagree about anything related to the child's education, including eligibility and assessments.

The importance of school districts' following rules and procedures cannot be overemphasized; being aware of those rules and what to do when they are not followed may be crucial to your child's case. (Please see Chapter 8 for a full discussion of possible school procedural violations and how they may affect your child's education and case.) We'll discuss some of these rules below.

TIP

Get involved. Like many laws, after its initial passage the IDEA was revisited and reapproved by Congress, in what's known as "reauthorization." Reauthorization does not happen every year, but when it does, it's a good time for advocates and others to change the IDEA by improving it. If you are interested in that process, contact an advocacy group (you'll find a list in Appendix B on this book's Companion Page on www.nolo.com; see Chapter 16 for the link).

Eligibility and Evaluations

Every school district has the legal duty to identify, locate, and evaluate children who may be in need of special education. This includes wards of the court, children who have no fixed address (such as migrant or homeless children), and children who may be advancing from grade to grade but nonetheless may need special education. (20 U.S.C. § 1412(a)(3).) Once a child is identified and located, the school district must find him or her eligible for special education through an evaluation and IEP process before specific programs and services can be provided.

Eligibility and Evaluation
In 2004, the IDEA provided these key changes to eligibility and evaluation: • Your child's school district must conduct the initial evaluation to determine whether your child is eligible for special education within 60 days of receiving your consent.   • The IDEA encourages states to eliminate the requirement for a "severe discrepancy" between achievement and intellectual ability.   • Parents can no longer unilaterally request more than one evaluation in a school year. A second (or third or fourth) evaluation in one school year now requires the agreement of the parent and the school district.   We discuss the details of these and many other rules about evaluation and eligibility in Chapters 6 and 7.

The IDEA defines "children with disabilities" as individuals between the ages of three and 22 who have one or more of the following conditions (20 U.S.C. § 1401(3) and (30); see also IDEA regulations at 34 C.F.R. § 300.8):

- intellectual disability (formerly known as mental retardation)
- hearing impairment (including deafness)
- speech or language impairment
- visual impairment (including blindness)

- serious emotional disturbance
- orthopedic impairment
- autism
- traumatic brain injury
- deaf-blindness
- multiple disabilities
- specific learning disability, and
- other health impairment, which may include ADD (Attention Deficit Disorder)/ADHD (Attention Deficit Hyperactivity Disorder).

For your child to qualify for special education under the IDEA, it is not enough that he or she has one of these disabilities. In addition, there must be evidence that your child's disability adversely affects his or her educational performance.

Your child has a right to an initial evaluation, with subsequent evaluations at least every three years. If you are not satisfied with the initial evaluation or you feel that your child's disability or special education needs have changed, you have the right to request an additional evaluation, and even an independent evaluation conducted by someone other than a district employee. (20 U.S.C. §§ 1414 and 1415(b)(1).) If you ask for more than one evaluation per year, however, the school district must give its consent. (20 U.S.C. § 1414(a)(2).) The school district can also dispute whether it should pay for an independent evaluation. (34 C.F.R. § 300.502.)

Evaluations Versus Assessments

The IDEA makes a distinction between "evaluations," which are the tests and other methods used to determine your child's eligibility for special education and to design your child's educational program, and "assessments," which refer to the tests your state uses to measure the performance of *all* children in school. Prior to the rising popularity of statewide assessments, however, these two terms were often used interchangeably (even in previous editions of this book), so don't be surprised if your school district continues to do so. Chapter 6 provides detailed information on special education evaluations.

The Flexible Concept of "Eligibility"

As you have seen, the IDEA is often less than crystal clear in terms of what conditions it covers. In addition, state laws that parallel the IDEA have their own rules for who is eligible for special education. For example:

- In one case, the court noted that although the student had no "academic" needs or problems, her education was "adversely affected" because depression, distractibility, and suicidal thoughts affected her attendance and emotional state. (*NG v. District of Columbia*, 556 F.Supp.2d 11 (D. D.C., 2008).)

- The state of Arkansas defines "adverse effect" to include an impact on "affective, behavioral and physical characteristics," further enforcing the view that an "education" is not just grades.

- Although an "emotional disturbance" can be a disabling condition, the line between emotional problems and social maladjustment (which is not legally disabling) is not easy to draw. In *Springer v. Fairfax County School Board*, 134 F.3d. 659 (4th Cir. 1998), the court noted that the population targeted by the emotional disturbance category can be a "wild and unruly bunch .... adolescence is, almost by definition, a time of social maladjustment." If emotional disturbance included a "bad conduct" definition, then almost every teenage student would meet the eligibility criteria. On the other hand, some courts have sided with the court in *Mr. and Mrs. I. v. Maine School Administrative Dist. No. 55*, 2005 WL 1389135, which noted that a student who is anxious, sad, or being teased and not relating to peers can qualify. The line between a social maladjustment and a qualifying "emotional disturbance" will depend on the specific evidence and, frankly, on how the judge views social norms.

RELATED TOPIC

Eligibility for special education services is discussed in detail in Chapters 6 and 7. The very specific rules regarding the initial and subsequent evaluations are described in Chapter 6.

Nature of the Education

Under the IDEA, your child is entitled to the following fundamental educational rights (20 U.S.C. §§ 1401(9) and (29)):

- **Free appropriate public education (FAPE).** Your child is entitled to an *appropriate* education at no cost to you.
- **Special education.** Your child is entitled to an education *specially designed* to meet his or her *unique* needs.

RELATED TOPIC

Chapter 5 discusses how to develop a blueprint of your child's program and service needs.

The IDEA fundamentally requires the educational program to fit your child, not the other way around. For example, it is not appropriate for a school district to place a deaf child in a class for developmentally disabled children or a learning-disabled child in a class for emotionally disturbed students. These would not be individually tailored IEPs and would not be appropriate. "Appropriateness" is the standard for evaluating all IEP components—the goals, services, and placement.

Appropriate Does Not Necessarily Mean the Very Best

The law does not require your school district to provide the best possible education, but only an appropriate education. "Appropriate" is an elusive but tremendously important concept. It is used throughout the IDEA and frequently in the IEP process. For one child, an appropriate education may mean a regular class with minor support services, while a hospital placement might be appropriate for another.

What is a "free appropriate public education?" Perhaps the most difficult question to answer since the enactment of the IDEA in 1975 is what constitutes an "appropriate" education and what are the duties of a school district to provide it?

The question actually has two parts:

- Since "appropriate" is directly related to educational benefit, how is that benefit measured so as to determine whether the IEP offered your child is appropriate?
- What constitutes an education—is it only academic/scholastic work or does it include things like social and emotional growth?

Courts have attempted to provide some direction as to what is meant by an "appropriate" education and therefore what are the duties of your school district to provide an education that has value to your child. In 1982, the U.S. Supreme Court in a case called *Board of Education of the Hendrick Hudson School District v. Rowley* said that an appropriate education is one that "opens the door of public education" to a child with a disability, but does not guarantee any "particular outcome" and has no requirement to "maximize" a child's potential.

This set a low bar for what a parent could expect a district to provide and what outcomes were reasonable. A child with a disability should receive "some" educational benefit but there were no standards for what "some" meant.

The *Rowley* standard has been significantly altered since 1982 by courts all over the nation. Courts have ruled that an "appropriate" education is one in which "more than a trivial amount of educational benefit" is required, that "educational benefit" must be meaningful," that your child "progress academically," that learning be "significant and meaningful," and the benefit must be "gauged in relation to a child's potential [not full potential]." A child with a disability should also make "measurable and adequate gains in the classroom."

The concepts of "appropriate" and educational benefit are still more vague than not (for example, what is "significant" learning?), and subject to your child's individual needs. The language courts have come up with is important to be aware of, but will not automatically mean when you tell your school district that your child needs X or Y to receive "significant" benefit, the district will agree. But it also means that appropriate no longer means the minimum effort, or a weak effort, at providing "something" for your child. That said, there is still no requirement to "maximize" your child's potential or that he receive the "best" or "most" appropriate

Educational Benefit Under the IDEA

The issue that has bedeviled parents, students, school districts, and courts since the passage of the IDEA in 1975—what constitutes a sufficient "educational benefit" under the IDEA, or how much educational benefit does the district have to provide to meet its legal mandate to provide a child with a disability an "appropriate" education—is about to be addressed by the Supreme Court.

Back in the *Rowley* case (1982), the Supreme Court said that that passing from grade to grade might represent enough educational benefit, regardless of actual educational progress or potential. The Court famously (or infamously depending on where you sit at the IEP table) stated that "the intent of the Act was more to open the door of public education to handicapped children than to guarantee any particular level of education once inside."

When the IDEA was reauthorized in 2007, Congress appeared to expand the *Rowley* standard of educational benefit, noting that implementation of the IDEA was "impeded by low expectations" and that children with disabilities are entitled to "high expectations" and, "to the maximum extent possible," to meet the challenging expectations that are established for all children.

Just as we go to press, the U.S. Supreme Court has issued an important ruling that clarifies and enlarges upon what constitutes educational benefit for children with disabilities. The decision was unanimous and is a positive development for your child. In the case *Endrew F. v. Douglas County School District* (issued March 22, 2017), Endrew F. was a child with autism. His parents believed he had not progressed and it appeared that he still exhibited "multiple behaviors that inhibited his ability to access learning in the classroom."

The Supreme Court rejected the lower court's language that "merely more than de minimis" [minimal] progress was sufficient to prove there was educational benefit. The key findings by the Supreme Court were that a child's IEP/program must be "appropriately ambitious" and "calculated to allow a child to make progress appropriate in light of the child's circumstances." In addition, a child's IEP/program should be measured against the broader requirement from *Rowley* that, when a child is in a

Educational Benefit Under the IDEA (continued)

regular classroom, grade level advancement is required. If a child in a regular classroom is entitled to educational benefit as reflected in grade advancement, other children in special education in other placements are entitled to similarly positive opportunities.

While the Supreme Court noted the expertise of local educators in framing the issue of appropriate and did not elaborate on what "appropriate progress will look like from case to case," the court was clear that it was raising the *Rowley* standard. The court stated that a merely minimal education is hardly an education at all and is aimed so low as to be "tantamount to 'sitting idly'... awaiting the time when they were old enough to 'drop out.'"

While there is still and likely always will be vagueness about any language that tries to define appropriate, a phrase like "appropriately ambitious" in allowing for progress is indeed a higher standard than the standard that was established by *Rowley*.

As you plan for your next IEP, a key will be that your child is entitled by law to a program that is sufficiently "ambitious" as to allow progress consistent with your child's circumstances. In reality, what does that mean? Where is your child now in all the areas of need, what would be a reasonable and appropriate level of improvement, and what does he or she need in program, services, and strategies to accomplish that ambitious advancement?

education. That is why we will remind you repeatedly that when describing a program or service you want for your child, never use the words "best," "maximum," or similar adjectives. You want an "appropriate" education as reflected in the detail of your child's blueprint.

The second issue in considering what is FAPE is what constitutes an education? Most state law, federal policy, and court decisions acknowledge that an "education" is more than grades, more than academic work and progress. You can and should insist that the IEP team consider your child's emotional, linguistic, social, behavioral, and other nontraditional academic/scholastic needs. As one court said, the IDEA wants to "foster self-sufficiency" in students. If your school district says that an "appropriate" education is one that only focuses on standard academics, ask them where it says that in the law, where FAPE is defined that way. And remind them that the IEP process talks about goals and objectives, not specific academic classes, and further states that the IEP team must consider the "strengths of the child and the concerns of the parents for enhancing the education of their child...." (34 C.F.R. § 300.324; see also 34 C.F.R. § 300.323.)

Do you have to accept special education or related services? The 2004 amendments to the IDEA make clear that you have the right to reject special education and related services. As Congress said, you have the "ultimate choice" in these matters; the school district cannot force anything on your child if you don't want it.

How Your State Law Defines an Appropriate Education

It is important to try to have some understanding of your state's special education laws. While some state special education laws duplicate federal special education laws verbatim, many states add a good deal to the requirements of school district. (Remember, state law must parallel federal special education law, but can provide greater protection and more rights for your child.) For example, in relation to what is meant by an "appropriate education," North Carolina has state policy that requires that every child must have fair and full opportunity to reach her "full potential."

In terms of what is meant by an education, Maine goes far beyond the federal government in its definition. Maine defines "educational performance" to include academic areas (reading, math, and so on), but also nonacademic areas (daily life activities, mobility, etc.) and extracurricular activities as well as six guiding principles for what students should become:

- clear and effective communicators
- self-directed and lifelong learners
- creative and practical problem solvers
- responsible and involved citizens
- collaborative and quality workers, and
- integrative and informed thinkers.

(Maine Department of Education Regulation 132.)

Educational Placement or Program

Decisions about your child's educational placement or program, along with related services (discussed below), will take center stage in the IEP process.

Least Restrictive Environment

IDEA does not tell you or the school what specific program or class your child should be in; that is a decision for the IEP team. The IDEA does require school districts to place disabled children in the least restrictive environment (LRE) that meets their individual needs. A child's LRE will depend on that child's abilities and disabilities. Although Congress expressed a strong preference for mainstreaming (placing a child in a regular classroom), it used the term LRE to ensure that individual needs would determine each individual placement—and that children who really need a more restrictive placement (such as a special school) would have one.

It is important you understand the difference between the concept of LRE and a specific placement for a specific child. The IDEA requires that each school district have a variety of placement options for your child, called the "continuum of placement options" (see "Range of Placements," below). One of those options is indeed a regular classroom (often referred to as "mainstreaming" or "inclusion") and it is the placement Congress preferred when it enacted the IDEA. There are however, other options including separate classes, schools, and even residential placement. The decision on which placement is right for your child should take into account all of his or her needs. For one child, the LRE may and should be a regular classroom; for another it may and should be a separate class or school.

There is a good deal of debate about the LRE requirement in the national special education community. There are those who believe that all children regardless of their needs and challenges should be mainstreamed. This represents a long-standing commitment of our nation to remove any form of "segregation" from our educational system. There are those who are equally passionate and believe that there are children for whom a regular classroom would actually be more restrictive;

for example, a deaf child who uses sign language or a child with significant emotional challenges who needs to be in a very small class on a very small and sheltered campus. As an attorney, my first and only responsibility is to my clients' specific needs and not some generic goal. You, of course, have only one goal, the best placement for your child.

How is the least restrictive environment selected? The preference for a regular classroom placement is found in the language of the IDEA, Section 300.114. This section says that the school district must ensure that, to the "maximum extent appropriate, children with disabilities … are educated with children who are nondisabled" and that removal of children with disabilities from the regular classroom should occur only if "the nature of the disability is such that education in regular classes with the use of supplementary aids and services cannot be achieved satisfactorily."

This language suggests that a child should always begin in a regular class and only after it is demonstrated that he or she cannot receive an appropriate education there, should he or she be "removed" to a more restrictive placement. In reality, of course, this does not always happen and in some cases a regular classroom placement could actually be harmful for a child. Again consider a deaf child who communicates through sign language who would be fully isolated in a regular class or a child who is afraid of a large class. It would be cruel to place this child in a regular class first. (The IDEA does add that when an IEP team selects the LRE for a child, the team must consider any potential harmful effect on the child or on the quality of services that he or she needs. 34 C.F.R. § 300.116.)

To sum up, the LRE rules demonstrate:

- a strong preference for mainstreaming, including the requirement to provide aides and services before a child can be removed from a regular class
- a recognition that a different placement may be necessary, depending on the child's individual needs and challenges, and
- LRE is not a specific place but a determination that one of the continuum of placement options is the "least restrictive" for an individual child.

What Is Right for Your Child

In my practice over many decades, I have found that many school districts—not all, but many—have a rigid sense of LRE and apply it rigidly. School districts have rightfully accepted that Congress placed a high premium on placing children with disabilities in regular educational settings, but they do not always understand that LRE is fluid and individually determined. For example, I have had many student clients who had severe emotional challenges and could not access their education in any placement but a residential treatment center. The district would counter, "That is not LRE." I had to explain, and you may have to explain, that LRE is determined by individual need, not a generic rule for all children. This view is reinforced by the existence of the continuum of placement options. If Congress felt there was only one option—only one "LRE"—it would not have included the continuum.

Court decisions on LRE. Federal courts throughout the country have long struggled with the tension between the specialized needs of children under the IDEA and the requirement to place those children in the least restrictive environment. *Daniel R.R. v. State Board of Education*, 874 F.2d 1036 (5th Cir. 1989), is a significant case that balanced the right to be in a regular classroom versus the need for highly detailed services that might preclude mainstreaming. The court held that a school district must consider the following before removing a child from a regular placement:

- If the student can benefit from mainstreaming, the fact that the child may not gain as much as other students cannot be the basis for denying a regular classroom placement.
- The benefits of mainstreaming are not merely educational, but may be social, linguistic, and more. When analyzing the benefit of mainstreaming, these noneducational factors must be considered.
- The student's impact on other students must be considered.

- The child should be mainstreamed to the "maximum extent appropriate," even if the student must be placed in a nonregular education program (such as mainstreaming for part of the school day).

What is clear from the court decisions and due process hearing decisions that have dealt with this issue is that judges pay close attention to the circumstances of each case. For example, a federal court found that placing a child with Down Syndrome in a special classroom for core academic classes, but in general education classes for electives, was the least restrictive environment based on his needs. *Dick-Friedman ex rel. Friedman v. Board of Educ. of West Bloomfield Public Schools,* 427 F.Supp.2d 768 (E.D. Mich. 2006). Another judge concluded that 13-year-old twins with Rett Syndrome (who had six-month-old motor skills and 17-month-old cognitive-functioning skills) did not need to be mainstreamed because they would receive limited or no value from placement in a regular classroom. (*Kerry M. v. Manhattan School Dist. #114,* 46 IDELR 194 (N.D. Ill. 2006).)

Placement Versus Program

The terms placement and program are often used interchangeably, but there are some differences in meaning. As used in the IDEA, placement refers to the various classrooms or schools where a child may be physically placed. Program has a broader connotation: It includes not only where the program is located, but also the components of that program, including extra services, curricula, teaching methods, class makeup, and so on. Placement and program components should both be addressed in your child's IEP.

The IDEA states that a child should be in the regular classroom unless the child cannot be educated satisfactorily there, even with the "use of supplementary aids and services." (20 U.S.C. § 1412(a)(5).) LRE further requires that a child should be educated as close to home as possible and in the class he or she would attend if nondisabled. (IDEA regulations at 34 C.F.R. §§ 300.114–120.) In an interesting case out of Arizona, a school district wanted to place a deaf student in the State School for the Deaf, two hundred miles from his home and against the wishes of his parents. The court concluded that the child's language skills were so minimal and his education so impeded that the LRE environment was indeed the state school, not a regular classroom or even regular school. (*Poolaw v. Bishop*, 67 F.3d 830 (9th Cir. 1995).)

If a child will not participate with nondisabled children in a regular classroom and in other school activities, the IEP team must explain why. (20 U.S.C. § 1414(d)(1)(A).)

Range of Placements

While the IDEA expresses a preference for regular education, it recognizes that some children with disabilities should not be in a regular class. Individual need determines the appropriateness of a placement. If regular classroom placement is not appropriate, the IDEA requires that the school district provide a range of alternative placements—called a continuum of placement options—including the following:

- regular classes for part of the school day
- special classes in regular schools—for example, a special class for children with developmental disabilities
- special public or private schools for children with significant difficulties, such as a school for emotionally troubled students
- charter schools
- residential programs
- home instruction, and
- hospital and institutional placement.

If a child's unique needs dictate an alternative to a regular classroom, the continuum requirement ensures that the school district will make different placement options available. No matter where children are placed, however, the IDEA requires every child to have access to the general curriculum taught in the regular classroom. The IEP must specifically address how this requirement will be met. (20 U.S.C. § 1414(d)(1)(A).)

Is Mainstreaming a Requirement?

Court decisions interpreting the least restrictive environment rule have been as varied as the children in special education. Some court opinions have concluded that mainstreaming is a requirement of IDEA; other judges have ruled that it is "a goal subordinate to the requirement that disabled children receive educational benefit." (*Hartmann by Hartmann v. Loudoun County Bd. of Educ.*, 118 F.3d 996, 1002 (4th Cir. 1997).)

A common example of the possible conflict between mainstreaming and an appropriate educational setting occurs with a child who needs very specialized curricula, intense services, specialized staff, or a protected environment. The child's unique needs may conflict with the right to be mainstreamed.

This does not mean that children should necessarily be removed from a regular classroom when they do not perform as well as their peers. But if the student cannot receive a meaningful education even with the use of supplementary aids and services, then a more restrictive environment is appropriate. The more complex the needs, the more likely the scale will tip toward a nonmainstreamed placement.

Charter Schools

Charter schools are public schools generally like traditional public schools, but depending on state law, they may have more freedom from state regulations. Charter schools must follow all federal law, however. Therefore, charter schools must meet all the requirements of the IDEA, including "child find," assessments, IEPs, and due process.

A charter school, again depending on state law, may either be an "independent" educational agency, which means the school is its own school district and has direct responsibility for special education, or may be dependent on and formally part of a school district. In this second case, it is the district that is ultimately responsible for all IDEA requirements. In this situation, think of the charter school as merely one other placement option within the district.

Charter schools are intended to give parents more choice as to where to send their children. There is, of course, significant debate about charter schools; there are those who point to significant gains for children in charter schools, while other academicians suggest little or no change in scores whether a child goes to a charter school or a traditional public school. Other concerns about charter schools include anecdotal information that they are less inclined to provide full special education services, may not have qualified staff, and do not know the complex special education procedures. A recent report out of Oakland, California, indicated that charter schools there did not provide the level of special education and related services that public schools normally do. This is not to say charter schools are not worth an investigation, but it is crucial that you fully investigate any charter school:

- Are the teachers credentialed?
- What experience has the school had with special education?
- Is there a special education administrator?
- Is there other staff with the kind of knowledge and training your child deserves?
- Is there any financial incentive for the charter school to limit its programs and services for children with disabilities?

Depending on the state, a charter school may be able to follow different rules regarding teacher certification. This can affect a child's special education possibilities. Since at a regular school, special education teachers and specialists almost always have state requirements in terms of education and demonstration of specific proficiencies in an area of special education, placement in a program where there are lesser requirements can be concerning and often quite serious in terms of the delivery of an appropriate education for your child.

If you have a child in a charter school, you and your child have all the same rights under the IDEA that apply to those in a regular school, regardless of whether the charter school is an independent school or within a specific school district. That also means that the charter school has all the responsibilities under the IDEA discussed throughout this book. But the fact that the IEP/IDEA requirements for charter schools are the same does not mean that the schools may not misunderstand or ignore those requirements. For example, one federal court made it clear that a charter school can be found to violate the requirements of the IDEA, in this case, a change of placement without an IEP. The court in *R.B. v. Mastery Charter Sch.,* 762 F.Supp.2d 745 (E.D. Pa. 2010), stated that the charter school's "attempt to evade its obligations under the IDEA by passing the buck—in this case, a special-needs student's education—to the District is troubling.... [the school] is bound by all the obligations of IDEA."

Private School Placement Before a Public School Program

Although the IDEA provides that there are circumstances when a public school must place or pay for a child's placement in a private school, it hasn't always been clear whether a child must *first* receive public school services (or be placed in a public school) before the school district must pay for or place the child in a private educational setting. The U.S. Supreme Court addressed this question in *Forest Grove School District v. T.A.,* 129 S.Ct. 987 (2009). In that case, the parents enrolled their child in a private school before the district had offered any of their own services. The district didn't want to pay for the education. But because the school district had known that the child was having difficulties but failed to offer any services, the court concluded that it couldn't avoid paying for private placement.

The Difference Between Non-Public Schools and Private Schools

If you are thinking about a non-public school for your child, please note that there are usually two kinds of private schools available: a *non-public school* certified as a special education program by your state and a *common private school*, which is not certified as a special education program.

As with all placement issues, you will have to show that the public school IEP option is not appropriate for your child and the non-public option is. Rules may vary from state to state, but while it is much harder to get a school district to agree to placement in a purely private school, as opposed to a certified non-public school, it does happen. You will, however, have a more difficult case if the private school does not have any special education staff and/or overall expertise and understanding of special education needs. While I have been able to convince districts to pay for a private school, it is much easier if the non-public school is certified in special education.

Support or Related Services

Support or related services are the additional help your child needs to meet his or her IEP goals. These services are not educational per se—they are the psychological, occupational, therapeutic, or practical assistance your child needs to succeed. The IDEA requires schools to provide related services for two reasons:

- to help your child benefit from special education, and
- to ensure that your child has the chance to "achieve satisfactorily" in a regular classroom.

Under the IDEA, related services include the following:

- speech-language pathology and audiology services
- psychological services
- physical and occupational therapy
- recreation, including therapeutic recreation
- social work services
- counseling services, including rehabilitation counseling

- orientation and mobility services
- medical services for diagnostic and evaluation purposes
- interpreting services
- one-on-one instructional aide
- transportation
- technological devices, such as FM/AM systems or special computers, and
- school nurse services. (20 U.S.C. § 1401(26).)

This is not an exhaustive list. Because everything under the IDEA is driven by a child's individual needs, the IEP team has the authority to provide any service your child needs, even if it's not listed specifically under the IDEA.

Rules for Related Services

When Congress amended the IDEA in 2004, it made a few changes to the list of related services. Here are the key changes:

- **Interpreting services.** Congress added "interpreting services," although it did not specify whether sign language interpreters must be certified, an important issue for deaf and hard of hearing children.
- **School nurse services.** Congress also added "school nurse services designed to enable a child with a disability to receive a free appropriate public education." (See "Is a Medical Service a Related Service?" above for more information.)
- **Surgically implanted device.** Congress also specified that a surgically implanted medical device, or the replacement of such a device, is *not* a related service. (20 U.S.C. § 1401(26).) This language refers to cochlear implants.
- **Peer-reviewed research.** The latest version of the law also requires that the related services listed in the IEP be "based on peer-reviewed research to the extent practicable." (20 U.S.C. § 1414(d)(1)(A).) See Chapter 10 for more information on this requirement.

Is a Medical Service a Related Service?

The question of what constitutes a related service has been debated since the IDEA was enacted in 1975. One particularly difficult issue has been whether a medical service constitutes a related service if it is needed for a child to benefit from special education. In 1999, the U.S. Supreme Court confirmed that a medical service is a related service if it is limited to "diagnostic and evaluation purposes."

The Court also ruled, however, that other medical services might constitute related services under the rules of the IDEA if they can be performed by a nonphysician. In the case heard by the Court, the child needed and was granted the services of a nurse to provide, among other things, daily catheterization, suctioning of a tracheotomy, and blood pressure monitoring. (*Cedar Rapids Community School Dist. v. Garret F. ex rel. Charlene F.*, 119 S.Ct. 992 (1999).)

Congress codified the *Cedar Rapids* ruling when it amended the IDEA in 2004. The law now provides that school nurse services qualify as a related service. (20 U.S.C. § 1401(26).) (Oddly, a few courts have flipped the *Cedar Rapids* logic on its head. In *Max M. v. Thompson*, 592 F.Supp. 1437 (N.D. Ill. 1984), a child was receiving psychiatric care from a psychiatrist (a psychiatrist is a physician). The court ruled that this was a related service because the therapy could also be provided by a nonphysician.)

Parents will always have to show that a particular related service is necessary to their child's education, but there is no longer any dispute that services that can be performed by nurses can be required under the IDEA. Finally, keep in mind that normal medical services, such as check-ups and normal diagnostic or other procedures (like an appendectomy) are well beyond the reach of IDEA requirements.

Assistive Technology

The IDEA requires that a child be provided with assistive technology services. These services include:

- evaluating how the child functions in his or her customary environment
- leasing or purchasing assistive technology devices

- fitting, maintaining, and replacing assistive technology devices
- using and coordinating other therapies, interventions, or services in conjunction with such technology, and
- training and technical assistance for the child, the child's family, and the educational staff.

Technological devices are defined as any item, piece of equipment, or system acquired, modified, or customized to maintain, increase, or improve the functional capabilities of a child with a disability. An assistive technology device or service might be an augmentative communication system, a computer, an FM trainer, computer software, pulmonary devices, a touch screen, a calculator, a tape recorder, a spell-checker, books on tape, and even items such as oxygen tanks. (20 U.S.C. § 1401(1) and (2), and 34 C.F.R. §§ 300.5, 300.6, and 300.105.)

Transition Services

The IDEA requires the IEP team to develop a transition plan to be included in the first IEP in effect when your child turns 16 or at an earlier age if the IEP team determines that to be appropriate. (20 U.S.C. § 1414(d), 34 C.F.R. § 300.320(b).)

In the transition plan, you and the IEP team must spell out how your child will proceed after high school, whether to college, to work, to a training program, or to develop the skills necessary to live independently as an adult. (20 U.S.C. § 1414(d)(1)(A).) The plan must include "appropriate measurable postsecondary goals," based on appropriate transition assessments focused on training, employment, education, and independent living skills. The IEP must also list the specific transition services that will be required to help your child reach these transition goals.

Due Process

In law, "due process" generally refers to the right to a fair procedure for determining individual rights and responsibilities. Under the IDEA, and as used in this book, due process means your child's right to be evaluated, receive an appropriate education, be educated in the LRE, have an IEP, and be given notice of any changes in the IEP.

Due process also refers to your specific right to take any dispute you have with your child's school district—whether a disagreement about an evaluation, eligibility, or any part of the IEP, including the specific placement and related services—to a neutral third party to help you resolve your dispute. These rights are unique; only children in special education have them.

Rules for Due Process

When Congress amended the IDEA in 2004, it made several important changes:

- **Filing deadline.** Parents must file for due process within two years after they knew, or should have known, of the underlying dispute. If your state has its own deadline, the state rule will apply.
- **Times of response.** Once a due process request has been filed, the other party has ten days to respond.
- **Resolution meeting.** Within 15 days after receiving a due process request, the school district must convene a meeting to try to resolve the dispute. The school district cannot have an attorney at this meeting unless the parents bring one.
- **Attorneys' fees.** If parents bring a due process action for any improper purpose, "such as to harass, to cause unnecessary delay, or to needlessly increase the cost of litigation," they may have to pay the school district's attorneys' fees. (20 U.S.C. § 1415.)

You can find details on each of these changes in Chapter 12.

There are two options for resolving disputes through due process: mediation and a due process hearing. In mediation, you and the school district meet with a neutral third party who helps you come to an agreement. The mediator has the power of persuasion, but no authority to impose a decision on you.

"Let's Sue Them"

Many of my clients are deeply frustrated with their child's school district, understandably so. It does not surprise me then, when they urge me to "sue them!" A word on suing school districts: as discussed above, there is an existing procedure that's required in almost all cases—due process—which you must use before you can go into court.

There are some exceptions, such as when there is an emergency situation that must be addressed well before there can be a due process hearing. For example, assume your child with a learning disability also needs one-on-one nursing services and, without them, your child would be in danger. But the school district does not agree and you cannot wait to go through the hearing process. (Once you ask for a due process hearing, the law gives your state 45 days to issue a decision, and that timeline is often extended.) In this case, a court may very well step in to issue an emergency order regarding the nursing services rather than have your child wait for a due process hearing. For more information, see Chapter 12 section titled, "When You Can Go Straight to Court Instead of Using the Due Process Hearing. "

The other exception is for a problem that is outside of special education, most notably if your child has been injured or otherwise harmed at school. Say your daughter is hit by another student or has been so badly bullied that she has suffered an emotional breakdown. The school would likely have a responsibility to prevent these harms and would possibly be negligent since they did not. The child may have a legal claim for damages (money compensation), and this claim would be raised in a court of law and not in a due process hearing. Using this option requires great care, and you should contact a local personal injury lawyer with experience in taking action against educational institutions if you find your child in this situation.

Suing often sounds appealing, but it is often a long and challenging process and usually involves major failures by the school district, not just minor infractions. Think very carefully before you make your child subject to a lawsuit against the district. Your child may have to testify and be exposed to the bruising nature of litigation.

If you cannot reach an agreement in mediation (or prefer to skip mediation altogether), you can request a hearing. There, you and the school district present written and oral testimony about the disputed issues before a neutral administrative judge. The judge will decide who is right and issue an order imposing a decision. Either you or the school district can appeal to a federal or state court, all the way to the U.S. Supreme Court. But before you conjure up images of walking up the marble stairs to the highest court in the land, you should know that most disputes with school districts are resolved before a hearing and certainly before you find yourself in a courtroom.

If you believe that your school has violated a legal rule—for example, by failing to hold an IEP meeting—you should file a complaint (discussed in Chapter 13). The complaint process is quite different from due process (covered in more detail in Chapter 12). A due process matter involves a factual dispute between you and the school district. A complaint involves a failure by the district to follow the law.

Suspension and Expulsion

Some children with disabilities have trouble behaving themselves in school. Like all other kids, children with disabilities sometimes act out, try to get attention in the wrong ways, or are more interested in their friends than their schoolwork. But sometimes, these children have behavioral problems that are directly related to their disabilities. A child with ADD who can't pay attention in class, a child whose developmental delays lead to immense frustration, or a child whose autism makes it hard to follow a teacher's instructions can create disciplinary problems. A child who has secondary emotional difficulties because of a disability may be disruptive or even get into fights. How can schools balance their responsibility to maintain order with their duty to provide an appropriate education for children with disabilities?

Most states have laws and procedures about disciplinary action—including suspension and expulsion—quite separate from special education laws and procedures. These disciplinary rules apply to all students within a school district. For special education students, however, these rules must be applied in conjunction with the laws and procedures of the IDEA, including specific protections that apply when a child with a disability is subject to suspension or expulsion. Like all children in school, your child must follow the rules; otherwise, he or she may be suspended or expelled. Before the school district can take this type of action, however, the IDEA requires a very careful analysis of whether the disability played a role in your child's behavior and, if so, whether suspension or expulsion is really justified.

In 1997, Congress added many new rules to the IDEA regarding the suspension and expulsion of special education students. Although these rules provide specific rights and procedures for children in special education who are subject to discipline, Congress clearly intended to allow school districts to remove students who misbehave or are dangerous.

> ⓘ CAUTION
> **Get some help if your child is in trouble.** The IDEA rules and procedures applicable to suspensions and expulsions are complicated—and the stakes for your child in these situations are very high. This section provides an overview, but you'll probably want to contact a parent support group or special education lawyer if your child faces serious disciplinary action. This is one situation in which you shouldn't try to go it alone.

The IDEA and Disciplinary Action

The IDEA provides that a student with an IEP cannot have his or her program, placement, or services changed unless the school district and the child's parents agree to the change. Absent such an agreement, the child is entitled to remain or "stay put" in the current program until either a new IEP is signed or a hearing officer decides that the child's program can be changed. (20 U.S.C. § 1415(j).) The school district cannot remove your child or unilaterally change your child's program— if it tries to do so, you can assert your child's right to stay put in the current placement until a new IEP is in place or a hearing officer approves the change. This very broad rule is intended to prevent a school from moving a child without parental approval.

A proposed suspension or expulsion clearly constitutes a change in placement, and this is where state laws on suspension and expulsion run directly into IDEA requirements. Can a school district suspend or expel (remove the child from school) without violating the stay-put rule? The answer is, as you probably expected, yes and no. The law clearly states that a child with disabilities can be suspended or expelled, but the suspension or expulsion cannot take place unless certain IDEA procedures are followed. (20 U.S.C. § 1415(j) and (k); these rules are further explained in the IDEA regulations at 34 C.F.R. §§ 300.530–537.)

Congress created different rules depending on the length of the suspension or expulsion. This part of the IDEA is fairly complex, but generally, children who are facing more than ten days out of school have more procedural protections under the law.

Suspensions or Expulsions for Up to Ten Days

Any special education child removed from school *for up to ten consecutive days* is not entitled to the IDEA procedures and protections. Because such a removal does not constitute a "change in placement," the child cannot claim the right to stay put. Because many suspensions are for fewer than ten consecutive days, most special education students who are suspended do not have the right to contest that removal based either on the IDEA's stay-put rule or on the IDEA's specific disciplinary procedures. In short, a child with disabilities can be suspended from school for up to ten days just like any other student.

Suspensions or Expulsions Exceeding Ten Days

If a school district intends to suspend or expel a special education student for more than ten consecutive days, that *might* constitute a change in placement. In these situations, additional IDEA procedures kick in before the child can be removed. These procedures might also apply to a child who is removed from school for more than ten nonconsecutive days.

Within ten school days of a decision to change a student's placement, an IEP team must hold a "manifestation determination" review. If the IEP team determines that the misbehavior was caused by the child's disability or by the district's failure to implement the IEP, certain steps are required. The district must either develop a behavioral intervention plan for the child, or modify the child's existing plan. The district is required to return the student to the original placement unless the parent and the district agree to a change of placement as part of modifying the student's behavioral intervention plan. (You can find these requirements at 34 C.F.R. § 300.530(e).)

Dangerous Behavior

The IDEA makes an exception to the ten-day rule for disciplinary problems involving weapons or drugs. A special education student who brings a weapon to school or possesses, uses, sells, or solicits the sale of drugs at school or during a school function can be removed for up to 45 days without parental agreement. This means the student cannot assert the right to remain in the current placement pending the conclusion of the required IDEA disciplinary procedures. The student is entitled, however, to an "interim alternative" placement as determined by the IEP team.

Related Requirements

As a general rule, the IDEA requires the IEP team to develop a "behavioral intervention" plan for students whose behavior impedes their own learning or that of others. (34 C.F.R. § 300.324(a)(2)(i).) It would not be surprising if a special education student facing suspension or expulsion had such a plan in his or her IEP. As mentioned above, if a student is removed for more than ten days, and the IEP team determines that the student's behavior was a manifestation of his or her disability, the IDEA requires the IEP team to do a "functional behavioral assessment" and implement a "behavioral intervention plan" if one is not already in place.

For a child whose disability impairs his or her ability to relate to others or behave appropriately, the plan should address those needs and provide strategies for helping improve peer relationships and/or school behavior. For example, a child who takes out the frustration of a disability by lashing out at other students might be taught alternative methods to express frustration, such as talking to a counselor, taking a "timeout," or expressing anger more constructively ("I don't like it when you interrupt me when I'm speaking in class").

RESOURCE

Need more information on discipline? The Center for Effective Collaboration and Practice (a group dedicated to helping students, teachers, and parents address emotional and behavioral concerns) has lots of great ideas on dealing with disciplinary and behavior problems, as well as detailed information on drafting behavioral intervention plans. You can find this material at www.air.org (the center is a branch of the American Institutes for Research).

Additional IDEA Rights

The IDEA provides for many rights for students, including the following additional mandates.

Summer School

The IDEA regulations require the school district to provide children with summer school or an "extended school year" (ESY) if necessary to meet their needs. (34 C.F.R. § 300.106.)

The general rule applied to whether a school district must provide ESY is whether your child will "likely regress" without it. That rule has expanded somewhat: the U.S Department of Education, Office of Special Education Programs, has written that if the child will too slowly "recoup" what was lost without ESY, then ESY must be provided.

Private School

The IDEA gives your child the right to be placed in a nonprofit or private (including parochial) school if your school district cannot provide an appropriate program. (20 U.S.C. § 1412(a)(10).)

There must be an IEP agreement or due process or court ruling that the private school is appropriate before the school district is required to pay for a private school placement. If you place your child in a private school unilaterally—on your own—your school district is not required to pay.

Although the school district does not have to pay tuition costs for children whose parents place them in private school, it must offer special education and related services to these children. The school district need not provide these services at the private school (although it can choose to do so), nor does it have to provide any services different from or in addition to those that would be available if the child were in public school.

Under the 2004 amendments to the IDEA, school districts must consult with private schools about whether and how special education and related services will be provided to children whose parents placed them in private school. The private school can file a complaint with the state educational agency if it feels the district is not complying with this "consultation" requirement in a timely and meaningful manner. (20 U.S.C. § 1412(a)(10).) The school district does not have to provide services at the private school, so this consultation or "right to talk" requirement doesn't create or expand rights for children whose parents place them in private school.

IDEA Notice Requirements and Private School Placements

If you plan to remove your child to a private program, you must notify the school district of your intent either:

- at the most recent IEP meeting you attended prior to removing your child from public school, or
- by written notice at least ten business days before the actual removal. (20 U.S.C. § 1412(a)(10)(C).)

If you don't provide this notice, and then pursue due process to seek reimbursement for your child's placement in a private school, reimbursement may be denied, or you may receive only partial payment.

Special Education in Prison

Imprisoned children between the ages of 18 and 21 who were identified and had an IEP prior to incarceration are also entitled to a free, appropriate public education. (20 U.S.C. § 1414(d)(7).) Children who are convicted as adults and incarcerated in adult prisons, however, do not have certain protections, such as those relating to general assessments and transition planning.

Individualized Education Program

An IEP may seem complicated—it is a meeting, a document, and a description of your child's entire educational program. While the IEP meeting is discussed in detail in Chapters 10 and 11, here are a few introductory concepts:

- By law, you are an equal partner in the IEP process. As a general rule, no part of the IEP can be implemented without your approval.
- Your child's first time in special education will follow an initial eligibility IEP. Thereafter, IEP meetings will be held yearly, focusing on the specifics of your child's current educational program and what next year's IEP will look like. While the procedures for these two kinds of IEPs (called eligibility and program IEPs) are the same, there are some important differences—see Chapters 7, 10, and 11.
- You and the school district must agree to and sign an IEP before your child begins special education initially, and at least once each school year after that.
- Whenever you or your child's school district want to change your child's current IEP, the district must schedule a new IEP meeting and develop a new written IEP. You and the school district can agree to hold the meeting via video conference or conference call, or agree to make changes in the written IEP without an IEP meeting. (See "Rules for IEP Meetings," below.)
- You are entitled to an IEP meeting whenever you feel one is needed—for example, if you have concerns about your child's progress, there are classroom problems, or a related service or placement is not working.
- The IEP, once signed by you and the school district, is binding; the school district must provide everything included in that IEP.

This section provides details about the written IEP. Every IEP, in every school district in every state, must include the same information (although forms will vary).

Current Educational Status

The IEP must include a description of your child's current status in school in the areas of cognitive skills, linguistic ability, emotional behavior, social skills and behavior, and physical ability. (20 U.S.C. § 1414(d)(1)(A)(i).) Current functioning may be reflected in testing data, grades, reports, or anecdotal information, such as teacher observations. The IDEA calls this the "present levels of academic achievement and functional performance." This part of the IEP must describe how your child's disability affects his or her involvement and progress in the general curriculum. Formal testing or assessments of your child will provide a good deal of information.

RELATED TOPIC

Chapters 6 and 8 cover evaluations and other ways to develop useful evidence of your child's educational status and needs.

Rules for IEP Meetings

The 2004 amendments changed some of the rules for IEP meetings. Here are some of the 2004 provisions (Chapters 10 and 11 cover IEP meetings in detail):

- Changes to the IEP can now be made without a meeting, if both the parent and the school district agree and the changes are made in writing. If you decide to forgo an IEP meeting, you should make sure you understand the changes and that the written agreement reflects them accurately. (34 C.F.R. § 300.324(a)(4).)
- IEP meetings can now be held by video conference or conference call rather than in person. (34 C.F.R. § 300.328.)
- Members of the IEP team can be excused from attending in certain circumstances, if you agree to their absence. (34 C.F.R. § 300.321(e).)
- If a child transfers from one school district to another (in or out of state), the new school district must initially provide a program "comparable" to the one described in the existing IEP. (34 C.F.R. § 300.323.)

Measurable Annual Goals

Goals are the nuts and bolts of your child's daily program as detailed in the IEP. They generally refer to academic, linguistic, and other cognitive activities, such as reading or math.

> **EXAMPLE:**
> **Goal:** John will read a three-paragraph story and answer eight out of ten questions about the story correctly.

While goals are usually academic and cognitive in nature, there is no restriction on what goals may cover or say. They should reflect whatever the IEP team determines is important to your child's education. Goals can relate to physical education, how your child socializes with peers, even how your child will move about the school.

The IDEA refers to "measurable annual goals, including academic and functional goals" designed to meet your child's educational and other needs and enable him or her to be "involved in and make progress in the general education curriculum." The law requires your child's IEP to describe how yearly progress toward meeting these goals will be measured. (20 U.S.C. § 1414(d)(1)(A).) This is a change from the former version of the IDEA, which required the IEP team to come up with "benchmarks"—short-term objectives that would help a child achieve these larger goals. The new language seems broad enough to encompass short-term, specific objectives (although they won't be called by that name) as well as long-term goals. As to the term "measurable," an annual goal can be measured numerically, by teacher report, or any other method that is appropriate.

Whether your child is receiving a free appropriate public education (FAPE) may depend on whether the program offered by the school district can help him or her achieve the goals in the IEP. If you and the school district disagree about whether a specific placement or service is appropriate, one key issue will be whether your child's goals can be met without it.

RELATED TOPIC

Chapter 9 shows you how to write goals that support your child's placement and service needs.

Instructional Setting or Placement

The IEP must include information about the appropriate instructional setting or placement for your child. Here are a few examples of specific IEP placements:

EXAMPLES:

- A child with significant physical disabilities or learning disabilities might be placed in a regular classroom with support services.

- A child with significant language and cognitive delays might be placed in a special class.

- A child who is terrified of large spaces and crowds could be placed in a small, protected nonregular school.

- A child with serious emotional difficulties might be placed in a residential program.

Related Services

As discussed above, related services are the developmental, corrective, or supportive services necessary to facilitate your child's placement in a regular class or to allow your child to benefit from special education. These must be included specifically in the IEP.

Once the IEP team determines the appropriate related support services, the team should specify the nature of each service, including:

- when it begins
- the amount (such as all day, once a day, twice a week, once a week, or once a month)
- the duration (such as 15, 30, 45, or 60 minutes per session)
- the ratio of pupils to related service providers, and
- the qualifications of the service provider.

As noted earlier in this chapter under "Support or Related Services," the IDEA provides a specific list of possible related services (20 U.S.C. § 1401(26) and 34 C.F.R. § 300.34). It is certainly helpful that a specific service your child needs is on the list, but it's not absolutely necessary for a service to be listed. If you can prove that your child needs something not listed in order to benefit from and access his or her education, then the school district should provide it. One example might be equine therapy, which is not listed but has been shown to be of real benefit for children with special needs.

Other Required IEP Components

The IEP must also specifically address:
- how your child's disability affects his or her involvement and progress in the general curriculum used in the regular classroom
- how your child's need to be involved in the general curriculum will be met
- how special education and related services will help your child: advance toward attaining annual goals; be involved in the general curriculum, extracurricular, and nonacademic activities; and participate with children with and without disabilities
- whether any program modifications or supports for school personnel are necessary for your child to benefit from special education
- how you will be regularly informed of your child's progress
- how your child will participate in any district or statewide assessment of student achievement used for the general education population, and whether any modifications or accommodations will be necessary
- how your child's transition services will be provided (once your child is 16 years old), and
- how your child's need for assistive technology will be met.

For blind and visually impaired students, the IEP team must provide for instruction in Braille and the use of Braille, unless the IEP determines that Braille is not appropriate. (20 U.S.C. § 1414(d)(3)(B)(iii).)

In addition, IDEA requires that the IEP team "consider" the following:

- strategies, including positive behavioral interventions, to address the needs of children with behavior difficulties (20 U.S.C. § 1414(d)(3)(B)(i))
- the language needs of children with limited English proficiency (20 U.S.C. § 1414(d)(3)(B)(ii)), and
- the communication needs of deaf and hard of hearing children, including opportunities for direct communication with peers and staff, and instruction in the child's language and communication mode. (20 U.S.C. § 1414(d)(3)(B)(iv).)

For more details, contact your school district, your state department of education, or a disability group (Appendix B). See Appendix C for a sample IEP that includes these provisions. The appendixes are available on this book's Companion Page on Nolo.com. See Chapter 16 for the link.

Optional Components

The IEP may include other components, such as specific teaching methods, particular class subjects, or anything else the IEP team agrees should be included. (20 U.S.C. § 1414(d)(1)(A).)

EXAMPLES:

- An autistic child may be instructed in a method called Lovaas.

- A deaf child may be taught in American Sign Language.

The Importance of "Process"

The IDEA has very specific rules for assessments, eligibility determination, or notifying parents of their rights—basically, for the entire IEP process. Congress believed that establishing a clear procedure was as important, if not more important, than dictating specific IEP solutions for various situations. For example, instead of trying to anticipate and answer every possible special education scenario—"School district, follow this plan for a 14-year-old learning-disabled child, use this one for a seven-year-old learning-disabled student, and implement this one for a five-year-old vision-impaired student …"—the lawmakers decided that a clear diagnostic process would result in tailored plans that would better serve children with disabilities.

When Process Matters

A school district's refusal or failure to follow the rules can result in victories for the child. Here are some examples. Keep in mind that each case is heavily dependent on the precise facts presented to the judge—and no two cases are precisely alike.

In *Deal v. Hamilton*, 392 F.3d 840 (6th Cir. 2004), the school district had determined before the IEP meeting that the Lovaas method (a strategy for assisting autistic children) was "too expensive;" and also had issued an internal memo that this case was a "sensitive" one. A federal appellate court concluded that the district had predetermined it would not consider the Lovaas method, thereby depriving the parents of the opportunity to have a meaningful involvement in the development of their child's IEP.

In *W. G. v. Target Range*, 960 F.2d 1479 (9th Cir. 1992), the school district failed to reconvene to reconsider a student's eligibility for more than two years, and at the belated meeting, provided an already prepared IEP document. The appellate court concluded that these procedural violations were so significant that there was no need to go into whether the private school placement was appropriate.

Courts have handled many more cases involving procedural violations, including the failure to have a regular education teacher at the IEP meeting (as required by 34 C.F.R. § 300.321(a)(2)). For example, in *M.L. v. Federal Way School District*, 394 F.3d. 634 (9th Cir. 2004), the absence of a regular education teacher at the IEP meeting, and the failure of the IEP administrator in charge of making IEP decisions to have ever seen the child, were so serious as to render the process ineffective.

Keep in mind that in just as many cases, the facts did not support a finding of a procedural violation. And sometimes, even when a court finds that a violation has taken place, it concludes that the violation was not significant enough to trigger the "procedural rule."

But sometimes school districts fail to follow these rules. For example, school districts may fail to seek permission to assess a child, neglect to hold an IEP meeting every year as required, not provide a fair and open chance to discuss anything regarding your child at the IEP meeting, and fail to inform parents of placement options in the district. The district might not have the appropriate professionals at the IEP meeting; sometimes, even before the IEP meeting, they prematurely decide what they will provide.

When a school district violates any of the procedures of the IDEA, the violation itself may mean that the district has to do what you want for your child, regardless of whether you have sufficient evidence to prove your child needs the specific education program or services you're requesting. For example, suppose your child needs a particular related service and at the IEP meeting, the district representative says something like, "We don't offer those services," or "We've already decided your child does not need those services," or "No, we don't need to see the outside evaluation you had done about those services." These "the door is shut" statements violate the IEP's requirement that the meeting allow you a full and open chance to discuss your child's needs, without any predetermination by the district.

Or, perhaps you write the district to tell them that your child is having problems, and you would like them to evaluate her to determine whether she is eligible for special education. If the district refuses to assess her (or assesses her without your permission), those violations may be significant enough that your child would be found eligible, regardless of what the evidence showed. Violations are further discussed in Chapter 13.

When you have a dispute with your school district about some aspect of your child's IEP/education, it may be that you don't have a strong case. For example, you may want your child to have more of a particular related service, more time in a regular class, or even placement in a nonpublic school, and yet the evidence supporting that may not be strong. You may not be out of luck. A significant failure by your school or district to follow the "process" can render any dispute over educational services secondary. I want to stress the word "significant," because to result in your getting what you want for your child, the violation of process must directly impact your child's right to have an appropriate education or directly impact your ability to be part of the IEP process.

People often say that attorneys are always looking for technical failures to win a case, suggesting that the real "truth" of the dispute is never reached. We've all heard about the criminal who gets off on a technicality. But there are important reasons for focusing on procedural or "technical" requirements. This is particularly true in special education because the failure to provide the full "procedure" can have a very direct impact on your child's education.

Here are two examples of procedural violations, one not significant, the other significant.

> EXAMPLE 1. The school district provides a thorough IEP but a box is not correctly checked on a form. This is not likely going to be a significant procedural violation.

> EXAMPLE 2. You want your child placed in a regular classroom with an aide for the start of the new school year. The district does not hold an IEP meeting until midyear even though you have requested one over and over. Your child is unable to access the regular classroom for a significant amount of time. The procedural violation is significant and has had a direct educational consequence of importance.

Compensatory Education

When a school district fails to provide a child with a "free appropriate public education," including the placement, program, and/or services needed, the child may be entitled to "compensatory" education; that is, additional assistance to make up for the original failure. Compensatory education is not applicable when there is a disagreement between you and the district about some component of your child's IEP, but when the district fails to provide the IEP or violates IDEA procedures.

Compensatory education can take many forms and should relate directly to the child's individual needs. Compensatory ed. represents "replacement of educational services the child should have received in the first place" to place the child in the same position he or she would have been in if it weren't for the school's failure. (*Reid v. District of Columbia*, 365 U.S. App. D.C. 234, 401 F.3d 516, 518 [578] (D.C. Cir. 2005).)

Budgets and Cost Considerations Under the IDEA

The national education budget in the first decade of the 21st century was in the $800 billion range, with $110+ billion for special education. Approximately $12,000 was spent on average for a child in special education compared to $6,000 for students in regular education. The federal government covered only about $1,800 for each special education student, clearly way below the $12,000 average cost. In 2012, however, approximately $600 million was slashed from the federal special education budget due to sequestration.

Another sad truth is that state governments are facing rising deficits, which means that funding for schools is on the chopping block. As spending for education has decreased, many schools have had to cut back on educational programs and staff. Unfortunately, this means that some districts will make IEP decisions based on budgetary constraints rather than on educational need. While you need not be swayed by arguments about funding, don't be surprised to hear them.

This problem will only get worse until federal and state governments start funding education and special education commensurate with their importance in our society. Even as laws that impose stricter standards for students, teachers, and classroom size go into effect, schools aren't given the funding they need to implement these new requirements. Until parents and professionals unite to address this funding problem, legislators will continue to give education the short end of the fiscal stick.

The IDEA requires that your child receive a "free appropriate public education" and "free" is a central condition of that mandate. How should you deal with cost issues if they arise? Generally, the cost of your child's education cannot be the basis for an IEP decision. If a school administrator says that something cannot be provided because it costs too much, it's not in the budget, or providing it will mean taking services away from other students, simply say, "We are sympathetic to your financial restraints, but you know that the IDEA requires a 'free' public education. It also requires that cost is not supposed to be a factor in any IEP decisions. We should discuss my child's needs for [the features of your IEP plan] based on just that—*need*—not cost."

Budgets and Cost Considerations Under the IDEA (continued)

Be aware, however, that numerous courts have ruled that some programs or services are simply too expensive to force a school district to pay for them. These rulings often involve complex, medically related cases where a child needs expensive, ongoing services. In addition, if you want your child in a private program and the school district has a program that is very similar, if not entirely identical, the cost of the private placement can be raised as a bar to that placement. In such cases, you will have to prove that there's a clear difference between the programs to eliminate the cost factor.

What should you do regarding this issue? The IDEA is fundamentally an individual law, which means decisions about your child should be based exclusively or almost exclusively on his or her needs and not the school district's budget. If you feel money has been a determinant and your child is not offered an appropriate education because of it, you can challenge that—see Chapter 12.

Compensatory education may be payment of private school tuition, one-on-one tutoring, a classroom aide, or assistive technology support (one court ordered a school district to provide 608 hours of compensatory education through tech support).

Compensatory education can be provided after the student turns 21, but compensatory damages—money—is not usually available to make up for the school's failure to provide special education. Note that a failure to follow the procedures—a procedural violation—can have the same effect on a child as failing to provide services, and therefore may justify compensatory education. For example, a school fails to hold a timely IEP meeting and the student loses out on two months' of support. This procedural violation caused an educational failure, justifying compensatory education.

In short, a school district's procedural failures can be important—be sure to keep track of what your district does, how they respond to you, and how they otherwise follow the requirements of the IDEA.

Special Education Vouchers

The school voucher system—where parents can use government funding to pay for a private school—has grown in the United States, but it remains controversial in many ways. Some people feel it provides more choice at a time when public education is under increasing fire and subject to decreased funding. There is great irony here, for the very cost of vouchers may relate directly to the reduction in funding for public special education programs. In Wisconsin, for example, in 2013, Governor Scott Walker presented a budget that provided zero increase in funding for public school students while increasing taxpayer funding for private voucher school students by $1,400 per student. Some argue that vouchers help students from poor communities, while others argue that, because vouchers do not always cover all costs, especially for special education students, it is not serving those communities. While there is anecdotal information from parents that their child's individual voucher experience was positive, there is no current objective or statistical evidence that tells us on a large scale the level of success or failure for these programs.

The Conference of State Legislatures reports that the following states have voucher programs: Arizona, Arkansas, Florida, Georgia, Indiana, Louisiana, Maine, Mississippi, North Carolina, Ohio, Oklahoma, Utah, Vermont, Wisconsin, and the District of Columbia. These state voucher programs vary as to eligibility rules; in some states, vouchers are available only to students with disabilities and/or IEPs, while in other states, vouchers may be available to all low-income students or students in failing school districts. Vouchers are mandated by state law, so you need to check your state to see if there is even a voucher system in place.

Many states now have voucher systems in place for special education students, though most still do not. But the move toward making special education students eligible for vouchers is a developing matter.

Each state that has a voucher system for special ed students has its own unique requirements, statutory language, and rules regarding special education students and vouchers. Not all states provide for vouchers for all IDEA eligibility categories. A few states limit voucher programs to students with autism, blindness or visual impairments, deafness or hearing impairments, intellectual disability, orthopedic impairments, or traumatic brain injury, leaving out students with emotional disturbances or ADD/ADHD.

If you are interested in a voucher for your child with special education needs, it is important you consider the following:

- **IDEA rights.** If you place your child in a private program via a voucher, you are almost certainly giving up your child's rights under the IDEA. Voucher schools are not required to follow or implement a child's IEP and they are not subject to the Individuals with Disabilities Education Act (IDEA). The U.S. Department of Education, Civil Rights Division, has confirmed that by accepting a voucher, families are giving up their IDEA rights. Some states, such as Georgia, require a formal and written waiver that you understand you are giving up your rights under the IDEA.

- **IEPs.** Voucher schools are not required to follow or implement a child's IEP. In Georgia, for example, the private school does not continue the child's IEP and has no retesting or eligibility requirements. But in Wisconsin, private schools participating in the voucher programs do need to provide assessments. You should ask whether the private school will honor and continue some or any of your child's existing public IEP.

- **ADA and assisted technology or therapy.** Some private schools may not be accountable for the requirements under the Americans with Disabilities Act, and may not be wheelchair accessible. And in Wisconsin, for example, private schools that accept voucher students are not required to provide any therapies or assisted technology.

- **Teacher qualifications.** Be sure to find out the qualifications, if any, of the private school's teachers and staff. In Indiana, for example, private schools accepting vouchers are not required to have a teacher certified to work with special education students. (The *Washington Post* reported that, of the 3,200 Indiana students eligible for vouchers, 80% chose to stay in public school.) Likewise, in Wisconsin, private schools that accept vouchers are not required to have qualified special educators or therapists on staff.

- **Oversight.** There is usually no state or other formal oversight of the private schools that take special education "voucher" students.
- **Voucher amounts.** Find out how much the available voucher is for and whether it will cover all of the tuition and costs. Georgia's vouchers, for example, average $5,396 per student; it may be that a private school that accepts vouchers costs a good deal more than the state allotment. In Ohio, parents are also liable for costs above the state allotment. Louisiana's voucher law covers only about 50% of private school costs for special education students. In that same state, 14 private schools that serve children with autism have fees above what the state provides; this particularly hits families with lower incomes.
- **Related services.** Be sure to find out if the voucher covers all related services. In Georgia, for instance, you, and not the public school district, are responsible for transportation to the private school. In Ohio, students with speech and language challenges can receive a voucher for related services but not for tuition.
- **Returning to public school.** Be sure to ask your school district what happens if you decide to return your child to a public school. Will the previous IEP be honored?
- **Proof of use of funds.** Voucher states may require proof of the use of public monies for a private school, including receipts.

It is this author's considered advice that you should do significant research, talk to your state department of education, and talk to other parents to be fully informed regarding all voucher issues. Like many "products" offered to the public, the fine print is not always front and center. Personally, I would also have concerns about any educational program that is run on a for-profit basis and employs less qualified, less well-paid teachers. You should also check on whether your state voucher program has been legally challenged. Some state courts have found their state's voucher law to be unconstitutional. Be thorough, vigilant, and fully educated on all aspects of your state's special education voucher law.

Working With Your School District

Most, if not all, of your dealings will be with your local public school district, which has the legal responsibility for your child's IEP. Sometimes, however, special education programs are the responsibility of a larger educational unit, such as a county office of education. This is often the case when a school district is small.

The agency that you will have to work with, whether it's your local school district or the county office of education, is referred to as the local educational agency (LEA), and it can vary from state to state. Always start with the school district in which you reside. It has the ultimate responsibility for your child, even if there is a larger, area-wide agency involved. As used in this book, the term "local school district" refers to whatever educational unit is involved.

Key Players in the IEP Process

The key participants in the IEP process are:
- you
- your child (if appropriate)
- your child's teacher (potentially the best ally or worst enemy you have in the IEP process), whether a regular teacher or a special education teacher
- a school administrator with responsibility for special education —a site principal or special education administrator
- specialists, such as a school psychologist, speech or occupational therapist, communications specialist, or physical education specialist, and
- anyone else you or the school want to participate, such as your child's physician, your lawyer, the school's evaluator, or an outside independent evaluator you selected.

RELATED TOPIC
Chapter 10 covers the IEP participants in detail, including who has the critical roles, who has authority, and who should attend the IEP meetings.

Teacher Certification Requirements

When Congress amended the IDEA in 2004, it added language to conform the requirements of the IDEA with the requirements of No Child Left Behind (NCLB), the education law passed in 2001. (For more on NCLB, see "No Child Left Behind," below.) The IDEA now provides that any public elementary or secondary school special education teacher in your state must have:

- obtained "full" state certification as a special education teacher
- passed the state special education licensing examination, or
- completed valid state "alternative" certification requirements and hold a license to teach in your state. (20 U.S.C. § 1401(10).)

This rule does not apply to special education teachers in private or charter schools.

More Information: Special Education Laws

Your school district is required by the IDEA to provide you with a copy of federal and state statutes and regulations, and any relevant policies. Be sure to request this information, along with the school's IEP form. Most school districts have some kind of parent guide, as do most states. Contact your school district for a copy.

You can find the addresses, phone numbers, and websites of state departments of education through the U.S. Department of Education website at www.ed.gov. I highly recommend that you get a copy of any publications explaining your legal rights from your state department of education (many are online). Ask about the state special education advisory commission—the IDEA requires that each state have one, composed of educators and parents.

Because laws and policies change, it is important to keep up to date, especially if you are involved in a dispute with your school. For more information on legal research, see Chapter 14.

The Realities of Schools and Special Education

School districts and their special education administrators are as varied as parents. Their programs, services, and budgets will differ, as will their personalities. All of these factors influence the programs school districts offer and how they deal with children and parents. Depending on the population breakdown in the district, there may be many special education programs or only a few. Philosophical differences may have an impact on programs and services. Some administrators believe very firmly that most, if not all, children with disabilities should be mainstreamed in regular education. Some administrators believe with equal vigor that special programs are important and that children with disabilities, more often than not, belong in special classes.

Demonizing the "Other" Side

It is not uncommon for parents to view school administrators and other staff as impediments rather than partners in the special education process. Sometimes school personnel return the favor by viewing parents as unreasonable and difficult.

While there are times when such viewpoints are justified, remember that a majority of educators are passionate, hard-working, and caring individuals. They teach in a complicated environment with too much paperwork, too many requirements, and not enough support or pay. Demonizing all teachers or administrators does little more than polarize everyone—and your child is the one who will suffer from these strained relationships. Viewing everyone associated with the school as an enemy is a poor strategy for getting your child's needs met. And in most cases, it's simply not fair.

Of course, you should be vigilant and stick up for your rights, but remember that most folks on the other side of the table are there because they believe in your child. In return, you should expect those hard-working educators to see you as the determined, loving, and concerned parent that you are.

Who Is to Blame?

I am a parent of two children who had enormous challenges in school and over many years. There were times that I felt the school had failed, did not understand, or was so lost in a hundred other issues that my children were not being fully served.

When you find yourself in a similar situation, it's important to be as objective as possible about the school district's failures. This can be a difficult matter for any parent of a child with a disability, especially when there are situations where a district has certainly failed abysmally and even took action or failed to take action that had a direct negative impact on a child. I can even point to a few situations where a school district, willingly or otherwise, deeply harmed a child and exacerbated the difficulties the child experienced. In short, the child did "get worse" because of those district failures.

However, it is rare that the entire picture that is the difficulties of your child (or mine) is due entirely to the school district's misfeasance or malfeasance. I have had clients who see their children's problems as 100% the fault of the district, refusing to take into account all the many components that make up any individual, including but not limited to biology, environment, early traumas, and so on. The complex story of your child and the "why" is not a zero-sum situation.

Ultimately, I believe that taking the view that your child's current condition is entirely and only due to the school will not only make it difficult to develop the right strategy for success and make the relationship with the district even more tenuous, but it might also obscure issues that need addressing.

Try your best to see things as objectively as possible and try not to demonize educators. Most educators that I have dealt with over many decades don't go into this field to do harm. They may be beaten down or even just nasty, but most are not trying to injure your child. Remembering this can help you get where you need to in the IEP process.

Finding out what programs are in your district, and what personalities and philosophies you'll face, is important. Ask around. Talk to your child's teacher and other parents; go to PTA meetings. Many school districts have community advisory committees for special education; the parents involved in that group can be invaluable resources and will likely know the specific programs and approaches in your school district.

> RELATED TOPIC
>
> Chapter 8 provides detailed advice on how to explore available school programs. Chapter 15 discusses parent groups.

Some Overriding IEP Principles

In any endeavor, the details—particularly technical matters and legal language—can be overwhelming: IEP, due process, least restrictive environment, related services. What do these terms really mean, and how can you use them to help your child?

As you go through this book and the IEP process, you will become more familiar and comfortable with IEP terms. Particularly in the early stages of your planning, keep your focus on the following key factors.

Your Child's Needs Dictate the Contents of the IEP

The IDEA uses the term "unique" to describe your child's needs. As emphasized in this chapter, the IEP must fit the child, not the other way around. Practically speaking, this means that if your child needs a small class (fewer than ten children), a teacher with specific skills, and a variety of support services, then your local school district is required to provide them. Always ask whether a particular goal, service, placement, or other IEP component is providing your child with a free appropriate public education as required by law, and is serving his or her unique needs.

Factors Determining Individual Need

Your child's age, disability, and specific needs—academic, social, linguistic, emotional, cognitive, and physical—are key elements in determining the IEP. Of course, other factors may come into play, including necessary educational strategies, methodologies, and curricula.

Specific Classroom and Instructional Services

Your child's needs must translate into specific support or related services and a specific class or program. All the discussion in the world about unique needs will be meaningless if you and the IEP team don't eventually discuss (and come to terms on) placement and services.

Broad Discretion in Determining the IEP

It is human nature to want specificity. At some level, we may have liked Congress to have said exactly what should be part of a special education program, and what should go into the IEP. But in passing the IDEA, Congress knew it could not say specifically what should be in an IEP for child #1 or #999 or #99,999. There are too many variables and too many individual considerations.

That is why the IDEA does not say that a child with disabilities will be placed in a particular program with particular services. Instead, the unique needs of each child must determine what specific program and services are required. Thus, the IEP team has broad discretion. This flexibility is good for you, but also requires hard work and preparation on your part.

Section 504 of the Rehabilitation Act of 1973

Separate from any rights under the IDEA, your child may also qualify for special services under the Rehabilitation Act of 1973 (29 U.S.C. § 794), more commonly known as Section 504. This is essentially an access law that prohibits a school district from denying your child access to an educational program or educational facilities. For more information on Section 504, see Chapter 7.

No Child Left Behind

In 2001, Congress passed education legislation called "No Child Left Behind" (NCLB). When amending the IDEA in 2004, Congress added language to align it with the requirements of NCLB, primarily by imposing standards for special education teacher qualifications and emphasizing the teaching of "core academic subjects": English, reading or language arts, math, science, foreign languages, civics and government, economics, arts, history, and geography.

NCLB's stated purpose was to increase "accountability" for schools by requiring rigorous state educational standards in reading and math and by mandating state testing to determine whether children are meeting those standards. Test results must be broken out by race, ethnicity, income, English proficiency, and disability. School districts that don't show yearly progress, as reflected in standards and testing, are subject to corrective action and possibly even forced restructuring. Children who attend schools that are not making yearly progress have the opportunity to transfer to other schools, including charter schools, and to obtain supplemental services.

The effects of NCLB remain uncertain because of its complex requirements and the federal government's failure to adequately fund the law. Some states have tried to "opt out" of NCLB's provisions, primarily because the law imposes major requirements without the funds necessary to implement them. Some advocates worry that the lack of funding provided for NCLB could result in fewer dollars available for all educational programs, including special education. It isn't clear exactly how NCLB's mandates will affect special education.

Further clarification of the meaning of NCLB has emerged as the U.S. Department of Education and courts have addressed the requirements of the law. Thus far, one court has decided that the NCLB rule that only 2% of the student population can take "alternative tests" is superior to the core IDEA rule that each child's IEP, including any testing, must be made on an individual basis. Unfortunately, this ruling limiting the number of students taking alternative tests to 2% will almost certainly exclude some special education students who need an alternative test, particularly because the special education population is about 10%. On another front, the U.S. Department of

No Child Left Behind (continued)

Education concluded that the NCLB requirement that a teacher be "highly qualified" applies to public, but not private, school teachers. If your child is in special education and was placed in a private program, the teachers in that private program need not be highly qualified. The majority of states have agreed to adopt certain education ideas, such as tying teacher evaluations to student test scores and flexibility from some of the basic mandates of the law.

Getting Started: Tips for All Parents

If your child has had a disability since birth or from a young age—perhaps he or she is in a wheelchair and needs support to access a regular classroom, is developmentally disabled, has difficulty writing, or has a hearing loss or reduced vision—you've probably known for a while that your child would need special education.

If you've just recently realized that your child is having difficulty in school—from a simple problem with reading or math to a profound problem involving cognitive functioning or emotional difficulties—you may not have given much thought to special education. Perhaps a teacher, pediatrician, neighbor, or friend has pointed something out to you. The recognition may come as a surprise or even a shock. What does this mean for your child's immediate educational experience? What does it mean for the future? Will your child now be labeled—as learning disabled, visually impaired, emotionally disturbed?

In any case, the process you are about to embark on can be hard and frustrating. There may be times when dealing with the school makes life tough. Your child's difficulties may persist or even get worse. Sometimes, the problems may seem insurmountable. There may be a teacher shortage, insufficient school funds, or flawed program options. For all your preparation, you may feel like you're getting nowhere.

You may ask yourself why this happened to your family. But if you plan, organize, and persevere, if you take small, daily steps (rather than try to solve the problem in one fell swoop), you will help your child. You may not make the school experience perfect, or even always tolerable, but your child will benefit from your efforts.

Whether you, your child's teacher, or another professional discovers the difficulty, your school district has a clear legal responsibility under the IDEA to ensure that all children with special education needs within the district are identified, located, and evaluated (see Chapter 2). Usually, this means (or should mean) that your child's teacher or the school principal, or perhaps the school psychologist, will contact you, indicate the areas of initial concern, and perhaps suggest a meeting to discuss these concerns. The school will then likely recommend an evaluation by a specialist in your child's disability. The evaluation is the first major step toward special education eligibility and the development of an IEP. (Chapter 6 discusses evaluations in detail.)

Parents of Children Between Three and Five Years Old

If your child is between ages three and five and is not yet enrolled in school, contact the local school district if you believe your child has a disability. Your child may be entitled to services under the IDEA even before starting school. To be eligible, your child must be experiencing delays in physical, cognitive, communication, social, emotional, or adaptive development. (20 U.S.C. § 1401(3)(B).) If your child is found eligible, the IDEA rules and IEP procedures outlined in this book will apply.

Even though your school district has the responsibility to start the process, you shouldn't wait for the school to contact you if you have concerns. If you suspect that your child has special education needs and you haven't heard from the school district, get in touch with them. This chapter will help you get things started.

SKIP AHEAD

If your child has already been found eligible for special education or you have had experience with the IEP process, you can skip "First Steps," below. Even if you have been through the IEP process, however, be sure to read the discussion in the subsequent section about securing your child's records. Many intelligent and determined parents who have been through numerous IEPs have not taken this important step.

First Steps

What's the first thing you should do if you believe your child is eligible for special education? This section provides some suggestions on how to get started.

Recognize Your Child's Special Needs

It is very common for parents to realize that their child has unique needs and simply not know what to do about it. It may be that your child's problems can be isolated and addressed very specifically, or the problems may be more serious. But don't assume the worst; let the information you gather determine how serious the matter is and what you should do about it.

Start by focusing on your child's specific difficulties. Think back and consider whether your child has experienced any of the following:

- academic problems in reading, spelling, or math
- delays in developmental areas, such as language or fine motor skills
- difficulties processing or retaining information, such as understanding simple instructions, or problems with short- or long-term memory
- social or emotional problems
- trouble sleeping, eating, or getting along with the family
- sustained difficulties in paying attention or staying focused
- inappropriate or hyperactive behavior, or
- delays in physical milestones or other physiological difficulties, such as hearing loss, sight problems, difficulties with mobility, or handwriting problems.

Write down what you can remember about your child's past behavior or what you've observed recently. Try to think clearly, focusing on specific behavior patterns. You may feel some emotional upheaval or fear; you may even worry that you have done something wrong. These feelings are normal. Almost everyone who has had a child in special education has felt exactly as you do right now.

A child who is having difficulty in school will not automatically qualify for special education. There may be interim steps or non-special-education solutions for your child. Those steps are discussed below.

At this stage, you may also want to contact the school principal to request information about special education.

FORM

A sample letter requesting information on special education is below; a blank downloadable copy is available on this book's Companion Page on www.nolo.com. See Chapter 16 for the link.

TIP

Get into the habit of writing. You can always request information about special education by calling the school principal, who is likely to either provide the information or refer you to the district's special education administrator. But it's better to make your request in writing. A letter is more formal, won't be forgotten as easily as a phone call, and creates a record of your contact with your school district. In this book, you will be reminded frequently of the importance of putting things in writing.

Make a Formal Request to Start the Special Education Process

At any time, you can formally ask to begin the process of special education evaluation. To start:

- Call your school and ask for the name and phone number of the special education administrator.
- Call the special education administrator and ask about the eligibility process in the district.
- Follow up your phone call with a written request (and keep a copy for your records).

FORM

A sample letter making a formal request to start the special education process and conduct an evaluation is below; a blank, downloadable copy is available on this book's Companion Page on www.nolo.com. See Chapter 16 for the link. Other sample letters in this chapter make slightly different requests. You can combine some or all of these requests into one letter, if you wish.

Gather Information

Whether you plan to begin the formal evaluation process right away or wait a bit, you should start gathering information on your child's situation. Here are some good ways to start.

Talk to Your Child's Teacher

Find out what your child's teacher thinks is going on and recommends as a possible solution. Here are a few specific questions to ask:

- What are the teacher's observations? What are the most outstanding and obvious problems, and how serious are they? Is it a problem with math, reading, or broader cognitive issues (processing information or memory lags)? Does the problem have social or emotional manifestations?
- Would some adjustments in the classroom help, such as extra attention from the teacher, after-school tutoring, or measures to address behavioral problems?
- What activities might be useful at home? Does the teacher think that you need to spend more time on homework, walking your child through certain subject matters?
- What are the observations, conclusions, and recommendations of other school personnel?
- Are your child's difficulties serious? Do they require more formal special education involvement? If so, what are the next steps?

If you and the school agree to go ahead with interim, non-special-education steps, be sure to monitor your child's progress closely so you can determine whether they are working. Chapter 8 provides suggestions about tracking your child's progress.

Talk to Your Child's Pediatrician

Your child may have an organic or medical problem. Although most pediatricians are not experts in special education, they can discuss a child's developmental stage, health-related matters that affect the educational experience, and other cognitive, physical, linguistic, and emotional factors that might impact special education eligibility and possible educational solutions.

Request for Information on Special Education

Date: February 20, 20xx

To: Ronald Pearl, Principal

Mesa Verde Elementary School

123 San Pablo Avenue

San Francisco, CA 94110

Re: Amber Jones, student in 2nd grade class

of Cynthia Rodriguez

I am writing to you because my child is experiencing difficulties in school. I understand there is a process for evaluating a child and determining eligibility for special education programs and services. Please send me any written information you have about that process. Please also send me information about how I can contact other parents and local support groups involved in special education.

Thank you very much for your kind assistance. I look forward to talking with you further about special education.

Sincerely,

Mary Jones

Mary Jones

243 Ocean Avenue

San Francisco, CA 94110

Phones: 555-1234 (home); 555-2678 (work)

Talk With Other Parents

The local PTA should have information on parents with special education children; most school districts also have advisory committees of parents with children in special education. Call the school principal to find out about these groups.

> **RELATED TOPIC**
> Chapter 15 explains how to find or start a parents' group. Appendix B on this book's Companion Page on www.nolo.com has information on various national special education support groups. See Chapter 16 for the link.

Do Some Research

Look for written materials on special education and your child's area of difficulty. A wealth of information is available online.

> **RELATED TOPIC**
> For information on special education materials and organizations, both general and disability specific, go to this book's Companion Page on www.nolo.com. See Chapter 16 for the link.

Obtain Your Child's School Records

As a part of your information gathering, it's important to find out what is in your child's school file and what effect it will have on the IEP process. You'll need this information to assess the seriousness of your child's difficulties and the possible need for special education. If your child is found eligible for special education, reviewing the school file will help you determine the services and programs that may be appropriate.

Whether you are new at this or have been through many IEPs, whether you anticipate a major change in your child's educational program or no change at all, and even if you're not sure that you want your child in special education in the first place, it is important to secure copies of your child's school file on a yearly basis. New and important items may be added each year.

Request to Begin Special Education Process and Evaluation

Date: _February 20, 20xx_

To: _Ronald Pearl, Principal_

mesa Verde Elementary School

123 San Pablo Avenue

San Francisco, CA 94110

Re: _Amber Jones, student in 2nd grade class_

of Cynthia Rodriguez

I am writing to you because my child is experiencing difficulties in school.

[Describe specific difficulties your child is exhibiting].

I am formally requesting that the school immediately begin its special education process, including initial evaluation for eligibility. I understand that you will send me an evaluation plan that explains the tests that may be given to my child. Because I realize the evaluation can take some time, I would appreciate receiving the evaluation plan within ten days. Once you receive my approval for the evaluation, please let me know when the evaluation will be scheduled.

I would also appreciate any other information you have regarding the evaluation process, how eligibility is determined, and general IEP procedures.

Thank you very much for your kind assistance. I look forward to working with you and your staff.

Sincerely,

Mary Jones

mary Jones

243 Ocean Avenue

San Francisco, CA 94110

Phones: 555-1234 (home); 555-2678 (work)

While the contents of your child's file may vary, it is likely it will contain:

- report cards and other progress reports
- medical data (immunization records, health reports)
- attendance records
- disciplinary reports
- testing data
- evaluations and other testing material
- teacher comments and other observations, and
- pictures of your child (it's fun to see the kindergarten picture, the second grade picture with the missing teeth, and so on).

Your child's file may or may not include emails about your child. While you should ask for all emails, there is no guarantee the district will provide them. In one case, the court ruled that the emails had to be "maintained" for them to be available and so, if they are removed from the file or the system, there is no duty to produce them. Of course, it never hurts to ask.

Your Right to Access Your Child's School File

You have a legal right to inspect and review any education records relating to your child. If your child is already in the special education system, you have this right under IDEA. (20 U.S.C. § 1415(b)(1).) The rules in this section refer to children already in the special education system.

> **TIP**
>
> **Getting records for kids who aren't in special education.** If your child has not yet been found eligible for special education, you still have a legal right to his or her file under the Family Educational Rights and Privacy Act (FERPA). (20 U.S.C. § 1232(g).) FERPA is a federal statute. The purposes of FERPA are twofold: to ensure that parents have access to their children's educational records and to protect the privacy rights of parents and children by limiting access to these records without parental consent. FERPA applies to all agencies and institutions that receive federal funds, including elementary and secondary schools, colleges, and universities.

State law may also provide a right to your child's file, separate from the IDEA or FERPA rights. State law can vary, however, and you should find out the specifics—such as how requests should be made and how much time the school has to provide you with the file. Call your state department of education or your school district for information regarding these rules.

How to Get Copies of Your Child's File

When seeking a copy of your child's school file, make a written request for *everything*. The written request should go to the administrator in your school district who is responsible for special education. That may be the school principal or a person in your district's central office. The site principal can refer you to the appropriate person.

FORM
A sample letter requesting your child's school file is below; a blank, downloadable copy is available on this book's Companion Page on www.nolo.com. See Chapter 16 for the link.

The IDEA requires your child's school to grant your request without unnecessary delay and before any IEP meeting. The school must send you the file within 45 days, although it can and should send it more quickly. (See 34 C.F.R. § 300.613(a) of the IDEA regulations.) The Family Educational Rights and Privacy Act includes the same 45-day deadline.

If you have any problem getting a copy of your child's school file in a timely manner:

- Call and write the appropriate administrator, indicating that the law requires the school to provide the records without "unnecessary delay."
- If the principal or administrator does not respond to your request, contact the school district superintendent and your state department of education. Failure to provide you with your child's records is a violation of the law. Chapter 13 covers procedures for handling legal violations by your district.

Request for Child's School File

Date: <u>March 3, 20xx</u>

To: <u>Ronald Pearl, Principal</u>

<u>Mesa Verde Elementary School</u>

<u>123 San Pablo Ave.</u>

<u>San Francisco, CA 94110</u>

Re: <u>Amber Jones, student in second-grade class</u>

<u>of Cynthia Rodriguez</u>

I would like a copy of my child's file, including all tests, reports, evaluations, grades, notes by teachers or other staff members, memoranda, photographs—in short, *everything* in my child's school file. I understand I have a right to these files under

<u>The IDEA, specifically 20 U.S.C. § 1415(b)(1) [or the Family</u>

<u>Educational Rights and Privacy Act (FERPA) (20 U.S.C. § 1232 (g)) if</u>

<u>your child has not yet been found eligible for special education].</u>

I would greatly appreciate having these files within the next five days. I would be happy to pick them up. I will call you to discuss how and when I will get the copies.

Thank you for your kind assistance.

Sincerely,

Mary Jones

<u>Mary Jones</u>

<u>243 Ocean Ave.</u>

<u>San Francisco, CA 94110</u>

<u>Phones: 555-1234 (home); 555-2678 (work)</u>

TIP

Some states have tighter deadlines. Your state special education law may give schools a shorter deadline to provide copies of your child's record than the 45-day limit provided by the IDEA. California schools, for example, must provide copies of the record within five business days of a parent's request. Get a copy of your state's special education laws from your department of education early on so you know your rights—and cite the law when you request your child's file.

Cost of Getting Files

Under IDEA regulations, the school may charge a fee for making copies of your child's records, as long as the fee "does not effectively prevent the parents from exercising their rights to inspect and review those records." (34 C.F.R. § 300.617.) This means that you cannot be charged an excessively high fee—or *any fee at all* if you can show you cannot afford it. In addition, the school cannot charge a fee for searching and retrieving records.

If your child is not in special education, any fee for records might violate the Rehabilitation Act of 1973 (29 U.S.C. § 794) and the federal Freedom of Information Act. At least one court (*Tallman v. Cheboygan Area Schools*, 454 N.W.2d 171 (Mich. App. 1990)) has said that charging a fee for search and retrieval would violate the Freedom of Information Act.

While some districts can be very uncooperative about providing free copies of your child's file, others provide them as a matter of course. If your district charges you an excessive fee for searching and retrieving the file or charges you when you can't afford to pay a fee, write a letter to your administrator.

Go for the Copies

The IDEA allows you to inspect and review your child's school file as well as receive copies. (34 C.F.R. § 300.613.) These are two different rights—and you should exercise them both. You should always get copies of your child's file. If you can, you should also go to the school and review the original file, just to make sure the school district gave you everything.

What to Look for in Your Child's School File

Items that you are likely to find in your child's file are listed at the beginning of this section. As you review those documents, look for any information about your child's performance and needs, as well as comments from teachers and other professionals.

Request for Reduction or Waiver of Fee Charged for Child's School File

---

Date: March 20, 20xx

To: Ronald Pearl, Principal
Mesa Verde Elementary School
123 San Pablo Ave.
San Francisco, CA 94110

Re: Amber Jones, student in second-grade class of Cynthia Rodriguez

On March 3, 20xx, I requested copies of everything in my child's school file. Your secretary called me on March 19, 20xx, and stated that there would be a fee for the copies [or an excessive fee, or a fee for searching and retrieving]. The IDEA specifically states that you cannot charge a fee if it prevents me from exercising my right to inspect and review my child's file. I am on a fixed income and I cannot afford the fee you are charging.

[or: The IDEA prohibits you from charging such a high fee. A fee of 15¢ a copy seems fair, not $1 a copy.]

[or: The IDEA specifically prohibits you from charging a fee for searching for and retrieving the files.]

Therefore, I would appreciate it if you would send me copies, at no cost, at once. Thank you for your kind attention to this matter.

Mary Jones
Mary Jones
243 Ocean Ave.
San Francisco, CA 94110
Phones: 555-1234 (home); 555-2678 (work)

RELATED TOPIC
Chapter 4 discusses in greater detail how to organize your child's records.

Amending Your Child's File

You have the right to request that any false, inaccurate, or misleading information, or information that violates the privacy or other rights of your child, be amended or removed from your child's school file. (34 C.F.R. § 300.618.)

Your child's file is confidential and any "personally identifiable data, information, and records collected or maintained" must be protected. (34 C.F.R. § 300.610.) Your school district also has to provide you with a list of the "types and locations" of those files. (34 C.F.R. § 300.616.)

If the school refuses to amend or remove the information, you have the right to a due process hearing on the issue. (See Chapter 12.)

FORM
A sample request to amend the child's school file is below; a blank, downloadable copy is available on this book's Companion Page on www.nolo.com. See Chapter 16 for the link.

Harassment

Student bullying and harassment have increased significantly over the last ten years, and students in special education have not been spared. There are several issues you should be aware of regarding student harassment and bullying:

The states and federal government have enacted laws that identify bullying as a problem and establish procedures for dealing with it.

Request to Amend Child's School File

Date: _April 2, 20xx_

To: Ronald Pearl, Principal

Mesa Verde Elementary School

123 San Pablo Ave.

San Francisco, CA 94110

Re: Amber Jones, student in second-grade class

of Cynthia Rodriguez

I recently reviewed a copy of my child's file and would like to have a portion of the file amended, specifically:

The memorandum from the school psychologist, Ms. Taylor, stating that my child had severe emotional problems is inaccurate and inappropriate because Ms. Taylor did no testing and only briefly observed my child. This is insufficient to support the conclusion she reached.

The IDEA gives me the right to request that all information that is "inaccurate or misleading or violates the privacy or other rights of [my] child" be amended. (34 C.F.R. § 300.618.) I feel that this is just such a case and, therefore, request that you rectify the situation immediately.

Please notify me in writing as soon as possible of your decision regarding this matter. Thank you.

Sincerely,

Mary Jones

Mary Jones

243 Ocean Ave.

San Francisco, CA 94110

Phones: 555-1234 (home); 555-2678 (work)

State laws include those that require school districts to have antibullying policies; for example, Maryland's antibullying law states that each county board must establish a policy "prohibiting bullying, harassment, and intimidation" in consultation with parents, school staff, school volunteers, students, and members of the community. (Md. Code Ann., Educ. § 7-424.1(c).)

States define what constitutes bullying. North Carolina's law provides that bullying or harassing behavior includes acts "reasonably perceived as being motivated by any actual or perceived differentiating characteristic, such as race, color, religion, ancestry, national origin, gender, socioeconomic status, academic status, gender identity, physical appearance, sexual orientation, or mental, physical, developmental, or sensory disability, or by association with a person who has or is perceived to have one or more of these characteristics." (N.C. Gen. Stat. § 115C-407.15(a).) California's law requires local education agencies to adopt policies prohibiting harassment, intimidation, and bullying and procedures for reporting and investigating complaints of such actions. (California Ed. Code § 234.1.)

States also create responsibilities for school districts to take specific action to identify bullying and establish procedures for taking appropriate action against the perpetrators of bullying. For example, in Massachusetts, the law requires that, after receiving a report that bullying occurred, the school principal or a designee must promptly conduct an investigation. If the school staff determines that bullying or retaliation has occurred, the staff member must take appropriate disciplinary action, notify the parents or guardians of a perpetrator, notify the parents or guardians of the victim, and notify the local law enforcement agency if the staff member believes that criminal charges may be pursued against a perpetrator. Also, to the extent consistent with state and federal law, the school must notify the parents of the victim of the action taken to prevent any further acts of bullying or retaliation. (Mass. Adv. Legis. Serv. Ch. No. 71.37O(g).)

States also have requirements for training, preventive education, monitoring, and reporting.

Bullying and harassment can be particularly serious for students with disabilities, who may be less equipped than others to understand

and deal effectively with bullying. The U.S. Department of Education has issued guidance on bullying ("USOSEP Dear Colleague: Bullying of Students with Disabilities") to ensure that students with disabilities who are subject to bullying continue to receive free appropriate public education (FAPE) under the IDEA.

It is important to stress here that bullying, in addition to being deleterious for a child, can directly impact whether he or she can benefit from education and therefore be provided a "free appropriate public education." In a New York case, the district court developed a four-part test to determine when bullying results in a denial of a FAPE (see the *T.K. v. New York City Dep't of Education* case in Chapter 14).

If your child is facing harassment or bullying, it is crucial to:
- secure up-to-date information about the harassment itself
- have an updated assessment to detail the impact of that harassment, and
- have an IEP meeting to develop very specific goals and procedures for ending the bullying but also to discuss a process for dealing immediately and effectively with ongoing bullying.

Your child's IEP should include who will be responsible for identifying and responding to the bullying, what supportive services will be available for your child, what procedures will be in place to deal with the perpetrators, and, perhaps as important, a clear and strong school training process whereby staff and students are trained in recognizing and understanding bullying.

There are increasing numbers of lawsuits by students who have suffered emotional reactions to bullying and even have committed suicide. In one case, a student was harassed daily until, sadly, he killed himself. The school district where the bullying occurred is being sued for $20 million dollars for failure to supervise.

There is a good deal of information on the Internet on the subject of bullying. For instance, see the National Bullying Prevention Center's website at www.pacer.org/bullying and Stomp Out Bullying's website at https://stompoutbullying.org. You can also find information online regarding bullying by staff, including teachers and coaches; see the Kids in the House website at www.kidsinthehouse.com/teenager/bullying.

Getting Organized

W hether you are entering special education for the first time or preparing for your child's tenth IEP, you will be dealing with many issues and tasks, and vast amounts of written material. This chapter will help you organize the information you'll need throughout the IEP process. It also explains how to most effectively plan your IEP year.

Gathering information, getting organized, and figuring out what should go into your child's program are all related. If you haven't yet read Chapter 3, be sure to review the section on securing your child's school file before proceeding. When you get to Chapter 5 on developing an IEP blueprint for your child's ideal program and services, you will use much of the information from this chapter.

Use the Forms in This Book

Nearly two dozen sample forms, checklists, and letters appear throughout this book, with blank, downloadable copies available on this book's Companion Page on www.nolo.com. See Chapter 16 for the link. You can simply print and insert the relevant forms into your IEP binder—either as a separate section or in one of the major sections listed below. The IEP blueprint (discussed in Chapter 5) is one key document you should include as a separate section in your binder. Another is the IEP Material Organizer Form (discussed in Chapter 10), which you'll use to highlight key information in your binder and easily access your materials during the IEP meeting. These and other forms have spaces for far more information than you'll be ready to provide right now. That's okay. You're just getting started. It's perfectly fine to leave many of the form sections blank. You can fill them in later, as you read this book and get into the IEP process.

Start an IEP Binder

Many parents have found a simple three-ring binder with clearly labeled sections to be an invaluable organizing tool. A binder allows you to keep everything in one convenient location—from report cards to IEP forms.

Include every important document in your IEP binder. What's an important document? Anything containing substantive information about your child or procedural information concerning how and when things happen in the IEP process. While certain items can probably go into a file drawer, if you have any doubt, add them to your binder.

Listed below are some of the most important materials for your binder. Make as many sections as necessary to help you easily locate the information you'll need throughout the IEP process.

Your Child's File and Relevant School Materials

Your child's school records will play a key role at the IEP meeting, in developing the IEP itself, and possibly at any due process mediation or hearing. As emphasized in Chapter 3, you should get copies of *everything* in your child's school file, including report cards, attendance and disciplinary records, evaluations and testing data, and teacher comments. Review the documents carefully and put important items in your binder.

You can put everything in one large section of your binder labeled "school records," or you can divide the material into several sections. You'll probably have an easier time locating the information if you break it down into categories.

In addition to your child's file, your binder should include other relevant school materials, such as:

- evaluations
- samples of your child's work
- notes from your child's teacher and other staff members
- correspondence to and from the school
- past IEPs
- emails, if available (see the discussion of emails in Chapter 3)
- your notes and information on available programs and services, including the qualifications of particular teachers or service providers within the school district (Chapter 8 discusses how to develop information on available school options), and

- forms and informational materials sent to you by the school district, such as the school's IEP form and copies of key statutes and regulations on special education. (As mentioned earlier, the school is required by the IDEA to provide you with a copy of federal and state statutes and regulations.)

TIP

Always get a copy of your school's IEP form. Whether you're new to the IEP process or you've been through it before, be sure to get a copy of the current local IEP form (this varies from district to district) and any school guidelines on the IEP process. Keep the form and related materials in your binder. (You can find an example of an IEP form on this book's Companion Page on www.nolo.com. See Chapter 16 for the link.)

Binder Versus File Drawer

As your child progresses in school, your binder could quickly become unwieldy. Consider developing a new one each year. You can keep a file drawer or box of dated materials—for example, "2007 evaluation" or "2008 report cards." Include in your binder only information that is relevant to the current IEP year.

Your Child's Health and Medical Records

Your child's school file will probably include some medical information, such as the results of hearing or vision tests done at school. Be sure your binder includes these as well as medical records and important letters from your child's pediatrician and other health professionals.

Independent Evaluations

As explained in Chapter 8, an independent evaluation may be the most important document supporting what you want for your child. You'll definitely want to keep a copy of all independent evaluations in your binder.

Information on Programs and Services Outside the School District

If you're exploring private programs or service options, such as a specialized school for children with autism, be sure to include details in your binder, such as suggestions made by other parents, notes of your conversations and visits, and school brochures. (Chapter 8 explains how to develop information on programs and services outside of your school district.)

Special Education Contacts

You'll want to have a list of the names, mailing addresses, phone and fax numbers, and email addresses of people you will deal with on a regular basis, such as your child's teacher, the district's special education administrator, your child's physician, the school nurse, staff members who provide related services, parents or parent groups, and the like.

Keep this list of contacts in a prominent place in the front of your binder. Also, keep a copy with you, should you need to phone or write any of your contacts when you're away from home.

FORM
A sample Special Education Contacts form is below; with blank, downloadable copies available on this book's Companion Page on www.nolo.com. See Chapter 16 for the link. Make as many copies as you need.

IEP Journal

The importance of keeping a record of all conversations, visits, and information-gathering activities, whether on the phone or in person, cannot be overemphasized. In particular, you want to note the following in an IEP journal:

- the date and time of the conversation or meeting
- the names and positions of all people who participated in the discussion, such as your child's teacher, other school staff, the special education administrator, your pediatrician, or another parent

Special Education Contacts

Name, Address, Phone and Fax Numbers, and Email Address

School Staff

School: Lewis Elementary, 123 Rose St., Chicago, 60611; 555-1234 (main phone), 555-5678 (fax)

David Werner, Principal, 555-9876, DWE@aol.com

Charlene Hanson, District Special Ed. Administrator, 4111 Main, Chicago, 60611 555-4201 (phone), 555-7451 (fax), chsed @dusd.edu

Thayer Walker, Carrie's teacher, 567 Elm Ave., Chicago, 60611 555-0111 (classroom), 555-0114 (home)

Dr. Judy Goffy, school psychologist, 555-4333 (phone), drjg@aol.com

Outside Professionals

Dr. Hugh Maloney, independent evaluator, 780 Spruce Lane, Chicago 60612, 555-5169 (phone), 555-5170 (fax), drhm @compuserv.com

Martha Brown, tutor, 2229 Franklin, Chicago, 60612, 555-1490

Other Parents

Kevin Jones (son Robert in Carrie's class), 7 Plainview Dr., Chicago, 60614 555-5115, Kj@aol.com

Melaney Harper, District Community Advisory Chair, 764 Rockly, Chicago 60610, 555-7777 (phone), 555-9299 (fax)

Support Groups

Chicago Learning Disabilities Association (contact: Mark Kelso), 775 Kelly Rd. Chicago, 60610, 555-6226 (phone), 555-7890 (fax), chldas@aol.com

State Department of Education

Special Ed. Office (contact: Dr. Lea Casper), State Department of Education 88 Capitol Row, Springfield, 61614, 217-555-8888 (phone) 217-555-9999 (fax), ilsped@worldnet.att.net

Other

Dr. Joan Landman, Carrie's pediatrician, 32 Ashford Rd., Chicago, 60611 555-2222 (phone), 555-0987 (fax)

Illinois Special Ed. Advocates (Steve Mill, Esq.), 642 Mill Dr., Chicago, 60611 555-4511(phone), 555-8709 (fax), spedatt@netcom.com

- what was said by whom (this is *really* important), and
- any necessary follow-up actions (for example, a person you should call).

You'll want to fill in your IEP journal just as soon as possible after a conversation or meeting has ended. The longer you wait, the more likely you are to forget certain details or confuse dates, times, and statements or promises made. Don't be shy about taking notes when you meet or talk with someone. To establish written verification of what you've been told, you'll want to send a confirming letter soon after your conversation. Confirming letters are covered below.

Key Legal Requirements

As you immerse yourself in the details of your child's situation and needs, you'll find it helpful to refer now and then to "the letter of the law"—the precise language the law uses to define or explain the issues you're dealing with. Doing so will help you remain focused on what you can, and can't, expect to achieve. And incidentally, it doesn't hurt to refer to specific legal language at an IEP meeting—it shows you know your stuff and have a working knowledge of the IDEA. Here are some key IDEA requirements; you may want to add more that relate specifically to the issues that affect your child:

- **The definition of your child's disability:** A "specific learning disability" is a "disorder in one or more of the basic psychological processes involved in understanding or in using language, spoken or written, that may manifest itself in the imperfect ability to listen, think, speak, read, write, spell or to do mathematical calculations...." (34 C.F.R. § 300.8(c)(10).)
- **Related services:** "transportation and such developmental, corrective, and other supportive services as required to assist a child with a disability to benefit from special education...." (34 C.F.R. § 300.34(a).)
- **Least restrictive environment:** "Special classes, separate schooling or other removal of children with disabilities from the regular educational environment occurs only if the nature or severity

of the disability is such that education in regular classes with the use of supplementary aids and services cannot be achieved satisfactorily." (34 C.F.R. § 300.114(a)(2)(ii).)

There are hundreds of such IDEA regulations—other important areas are assessments (34 C.F.R. §§ 300.301–320); IEPs (34 C.F.R. §§ 300.320–328); and procedural rights (34 C.F.R. §§ 300.500–520). If you anticipate specific disagreements with your school district, look for regulations that cover those issues, too.

FORM

A sample IEP Journal page is below; a blank, downloadable copy is available on this book's Companion Page on www.nolo.com. See Chapter 16 for the link. Print several copies and keep a few with you—to use if you make phone calls from work, for example. Use the Class Visitation Checklist in Chapter 8 to keep detailed notes on visits to school programs.

Confirming Letters

Confirming what someone has said to you creates some proof of that conversation. A confirming letter can provide useful evidence—of what was said, by whom, and when—for an IEP meeting or a due process hearing.

To be sure the school district receives confirming letters, send them certified mail, return receipt requested.

> EXAMPLE: Your son needs a good deal of one-on-one help. You believe that a qualified aide should sit with him to work on reading, math, and spelling at least half of the school day. Your child's teacher tells you during a classroom visit that he agrees that your son needs one-on-one help for much of the day. In addition, the special education administrator admits to you that the current amount of aide time your son is receiving is not enough. You note both of these conversations in your IEP journal and send the administrator a confirming letter. Later, at the IEP meeting, the administrator balks at providing your son with more aide time. Your confirming letter will be quite helpful in establishing that both your son's teacher and the school administrator told you your son needs more aide time.

IEP Journal

Date: ___11/3/08___ Time: ___4:30___ a.m./p.m.

Action: ☒ Phone call ___201-555-0105___ ☐ Meeting _____

☐ Other: _____

Person(s) Contacted: ___Dr. P. Brin (Sp. Ed. Administrator)___

Notes: ___I explained that Steve is having problems in reading,___

composition, and spelling, plus some social difficulties.

___I said Steve needs an aide.___

___Dr. B: "We can't do that now; wait until the IEP."___

___I said we need IEP at once.___

___Dr. B: "We just had one; can't schedule another for at least___

___two months."___

- -

IEP Journal

Date: ___11/5/08___ Time: ___2:10___ a.m./p.m.

Action: ☐ Phone call _____ ☒ Meeting ___Washington School___

☐ Other: _____

Person(s) Contacted: ___met w/ T. Walker (teacher)___

Notes: ___T. Walker said "Steve will need at least two hours per day___

___of a 1:1 aide next year."___

___I asked if he needs an aide now.___

___T. Walker: "Probably."___

_____

_____

_____

Sample Confirming Letter

Date: May 14, 20xx

To: Salvador Hale, Special Education Administrator
    Coconut County School District
    1003 South Dogwood Drive
    Oshkosh, WI 50000

Re: Rodney Brown, fourth grader at Woodrow Wilson School

I appreciated the chance to speak with you yesterday regarding Rodney's current problems with reading comprehension. I agree with your comment that he needs a one-on-one aide for at least half of the day. I look forward to our IEP meeting next week and to resolving Rodney's current difficulties in school.

Sincerely,

Martin Brown

Martin Brown
145 Splitleaf Lane
Oshkosh, WI 50000
Phones: 555-4545 (home); 555-2500 (work)

Calendars

The next section describes the tasks and events that typically take place during the yearly IEP process. Later in the chapter we explain how to keep track of these tasks and events on a monthly calendar. To stay organized, keep a copy of your calendar in your binder.

The Yearly IEP Cycle

Part of successful organizing is having a clear sense of when things happen in the IEP cycle. Once your child is evaluated and found eligible for special education, the yearly IEP process will involve three broad considerations:

- Review—how are things currently going?
- Reassess—what additional information is needed?
- Rebuild—will the program be the same next year, or does it need changing?

The IDEA requires that an IEP be in place before your child begins the school year. (20 U.S.C. § 1414(d)(2)(A).) To develop a complete initial IEP, you'll need to gather information, deal with evaluations, prove that your child is eligible for special education, prepare for the IEP meeting, attend the IEP meeting, and work out any disagreements you might have with the school. This means you'll have to start planning well in advance to make sure everything gets done in time.

The best way to think about the IEP cycle is to start from your final goal—an IEP in place by the start of the school year—and work backward.

Finish Before Summer

To make sure that all special education issues are resolved before the school year begins, you will want an IEP meeting in the spring of the preceding year. This will give you time to resolve any disputes before the next school year starts. Because school personnel are usually gone during the summer, plan for the IEP meeting in May—or better yet, April—in case there is a dispute that has to be resolved through due process.

Request Your Meeting During the Winter

To ensure that your child's IEP meeting takes place in the spring, put the school district on notice by submitting a written request in February or March stating that you want the annual IEP meeting in April or May.

Begin Planning in the Fall

You'll need to be well prepared for the spring IEP meeting. Don't start collecting information a few weeks or even a month or two in advance.

You'll need much more time than that. Start in the fall or early winter of the preceding year.

The Cycle Isn't Set in Stone

Let's say you've just discovered that your child's problems in school might require special education. It's October. You didn't participate in the IEP cycle the previous year because it wasn't an issue. You'd prefer not to wait until the spring to have an IEP meeting to develop a plan for the following year, as your child would lose almost a whole year of school. Or, you went through the IEP cycle the previous year, but the current program is not working. It's November, and you don't want to wait until spring for a new program. What do you do?

Speak up. Don't wait until spring to raise issues that need immediate attention. Start gathering information, and request an evaluation and IEP meeting ASAP. You should request an immediate IEP meeting if you need one.

> **CAUTION**
>
> **Annual midyear IEP meetings are a bad idea.** Many students' annual IEP meetings take place in December or January. While you can request an IEP meeting at any time (and you should when there is an immediate concern), it is generally not a good idea to have your IEPs in the middle of the school year. If you do, you'll be making decisions too far in advance of the next school year. The easiest way to get back on schedule is to indicate at the midyear IEP meeting that you want another one at the end of the school year, preferably in April or May. Follow up your request with a confirming letter.

Sample Year in the Life of Your Child's IEP

Let us assume you are planning for the school year that begins in the fall of 2018. Ideally, by starting your preparation a year ahead of time, in the fall of 2017, you will have enough time without rushing or facing last-minute problems.

The sections below follow the general IEP yearly calendar and are intended to give you an introduction to the IEP year. Specific tasks are listed in each section; you'll find the details in Chapters 5 through 11.

Step One. Information Gathering: Fall (September–December)

No matter how many times you have been through the special education process, the fall months are generally a good time to gather information and develop a sense of what your child's program should be. The specific tasks include the following:

- Talk to teachers, school staff, and other parents (Chapter 3).
- Request copies of your child's school records (Chapter 3).
- Request an evaluation of your child as appropriate (Chapter 6).
- Begin drafting your child's blueprint (Chapter 5).
- Schedule visits to your child's class or other programs you think might be viable (Chapter 8).
- Gather other information, such as letters from your pediatrician and your child's tutor (Chapter 8).

Step Two. Evaluation: Winter (January and February)

After the first few months of school, the key issues for your child should begin to crystallize for you. You will know whether your child needs to be in special education or, if already eligible for special education, what programmatic components make sense. Now is the time to assess what information you have or need to get to make a strong case for eligibility. Steps to take include the following:

- Assess the current information in your child's record and decide whether it supports your IEP goals for your child.
- Monitor the progress your child is making under the current program.
- Complete additional evaluations, if you need more supporting information (discussed in Chapters 6 and 8). Depending on who

will be doing any additional evaluations and their calendars, you may need to plan for them earlier in the year.

- Continue developing your child's IEP blueprint (Chapter 5).

Step Three. IEP Preparation and IEP Meeting: Spring (March–May)

Spring is when you focus on working toward getting an IEP program in place for your child. This may be the most labor-intensive time of the whole cycle. Tasks include the following:

- Finalize your child's IEP blueprint of program and service needs (Chapter 5).
- Draft goals for your child's IEP program (Chapter 9).
- Prepare for the IEP meeting and invite participants who will speak on your child's behalf (Chapter 10).
- Attend the IEP meeting (Chapter 11).

Step Four. Dispute Resolution: Spring-Summer (June–August)

If you did not reach an agreement with the school administrators on your child's IEP program, then you can, as discussed earlier, go to a due process mediation or hearing. It is important that this process is completed before the beginning of the new year. (See Chapter 12 for information on due process.)

Step Five. School Begins: Fall (September)

You've been through your first (or another) IEP cycle. You'll want to monitor your child's progress in school and see if the IEP program is working. Remember: If it's not, you can request another IEP meeting and try to come up with some changes that make sense.

Keep a Monthly Calendar

It is vitally important to keep track of details of IEP tasks (such as drafting goals) and events (such as evaluations, school visits, and the IEP meeting).

Write everything down on a monthly calendar (your own or the form provided here), including dates on which:

- you were told things would happen—for example, "Scott's school file should be mailed today"
- you need to schedule a meeting—for example, "Request IEP meeting no later than today"
- you need to call or meet with someone such as a teacher, a pediatrician, or another parent, or
- you need to start or complete a particular task, such as develop an IEP blueprint.

FORM

A sample Monthly IEP Calendar is below; a blank, downloadable copy is available on this book's Companion Page on www.nolo.com. See Chapter 16 for the link. Print copies for each month of the year.

Track Your Child's Progress

Whether your child is just entering special education or already has an IEP in place, it's vitally important that you keep track of his or her progress in school. Gauging how well your child is doing will help you in several ways:

- It will provide you with a basis for comparing one semester or year to the next, and one subject to the next. If you don't keep close tabs on your child's progress, you won't know whether he or she is improving or getting worse, whether certain subjects are posing more difficulty than others as time goes by, or whether a particular classroom, service, or teaching methodology is having a positive effect.

- It will help you make your case for eligibility. If your child is not yet in the special education system, you can use the materials you gather to show that your child's academic achievement is not what it should be, or that certain subjects are posing particular difficulty.
- It will help you draft effective goals. When you sit down with the IEP team to write goals for your child, you will know exactly what subjects give him or her trouble—and where he or she needs to work especially hard to see improvement. This will help you tailor the goals to your child's particular needs. (See Chapter 9 for more on goals.)
- It will help you argue for a particular placement or service. If your child is not making appropriate progress, you can argue that the current placement or related services need to be changed. Keeping track of how your child is doing in every subject will give you the information you need to evaluate your child's educational program.
- It will help you develop a positive relationship with your child's teacher. Most teachers welcome parents who want to play an active role in their child's education, as long as the parents are respectful of the teacher's time and experience. By keeping in touch with your child's teacher and weighing in on issues of special concern, you'll help the teacher do a better job educating your child. And there's a lot that parents can learn from teachers, too—including which teaching methods might be appropriate, or what exercises or activities you can do at home to reinforce classroom lessons.

Get into the habit of reviewing all of your child's homework, classroom assignments, tests, and teacher reports. (Be sure to keep any that seem to really illustrate your child's difficulties or successes for your IEP binder.) Plan to visit your child's classroom often—volunteer your time, serve as a class parent, or participate in planned activities for parents. This will give you a chance to see how your child does in the classroom environment.

Monthly IEP Calendar

Month and Year: Oct 20xx

1	2	3	4	5	6	7
		Call Dr. Brin re: math problems		Follow up eval. request if not received		
8	9	10	11	12	13	14
	meet w/ Janice re: her son's experiences			Call Dr. Pearl re: recomm. on auditory problem		
15	16	17 Call at 4p.m. T. Walker to discuss Steve's sign reading problem	18	19 Send school written request for evaluation	20	21
22	23	24	25	26	27	28
	Call J. Brown of parent group		4:15 p.m. meet w/ T. Walker			
29	30	31				
		Begin Steve's IEP blueprint				

Talk to the teacher to set up a reasonable schedule for brief updates or conversations about your child. Remember, most teachers have more work to do than they have hours to do it in, so don't expect to hear from the teacher every day or every week. Instead, ask for some communication twice a month or so, on a day and time that's convenient. Some teachers find it easiest to send parents a brief email report of their child's progress; others would rather have a phone conversation. (If the teacher prefers a conversation, make sure to take notes.)

Create a section in your IEP binder for documents relating to your child's progress. Save copies of written updates from the teacher and samples of your child's schoolwork here. For more information on keeping track of your child's progress with an existing IEP, see Chapter 8.

Calendaring a Due Process Request

When Congress reauthorized the IDEA in 2004, it added a requirement that you must file for a due process hearing within two years of when you "knew" of the dispute, unless your state has a different time period. See Chapter 12 for more detail. It is a good idea to note the date when the "dispute" materialized for you—usually at an IEP meeting. Make this note on your yearly calendar as well as on a calendar you might check more frequently.

Developing Your Child's IEP Blueprint

At some point in the IEP process, you'll need to describe in detail what you believe your child's educational program should look like, including the placement and support services your child needs. I call the specifics of this program a blueprint. Despite the fancy name, a blueprint is just a list of items or components that you want in your child's program.

Why create a blueprint? Primarily to help you be an effective advocate for your child. To convince others that your child needs particular services or assistance, you must first be able to articulate exactly what you want for your child and why it's appropriate.

There are a few other reasons for creating a blueprint:

- It forces you to be specific. For example, stating that your child needs help in reading is not as effective as saying your child needs a one-on-one reading specialist one hour per day, four days per week.

- You'll know exactly what documentation you will need to support your request at the IEP meeting. For example, if your blueprint includes a one-on-one reading specialist one hour per day, four days per week, you'll need information from your child's school record or a person at the IEP meeting to support that position.

- A blueprint helps you determine what may be missing from the program suggested by the school. The IDEA requires that the program fit the child, not the other way around. Just because the school district offers a particular class or program doesn't necessarily mean that it is appropriate for your child.

- The blueprint serves as a standard against which you can evaluate your child's existing program and options currently available to you.

- The blueprint provides you with a continual reference point as you talk with others about your child's needs and move toward the IEP meeting.

In essence, the blueprint represents your ideal IEP program. It is your starting point. If you could be the special education administrator for your school district for one day, this is the IEP program you would design for your child.

You may think it's too early to draft a blueprint. Perhaps your child was just evaluated and found eligible for special education, but hasn't been in special education yet. Or maybe your child has been in special education for some time, but is scheduled for a new evaluation in another month. It's possible a new special education administrator will take over in the spring, with promises of new program options about which you know little. In any of these situations, you may think you don't know enough. In truth, there's always more information you can gather. But you have to start sometime, and now is as good a time as any. Don't worry if your blueprint is skeletal at first; it's for your use only.

Even parents new to special education usually have some intuitive sense of what their child needs. Take a moment to think about it. By the time you finish this chapter, you'll have the beginnings of a useful blueprint, not just vague notions of what might help. And as you go through other chapters and gather information on your child's needs, you'll be able to develop a more complete blueprint.

Begin at the End: Define Your Child's Needs

It's the first day of school in the upcoming school year. Close your eyes and picture what your child's classroom will look like. Is there a tutor? A sign language interpreter? No more than ten kids in the room? Is it a regular classroom? A special education class in a neighboring school district? A special private school? Don't hold yourself back.

Sit down with a pad of paper and pen or in front of your computer, and write out the ideal program and services for your child. Remember that your blueprint is your wish list for your ideal IEP. Don't draft your blueprint to follow the school district's program if you think it's not appropriate.

Preparing an IEP Blueprint

This section covers the seven key components of a blueprint—the items you want included in your child's IEP. You can use the blueprint to develop your IEP form, although the two documents won't be identical. (Chapter 11 explains how to do this.)

Some components are quite general, such as ideal classroom setting; others are very specific, such as a particular class. Some of these seven components may not be relevant to your child's situation and may be ignored. You may not have enough information to complete each section now. As you know more, you can fill in the gaps.

An Appropriate Education

As you think about your child's needs, remember that while it is helpful for you to know what your ideal program and services for your child would be, the law requires only that the district provide an *appropriate* education for your child. The precise meaning of an "appropriate education" is hard to pin down. When Congress passed the IDEA in 1975, it was concerned with providing an education that would help students with disabilities become independent. Educators, parents, and courts have come up with various additional definitions. Some see an appropriate education as one in which the child has been given a basic floor of opportunity to learn, while others refer to an education that is reasonably calculated to provide meaningful educational opportunities.

FORM

A sample IEP Blueprint is below; a blank, downloadable copy is available on this book's Companion Page on www.nolo.com. See Chapter 16 for the link. Be sure to put your blueprint draft into your binder, along with supporting information and documents. (See Chapter 4.)

Classroom Setting and Peer Needs

In this section, specify the type of classroom you'd like for your child, including the kinds of peers he or she should have. Specific items to identify (when relevant) include:

- regular versus special education class
- partially or fully mainstreamed
- type of special education class (for example, for autistic students)
- number of children in the classroom
- ages and cognitive ranges of children in class
- kinds of students (with similar or dissimilar disabling conditions) and what behaviors might or might not be appropriate for your child—for example, a child with attention deficit disorder may need a classroom where other children do not act out, and
- language similarities—for example, a deaf child may need a class of children who use the same sign language.

Teacher and Staff Needs

Use this section to identify your desires concerning teachers and other classroom staff, such as:

- number of teachers and aides
- teacher-pupil ratio—for example, your child may require a ratio of no more than four students to one teacher
- experience, training, and expertise of the teacher—many special education classes are set up for children with specific disabilities; if your child has communicative disabilities or emotional problems, a class with a teacher for the learning disabled may not be appropriate, and
- experience, training, and expertise of aides.

Note that your child has no right to a specifically named teacher but rather staff members who are qualified.

Curricula and Teaching Methodology

In this section, identify the curricula and teaching method or methods you feel are appropriate for your child. You may have no idea right now. As you gather information, however, you will begin to learn about the various teaching methods, materials, strategies, and curricula used with children with disabilities.

Be as specific as possible. If you don't know what you *do* want, specify what you *don't* want. For example, an autistic child will require very different curricula and teaching methods from a child with hearing and speech impairments. A child in a regular classroom may require only a minor adjustment to the regular classroom curriculum.

Is There a Right to a Specific Methodology?

While the IDEA does not specifically require that a methodology or curriculum be included in the IEP and provided to the child, there is no prohibition against it. If a child needs a specific methodology to benefit from special education, then it is required; if you cannot prove that it's necessary, then the school district does not have to provide it.

Related Services

Include in your blueprint a list of necessary services, including the type and amount of services (such as number of times per week and length of time per session).

RELATED TOPIC

Chapters 2 and 8 provide details on related services, such as speech therapy, aide support, physical therapy, transportation, and psychological services.

Identified Programs

In Section 1 of the blueprint, you may have stated whether you want your child in a regular classroom or special education classroom. If you know about a program in a particular school that you think would work best for your child, be it in a regular classroom or a special education classroom, public or private, identify it here.

IEP Blueprint

The IEP blueprint represents the ideal IEP for your child. Use it as a guide to make and record the educational desires you have for your child.

Areas of the IEP	Ideal Situation for Your Child
1. Classroom Setting and Peer Needs—issues to consider:	
☐ regular versus special education class	_____ _____
☐ partially of fully mainstreamed	_____
☒ type of special education class	_____
☒ number of children in the classroom	_A class of no more than 10 students_ _____
☒ ages and cognitive ranges of children in class	_Age range 9–10; same cognitive range as Mark_
☐ kinds of students and behaviors that might or might not be appropriate for your child, and	_No behaviorally troubled students_ _No mixed "disability" class_ _____
☐ language similarities.	_____
2. Teacher and Staff Needs	
☒ number of teachers and aides	_1 teacher; 1 full–time aide_ _or 2 half–time aides_
☒ teacher-pupil ratio	_10:1 pupil–teacher ratio_
☒ experience, training, and expertise of the teacher, and	_Teacher with specific learning disability training, experience, credentials_
☒ training and experience of aides.	_Aide: previous experience working with L–D students_
3. Curricula and Teaching Methodology—be specific. If you don't know what you do want, specify what you don't want.	_Slingerland method_ _Teaching strategies that include significant repetition_

IEP Blueprint (continued)

Areas of the IEP	Ideal Situation for Your Child
4. Related Services—issues to consider:	
☒ specific needed services	1:1 aide two hours per day
☒ types of services	Speech and lang. therapy 3 times/week, 40 min. per session, 1:1
☒ frequency of services, and	30 minutes of psych. counseling once a week with psychologist experienced with children with learning disabilities and emotional overlay
☒ length of services	A class of no more than 10 students
5. Identified Programs—specify known programs that you think would work for your child, and the school that offers them	Special day class (5th grade) for learning disabled at Washington School (Ms. Flanagan)
6. Goals—your child's academic and functional aims.	Improve reading fluency and comprehension: Read three-paragraph story with 80% comprehension; complete reading within 10 minutes Improve peer relationships: Initiate five positive peer interactions/week
7. Classroom Environment and Other Features—issues to consider:	
☒ distance from home	No more than five miles and less than 30-minute bus ride to school
☐ transition plans for mainstreaming	

IEP Blueprint (continued)

Areas of the IEP	Ideal Situation for Your Child
☐ vocational needs	
☒ extracurricular and social needs, and	Involvement in after-school recreation and lunchtime sports activities
☒ environmental needs.	Small school (no more than 250 students); quiet classroom; protective environment (procedures to ensure students do not wander); acoustically treated classroom A class of no more than 10 students
8. Transition Services—higher education, independent living skills, job training; required before age 16.	Will learn the transportation system Will open a bank account Will learn how to keep track of daily expenses Will learn how to look for and apply for a job
9. Involvement in the General Curriculum/Other—to what extent will your child be involved in regular programs and curriculum, and what help will your child need to do it?	
☐ amount of time in regular education classroom (100%, 80%, none, etc.)	
☒ modification of general curriculum	Large-type materials Repeated review/drill 1:1 aide to work on reading comprehension
☒ statewide assessment exams: Will your child take them? Will accommodations be necessary?	Assessments: Large-print versions Additional time to complete testing Supervised breaks within test sections

Goals

The IDEA used to refer to a child's "goals and objectives" (and some school representatives may continue to use these terms): Goals were long range in nature, while objectives were generally more specific, short-term benchmarks that would help a child achieve the broader goal. When Congress amended the IDEA in 2004, however, it took out all references to objectives and benchmarks.

The law now refers to measurable annual goals including "academic and functional goals" designed to meet the child's disability-related and other educational needs. (20 U.S.C. § 1414(d)(1)(A).) Because the statutory language is very general, however, it gives the IEP team a lot of latitude when coming up with goals—and nothing in the law prevents the team from using specific, concrete goals (much like the objectives that used to be required).

Examples of goals include:
- improve reading comprehension or other academic skills, such as math, spelling, or writing
- improve social skills
- resolve a serious emotional difficulty that impedes school work
- improve fine or large motor skills
- develop greater language and speech skills
- develop independent living skills, or
- improve auditory or visual memory.

At each IEP meeting, the school district should review the previous year's goals and objectives and determine whether the previous goals were met. Each goal should be reviewed in detail and information should be added to the IEP as to whether the goal was met or partially met. For instance, "Bill was able to do 2-digit multiplication with 80% accuracy and, thus, this goal was met." This can be important information, particularly if your child has not met previous goals. Your child's not meeting a goal creates a rationale for a stronger IEP with more services and may provide evidence at a later date if you have a disagreement with the district—for example, you can point to the failure as the reason why you are asking for two extra hours of one-on-one work with a specialist.

RELATED TOPIC

Chapter 9 discusses how to prepare goals.

Classroom Environment and Other Features

Use your blueprint to identify any other features of the program you want for your child, such as:

- distance from home
- transition plans for mainstreaming
- vocational needs
- extracurricular and social needs, and
- environmental needs—protective environment, small class, small campus, acoustically treated classroom, and the like.

Involvement in the General Curriculum

In this section of the blueprint, you should describe the extent to which you want your child to be involved in regular school programs and curriculum. For example, if you want your child placed in a regular classroom using the regular curriculum, but your child will need some one-on-one time with an aide and some modifications to the regular classroom teaching methodologies, you should indicate that here.

You should also jot down any modifications you believe your child will need in order to take statewide assessment tests. As these tests become more common, school districts are having to accommodate children with disabilities—and the 2004 amendments to the IDEA state that the IEP should include any modifications a child will need to participate in these tests. There are a variety of possible accommodations, but not all are available and allowed in every state and for every test. (See, for example, the test variations available to California's statewide assessments, as listed in the sample IEP form in Appendix D on this book's Companion Page on Nolo.com. See Chapter 16 for the link.) This is your blueprint, so you should list the accommodations that would best ensure that the assessments measure your child's ability, not the effects of his or her disability. Be warned, however, that this is an area where school districts don't have much flexibility to deviate from the state's rules about what is and is not allowed as an accommodation.

Other Sources of Information for the Blueprint

Developing your blueprint is an important part of gathering information and gaining a sense of what your child needs. As you learn more about your child's needs from professionals and others and find out what services and programs are available, add to or change your blueprint as appropriate.

People who are trustworthy and know your child—such as other parents, your pediatrician, the classroom teacher, or a tutor—are excellent sources of information for your blueprint. Pose your question like this: "Terry is having some problems with reading (math, cognitive growth, language development, social issues, emotional conflicts, mobility, fine or gross motor activities, or whatever), and I'm wondering if I should look for a new program (or different related services). Do you have any suggestions of people I might talk to, or programs or services I might consider?"

RELATED TOPIC
Chapter 8 contains important information about gathering facts, visiting school programs, and developing supportive material, such as an independent evaluation. This information will help you work on your blueprint.

What's Next?

If you are new to special education, the next step is to learn about the evaluation and eligibility processes—how your child is evaluated and qualifies for special education. Review Chapters 6 and 7 carefully.

If you are not new to special education, your next step will depend on your child's situation. Your child may need an evaluation before the IEP meeting—if so, be sure to read Chapter 6. If your child does not need an immediate evaluation and has already been found eligible for special education, move on to Chapter 8.

Evaluations

E valuations are important tools that help you and the school district determine what your child's needs are and how they can be met. The school district will rely very heavily on the results of the evaluation to determine whether your child is eligible for special education and, if so, what the IEP will include.

Evaluations are observations, reports, and tests that provide specific information about your child's cognitive, academic, linguistic, social, and emotional status. Evaluations describe your child's current developmental level—how he or she reads, perceives information, processes information, performs physical tasks, calculates, remembers things, relates to other children, and uses language.

CAUTION

Evaluations or assessments? This chapter covers evaluations— the tests and other information-gathering methods used to determine a child's eligibility for, and progress in, special education. Many advocates use the term "evaluations" interchangeably with the term "assessments," but they have different legal meanings. Under the IDEA, assessments are the statewide tests that evaluate the progress of all schoolchildren (not just those in special education) toward meeting various academic and other standards. Don't worry if your school district or a teacher refers to eligibility testing as an "assessment"; just make sure you understand how they are using the term.

The evaluation report will be a key factor in decisions made at an IEP meeting about your child's program and services. Ideally, the report will support what you want included in the IEP. For example, if you feel your child needs placement in a specific special education program, your chances of securing that placement are increased if the evaluation report recommends it.

Special Education Evaluations Versus General Assessments

Most (if not all) states require schools to administer a variety of tests to measure how children are doing in school and whether they are meeting certain state standards. These tests—often called general assessments—measure a child's mastery of a specific subject matter, such as American history or algebra. Most children also take tests to graduate from high school and qualify for college. While special education evaluations often measure similar abilities or aptitudes, they are intended to be used for a different purpose: to determine whether a child is eligible for special education and which special education services will be helpful to a particular child.

Since 1997, the IDEA has required schools to include special education children in state- and district-wide assessments, with appropriate accommodations for each child's unique needs. When the IDEA was amended in 2004, Congress added language stating that children with disabilities must be provided with "appropriate accommodations and alternative assessments" if necessary. Any alternative assessments given must be aligned with state content standards—that is, they must be related to any state rules regarding required subject areas for testing. (20 U.S.C. § 1412(a)(16).)

Not all of these tests are sensitive to special education test-takers, however. For example, California requires high school seniors to pass an "exit exam" before they graduate, but the State Board of Education has generally ignored the needs of special education students and failed to make appropriate exit exam accommodations or modifications. The state was sued for this oversight but a settlement was reached in 2008 that does not exempt special education students from taking exit exams in order to graduate. You should carefully review any state or district tests in which your child participates to make sure that the test is appropriate and that your child receives any accommodations necessary to take the test.

RELATED TOPIC

This chapter covers evaluations done by local public school districts. You also have the right to have your child evaluated by someone outside of the school district, often referred to as a private or independent evaluation. As discussed in Chapter 8, such independent evaluations are very valuable when you disagree with the school district's evaluation or feel that an independent expert will provide an evaluation supportive of your child's blueprint.

CAUTION

IDEA regulations have changed. The current statutes and regulations are in Appendix A on this book's Companion Page on www.nolo.com. See Chapter 16 for the link. Regulations regarding evaluations are found at 34 C.F.R. §§ 300.300–311.

When Evaluations Are Done

There are two kinds of evaluations: an initial eligibility evaluation to determine whether you child qualifies for special education, and subsequent or follow-up evaluations to get up-to-date information on your child's status and progress. The initial evaluation must be done *before* your child can be found eligible for special education.

While you can wait for the school district to initiate the evaluation process, you don't want to delay unnecessarily. If you haven't heard from the school, make a formal request for an evaluation.

FORM

A sample Request to Begin Special Education Process and Evaluation is in Chapter 3; a blank, downloadable copy is available on this book's Companion Page on www.nolo.com. See Chapter 16 for the link.

The IDEA requires the school district to complete your child's first evaluation and determine whether your child is eligible for special education within *60 days* of receiving your consent to do the evaluation. And that's *60 calendar days*, not business or school days—weekends and holidays count toward the 60-day deadline. If your state has its own time frame for the initial evaluation and determination of eligibility, then that deadline will apply rather than the 60 days specified by the IDEA. (20 U.S.C. § 1414(a)(1)(C)(i)(I).) Remember, your school is required to provide you with an explanation of all applicable special education laws, whether federal or state.

The Evaluation Process, Step by Step

Here is how an evaluation process typically proceeds:

1. You request an evaluation, or the school identifies your child as possibly needing special education. (See Chapter 3.)
2. The school presents you with an evaluation plan listing all testing to be done on your child in order to determine eligibility for special education, or to assess your child's current status if already in special education.
3. You approve the plan (or ask that certain tests or evaluation tools be added and/or eliminated).
4. You meet with the evaluator to discuss specific concerns and your own evaluation of your child's problems, based on your personal observations, physician reports, and the like.
5. The school evaluates your child.
6. You receive a copy of the school's report.
7. You schedule independent evaluations if necessary. (See Chapter 8.)
8. You attend the IEP eligibility meeting (or the yearly IEP meeting, if your child is already in special education), where the evaluation results are discussed.

If you "repeatedly" fail or refuse to "produce" your child for the evaluation, then the school district will not be required to meet the 60-day deadline. If your child changes school districts before the previous district made an eligibility determination, the new district has a responsibility to make "sufficient progress" in meeting the 60-day deadline, but will not necessarily be bound to it. (20 U.S.C. § 1414(a)(1)(C)(ii).)

Once your child is found eligible for special education, he or she must be evaluated at least every three years, or more frequently if you or a teacher requests it. You have a right to have your child reevaluated at least once a year; if you want more frequent reevaluations, you will need the school district's consent. (20 U.S.C. § 1414(a)(2).) See the end of this chapter for more on reevaluations.

Legal Requirements for Evaluations

The IDEA guarantees every child certain rights in the evaluation process. An evaluation must:
- use a variety of evaluation tests, tools, and strategies to gather information about your child
- not be racially or culturally discriminatory
- be given in your child's native language or communication mode (such as sign language if your child is deaf or hard of hearing)
- validly determine your child's status—that is, it must include the right test for your child's suspected areas of disability
- be given by trained and knowledgeable personnel, in accordance with the instructions provided by the producer of the tests
- not be used only to determine intelligence
- if your child has impaired speaking or sensory skills, accurately reflect your child's aptitude or achievement level—not just your child's impairment
- evaluate your child in "all areas of suspected disability," including health, vision, hearing, social and emotional status, general intelligence, academic performance, communicative status, motor abilities, behavior, and cognitive, physical, and developmental abilities, and
- provide relevant information that will help determine your child's educational needs. (20 U.S.C. § 1414(b).)

In addition, the process must include other material on your child, such as information you provide (a doctor's letter or a statement of your observations), current classroom assessments and observations (objective tests or subjective teacher reports), and observations by other professionals. (20 U.S.C. § 1414(c)(1).)

Evaluation Components

Evaluations almost always include objective tests leading to numerical conclusions about a child. Depending on your child's disability, many tests are available—including ones to evaluate general intelligence, reading comprehension, psychological states, social development, and physical abilities. You may have already heard of some of them, such as the Wechsler Test, Kaufman Assessment, and Draw-a-Person. For each test, the report should include an explanation of the test and the test's results.

An evaluation need not be made up of only formal tests. It can also include supportive material that provides information or recommendations about your child's educational status, such as:

- a general description of your child
- teacher and parent reports
- full-scale evaluations by experts specializing in your child's disability
- letters from a family doctor or counselor
- daily or weekly school reports or diaries, and
- other evidence of school performance, including work samples.

Finally, the report should draw a conclusion about your child's eligibility for special education and make specific recommendations about strategies, curricula, interventions, related services, and programs needed for your child.

Evaluation Plans

Before the school district begins the formal evaluation process—either an initial evaluation or a reevaluation—it must send you a written evaluation plan and receive your written approval.

The evaluation plan must include:

- specifically named tests
- a section where you can request additional tests or other methods of evaluation, and
- a place for you to provide your written approval or disapproval.

The IDEA requires the school district to get your permission before it can evaluate your child. Your consent must be "informed," which means that you must understand fully what you are consenting to. If you don't give permission, the school district can still seek to evaluate your child, but it will have to go to due process and get an order from the hearing judge allowing it to proceed. If the school district doesn't force the issue, however, then it is not obligated to provide special education or hold an IEP meeting. (34 C.F.R. § 300.300(a)(3).)

The IDEA allows a teacher or specialist to "screen" children to determine appropriate teaching strategies "for curriculum implementation" without parental permission; such screenings are not considered evaluations to which you must consent. While this new rule seems like a sensible way to let teachers do their jobs, it may be hard to tell the difference between a screening and a full-fledged evaluation. You should certainly ask teachers and the special education administrator to give you detailed information on any such screenings they conduct. Then, if the school tries to use screening information during eligibility discussions at an IEP meeting, you can object that this information is not supposed to be part of the eligibility process. (20 U.S.C. § 1414(a)(1)(E).)

If your child is already in special education and you refuse to allow further evaluation, your child retains the right to his or her current program and services, but the district can take you to due process to get approval to reevaluate your child over your objections. (See Chapter 12 for more on due process.)

Evaluating the Tests

In almost all cases, a person in your school district who is knowledgeable about special education will determine which tests are to be given to your child. There's a very good chance that this person will also administer the tests or supervise whoever does the testing. How will you know if the proposed tests are appropriate for your child?

The best source of information is people who are familiar with special education testing. Likely candidates include the person who developed the evaluation plan, your child's teacher, other parents, and your pediatrician.

Other possibilities include independent special education evaluators you've worked with or school special education personnel you trust. You may also want to talk to organizations that represent the specific disability of your child, such as the Council for Exceptional Children or a state association for children with learning disabilities.

Testing Children With Limited English Proficiency

The 2004 amendments to the IDEA recognize an important change in American demographics: that the "limited English proficient population is the fastest growing in our Nation." (20 U.S.C. § 1400(11).) To address this issue, Congress has created rules about the evaluation of children with limited English proficiency. The district must administer evaluations in the child's native language, so that the tests will yield "accurate information on what the child knows and can do academically, developmentally, and functionally." (20 U.S.C. § 1414(b)(3).) Tests and evaluations that don't take this issue into consideration will not be considered "appropriate."

These protections also apply to deaf and hard-of-hearing children who may not be proficient in English. Many of these children not only have a different native language—American Sign Language, or ASL—but also use an entirely unique communication mode—visual or sign language.

RELATED TOPIC

Chapter 8 discusses independent evaluations. Appendix B on this book's Companion Page on www.nolo.com provides a list of advocacy, parent, and disability organizations you might consider contacting for information on different types of evaluations. It is available on this book's Companion Page on www.nolo.com. See Chapter 16 for the link.

Here's what you want to find out:

- whether the proposed tests are appropriate to assess your child's suspected disability

- what the tests generally measure, such as general cognitive skills or language abilities
- whether the tests' results are numeric scores or more descriptive statements about your child's performance (or both)
- whether the tests' results will provide a basis for specific recommendations about classroom strategies, teaching methods, and services and programs for your child
- how the tests are administered—for example, whether they are timed, and whether they are oral or written
- the evaluator's expertise, training, and experience in doing this kind of testing, and
- how the results are evaluated—for example, will your child score in a certain percentile ("Mary is in the 88th percentile") or will your child be given a different type of rating ("Mary scored at the second-grade level").

Adding to the Plan

If you have concerns about the plan submitted to you, you have every right to ask for changes. The IDEA states that the process should include evaluations and information provided by:

- the parents
- classroom-based, local, or state assessments
- classroom observations, and
- observations by teachers and related services providers.
  (20 U.S.C. § 1414(c) and 34 C.F.R. § 300.305(a)(1)(i)–(iii).)

You can also request that reports and other material from outside professionals be included (for example, a psychotherapist or a speech therapist working privately with your child).

You can request that specific tests be administered to your child, or that certain information (such as a formal interview with you, a review of your child's school work, a teacher's observations, or a pediatrician's report) be used to evaluate your child and be included as part of the report. Be as specific as possible in your request. For example, if your child has limited fine motor skills and problems with handwriting, ask the evaluator to analyze handwriting samples.

Many special education evaluators are not comfortable evaluating testing and other data that don't produce a numerical result. The plan you receive may consist primarily of standardized tests. The school district may object if you ask for an evaluation of subjective reports or anecdotal observations. Nevertheless, you have the right to insist that this information be included in your child's evaluation. Subjective reports and anecdotal observations may be key to coming up with the ultimate IEP program.

> **TIP**
>
> **What "other information" should be included in the plan?** By this time, you have probably gathered information about your child—secured the school file and talked to teachers, other parents, or experts—and have some sense of the key issues. Be sure to take a look at your blueprint, no matter how incomplete it may be, for ideas. See Chapter 5.

If the evaluator refuses to make the changes you request, send a letter to the school district's special education administrator. Explain that you are exercising your right under the IDEA (20 U.S.C. § 1414) to request that additional materials be added to your child's plan, and that the evaluator refused to do so. Describe exactly what you want included and the reasons the evaluator gave you for the refusal. As always, keep a copy of your correspondence.

Approving or Rejecting the Plan

Ultimately, you must sign the plan, indicating whether you accept or reject it. Signing the plan need not be an all-or-nothing proposition. You can:
- accept the plan
- accept the plan on condition, or
- reject the plan.

Accepting the Plan

If you accept the plan as submitted to you, mark the appropriate box—most evaluation plans have approval and disapproval boxes—sign and date it, and return it to the school district. If there is no acceptance box, write "plan accepted," sign and date it, and return it. Be sure to make a photocopy of the plan and add it to your IEP binder.

The IDEA requires that you give "informed" consent, which means you understand what you are consenting to. Therefore your district cannot hand you the plan describing tests you do not understand. You have a right to be told what is being done and why. Only then can you give an "informed" consent to the evaluation.

Your consent to the evaluation cannot be used or construed as consent for the provision of special education and related services. You have the right to separately consent to or contest those items. (34 C.F.R. § 300.300(a)(1)(ii).)

The district can proceed without your approval of a *reevaluation* provided they prove they could not secure your consent. Specifically, they must show that they made "reasonable efforts" to obtain your consent and you have failed to respond. (34 C.F.R. § 300.300(c)(2).)

Accepting the Plan on Condition

There are two possible reasons why you might accept the plan with a condition. First, you might accept the tests proposed, but want additional tests administered or additional information considered. In this situation, try to get the evaluator to agree informally, or ask for help from the school district. (See "Adding to the Plan," above.)

Second, you may not want certain proposed tests administered to your child—perhaps you believe that they aren't reliable or that they test for a problem that your child doesn't have. Whatever the reason, indicate your partial acceptance of the plan on the form as follows:

I approve only of the following tests:

Wrat, Kaufman

Date: _March 1, 20xx_

Signature: _Jan Stevens_

Rejecting the Plan

You have every right to reject the plan and force the evaluator or school district to work with you to find an acceptable plan. Your reasons for rejecting will probably fall into one or more of the following situations:

- the tests are not appropriate
- you want additional tests and materials as part of the evaluation, or
- the evaluator is not qualified.

Note, however, that if you reject the initial evaluation, the school district cannot then be found in violation of the law that requires they provide your child with a "free appropriate public education." In addition, when you reject the initial evaluation, the district is not required to hold an IEP meeting. (34 C.F.R. § 300.300(a)(3).)

To reject the plan, check the disapproval box, sign and date the form, and return it to the school district. If there is no box, write "evaluation plan rejected," sign and date the form, and return it. Keep a copy.

If the plan is not clear or does not give you enough room for your objections, you should attach a letter to the plan. A sample letter is provided. Use this as a model and adjust it depending on your specific situation.

After you submit your rejection (partial or complete) of the plan, the evaluator or school district will probably attempt to find a plan that meets your approval. If the district feels the evaluation should proceed under the plan you've rejected, it has the right to proceed to mediation or a due process hearing to force this issue, although this is rarely done (see Chapter 12).

Sample Letter Rejecting Evaluation Plan

Date: December 14, 20xx

To: Carolyn Ames, Administrator, Special Education
Central Valley School District
456 Main Street
Centerville, Michigan 47000

Re: Evaluation Plan for Michael Kreeskind

I am in receipt of the November 21, 20xx, evaluation plan for my son
Michael. I give my permission for you to administer the Vineland, PPVT-
III, and Wechsler tests, but not the rest of the ones on your list. I have
investigated them and feel they are too unreliable.

In addition, I am formally requesting that the plan reflect:

- that the evaluator will meet with me and my husband to review
  Michael's entire history and will include the issues raised during that
  meeting in the report, and

- that the evaluator will review samples of Michael's work and letters
  from professionals who have observed Michael.

I have one final concern. I have reviewed the credentials of Brett Forrest,
the evaluator selected by the district to evaluate Michael. I am concerned
that Mr. Forrest has no prior experience evaluating children with Michael's
disability. Specifically, I do not believe he is trained or knowledgeable about
the tests to be administered, as required under the IDEA (20 U.S.C. § 1414(b)
(3)(A)(iv).) Therefore, I do not approve of the assigned evaluator, Brett
Forrest. I request that an appropriate one be assigned and that proof of the
evaluator's qualifications be provided to us.

Thank you very much.

Michelle Kreeskind
Michelle Kreeskind
8 Rock Road
Centerville, Michigan 47000
Phones: 555-9876 (home); 555-5450 (work)

Evaluating the Evaluator

Your child's evaluation must be administered by trained and knowledgeable personnel in accordance with any instructions provided by the producer of the tests. (20 U.S.C. § 1414(b)(3).) How can you judge the qualifications of the evaluator?

- Ask the special education administrator for the credentials of the evaluator. If the administrator refuses, assert your right to know under the IDEA.
- Ask other parents and your child's teacher what they know about the evaluator.
- If you are working with an independent evaluator (see Chapter 8), ask if he or she knows the school's evaluator.
- If possible, meet with the evaluator prior to the testing (discussed below).

Can the District Force the Evaluation Against Your Wishes?

While it is not common, districts do have the right and on occasion can compel a child to be evaluated (either for the first time or a reevaluation) even if the parents reject the evaluation plan. In such cases the district is required to initiate and succeed at a due process hearing (see Chapter 12 on due process hearings). While the IDEA statutes and regulations do not tell us what a district must prove in order to convince the hearing officer to order the evaluation without parental consent, hearing officers are generally going to look for specific evidence proving that unless the child is evaluated, there will be negative educational consequences for the child. (34 C.F.R. § 300.300(a)(3).)

Meet With the Evaluator

After you accept the plan proposed by the school district, the evaluator will contact you to schedule the testing of your child. Now is the time to think ahead. In a few months, when you are at the IEP meeting planning your child's IEP program, the school district will pay the most attention to the evaluation done by its own evaluator. Therefore, you will want to take some time to establish a positive relationship with the evaluator before testing begins.

A good relationship is one in which the parties don't have preconceived ideas or view each other with hostility. Try to put aside negative comments you've heard from other people (or any bad experiences you've had with the evaluator in the past). Start with the assumption (or new attitude) that the evaluator is there to help your child get an appropriate education. Of course, this may not be an easy task. The evaluator may not be easy to talk to or may be put off by parents who want to play an active role. No matter what attitude the evaluator adopts, you should try to remain rational and pleasant.

Your job is to educate the evaluator about your child. The evaluator will have test results to evaluate and reports to read. But he or she doesn't live with your child or stand before your child in a classroom. To the extent possible, help the evaluator see your child from your perspective, particularly as it relates to the academic programs and services you feel are necessary. Ideally, you want the report to recommend eligibility and the specific program components you want for your child, as articulated in your blueprint (in Chapter 5).

So how do you go about getting your points across? If possible, meet with the evaluator before the testing is done. The law doesn't require an evaluator to meet with you, but the law does not prohibit it, either. Call up and ask for an appointment. State that you'd appreciate the chance to talk, are not familiar with all the tests, would like to find out how they are used, and would just feel a lot better if you could meet for ten to 15 minutes. If the evaluator cannot meet with you, ask for a brief phone consultation or consider sending a letter expressing your concerns.

Reality Check: The Evaluator Works for the School District

While you should assume that the evaluator wants to develop a good and appropriate educational plan for your child, don't lose sight of the fact that the evaluator is an employee of the school district. The evaluator probably knows what the school district will offer regarding your child's eligibility for special education or in terms of an IEP program, and the report may very well reflect the school's position. Some evaluators know exactly what a school district can provide and, unfortunately, tailor their reports accordingly, rather than prepare a report based on what a child truly needs.

On the other hand, just because the evaluator's report doesn't support what you want, it doesn't necessarily follow that the evaluator is acting against your child's best interests. The conclusions may be well reasoned and supported by the data. Be objective. Are the recommendations consistent with or contrary to the data? If you conclude that the evaluator is biased against you, request a new one. Remember, you always have the right to an outside or independent evaluation (see Chapter 8).

Whether you meet in person, talk on the phone, or state your concerns in a letter, you'll want to be clear and objective.

Eligibility evaluation. Let the evaluator know the specific problems your child is having in school, the material you have documenting those problems, and why you believe those problems qualify your child for special education.

> EXAMPLE: "Daniel has had a terrible time with reading. He's only in the second grade, but he is way behind. His teacher agrees—I have some notes of my conversation with her from last October. I could provide you with a copy of them if that would help. I'd greatly appreciate it if you could focus on Daniel's reading problem in your evaluation."

IEP program evaluation. If your child is already in special education or is likely to be found eligible, let the evaluator know of the IEP program components you believe are important. Here are a few examples.

EXAMPLES:

"Noah needs a small class where none of the children exhibit behavioral problems, with classroom strategies and methodology geared to children with his learning disability."

"Kayla needs the Lovaas method for autistic children. I would like you to evaluate the reports done by her doctor, her teacher, and the classroom aide, and address their suggestions in your recommendations section."

Be careful about how specific you get. The evaluator may think you're trying to take over and might not appreciate being told exactly what to include in the report. For example, a straight-out, "Please recommend that Megan have a full-time, one-on-one aide" or "Please write that Connor should be placed in the learning disability program at Center School" may be met with hostility. You may need to be less direct, such as, "The teacher wrote that Megan cannot learn to read without constant one-on-one attention. Please address that need in your report." Remember, your blueprint is a good guide here.

This part of the process is not easy. Don't be disappointed if the evaluator doesn't agree fully or even partially with what you are requesting. The best you can do is be clear about what your child's problem is, what you feel your child needs, and what materials support your conclusions. Ultimately, if the evaluator does not address your questions and you have good evidence to support those concerns, the value of the school's evaluation may be diminished.

Letter Requesting Evaluation Report

Date: <u>November 3, 20xx</u>

To: <u>Harvey Smith, Evaluation Team</u>

<u>Pine Hills Elementary School</u>

<u>234 Lincoln Road</u>

<u>Boston, MA 02000</u>

Re: <u>Robin Griffin, student in Sean Jordan's</u>

<u>1st grade class</u>

I appreciate your involvement in my child's evaluation and look forward to your report. Would you please:

1. Send me a copy of a draft of your report before you finalize it. As you can imagine, the process can be overwhelming for parents. It would be most helpful to me to see your report, because the proposed tests are complicated and I need time to analyze the results.

2. Send me your final report at least four weeks before the IEP meeting.

Again, thank you for your kind assistance.

Sincerely,

Lee Griffin

Lee Griffin

23 Hillcrest Road

Boston, MA 02000

Phones: 555-4321 (home); 555-9876 (work)

Reviewing the Report

After your child is evaluated, the evaluator will issue a report. Some issue their reports in two stages: a *draft* report and a *final* report. Ask how and when the evaluator plans to issue the report. Ideally, the evaluator will issue a draft report that you can review before the final report is submitted prior to the IEP meeting.

Even if the evaluator will issue only one version of the report, it is imperative that you see it before the IEP meeting. Under the IDEA, the school district must provide you with a copy of the evaluation report and with information documenting eligibility. (20 U.S.C. § 1414(b)(4)(B).)

By asking to see the report (preferably a draft of the report) ahead of time, you convey to the school district your intention to carefully review the evaluator's work. This will help you keep a sense of control over the process and prepare for the IEP meeting. It will also keep you from wasting valuable time at the IEP meeting.

FORM
A sample letter requesting the report is included here; a blank, downloadable copy is available on this book's Companion Page on www.nolo.com. See Chapter 16 for the link.

If you disagree with anything in the draft report or feel something is missing, ask the evaluator to make a change or add the missing information. Be prepared to point to material outside the report that supports your point of view. If the evaluator refuses, put your request in writing, with a copy to the special education administrator.

If the evaluator won't make the changes—or sends you only the final version—what can you do if you disagree with the final report? You can reject it. While you can express your disagreement before the IEP, it might be strategically wise to wait for the meeting and prepare your counterarguments with the evidence you have, including existing material and your independent evaluation (if any).

TIP

Don't forget independent evaluations. You have the right to have your child evaluated by someone outside of the school district, often referred to as a private or independent evaluation. Such independent evaluations are valuable when you disagree with the school district's evaluation. The independent evaluator can analyze the district's evaluation and point out its shortcomings. See Chapter 8 for more information on independent evaluations.

Reevaluations

In addition to the right to an initial eligibility evaluation, the IDEA also gives your child the right to periodic reevaluations. Your child must be reevaluated at least once every three years or when the school district determines that there is need for improved academic and functional performance. In addition, you, the school district, or your child's teacher can request a reevaluation once a year—and if you make this request, the school district must grant it.

You do not have a unilateral right to more than one reevaluation per year, however: The school district will have to consent to any additional yearly reevaluations. (20 U.S.C. § 1414(a)(2).) While it is certainly true that a student can be overevaluated, which can tax both your child's and the school district's stamina, there may simply be times when a second or third evaluation in one year is necessary. For example, if your child isn't progressing as you expected, teachers are raising concerns, IEP goals seem way out of reach, or for any other reason a significant change is necessary, it's probably time for a reevaluation. If you find yourself in this situation, put your request to the school district in writing, noting as specifically as possible why additional information is needed and why the current evaluation is not adequate, complete, or up to date.

Final Evaluations

A final evaluation is not required when your child's special education terminates. However, when those services end, the school district must provide you with a "summary" of your child's "academic achievement and functional performance" as well as "recommendations" regarding your child's "postsecondary goals." (34 C.F.R. § 300.305(e).)

Who Is Eligible for Special Education?

A ccording to the National Center on Educational Statistics, there were approximately 6,419,000 students age five to 21 in "served" special education in the 2010–2011 school year. When IDEA was first enacted, there were approximately 3,694,000 students "served." In 2010–2011, in special education, there were 2,357,000 with learning disabilities, 1,390,000 with speech and language delays, 417,000 students with autism, 381,000 with developmental delays, and 714,000 with "other health-impaired" issues.

SKIP AHEAD
If your child has already been found eligible for special education, skip ahead to Chapter 8.

Your child may be found eligible for special education for any number of reasons—for example, because of a learning disability, sensory or physical impairments, or psychological problems. To qualify, your child will have to meet the criteria discussed below.

CAUTION
Eligibility rules for children with learning disabilities have changed. When Congress amended the IDEA in 2004, it made important changes to the eligibility standards for children with learning disabilities. Briefly, the IDEA removed the previous requirement that there be a "severe discrepancy" between intellectual ability and achievement. (34 C.F.R. § 300.307.) The IDEA regulations define a learning disability as a disorder in one or more listed "psychological processes" (e.g., using language, doing mathematical calculations, etc.), and states that a child may be considered to have a learning disability if he or she does not "achieve adequately for the child's age or to meet State-approved grade-level standards" in one or more of eight listed areas. (34 C.F.R. §§ 300.8(c)(10) and 300.309.) For detailed information on these new rules, see *Nolo's IEP Guide: Learning Disabilities*, by Lawrence Siegel.

Eligibility Is Not an Annual Event

Once your child is found eligible for special education, he or she won't need to requalify each year. There are only three situations when your child's eligibility might be redetermined:
- Your child dropped out of special education and wants to reenter.
- You or the school district proposes a change from one eligibility category to another.
- There is evidence that your child no longer qualifies for special education. Reevaluation is not required if your child's eligibility status changes because he or she graduates from high school with a regular diploma or exceeds the age of eligibility (22 years old). (20 U.S.C. § 1414(c)(5)(B).)

Eligibility Requirements

In order to qualify for special education, your child must meet two eligibility requirements: (1) he or she must have a disabling condition, as defined in the IDEA, and (2) that condition must have an adverse effect on your child's education. In other words, it is not enough to show that your child has a disability—you must also show that your child's disability is causing enough problems to warrant special education help.

As you prepare for the eligibility process, understand that the IDEA uses many terms that are open to a variety of interpretations. For example, there's no precise definition of a "disabling condition," or the limits for "educational performance," or even an "education." Neither you nor the school district can consult a table or a list that will tell you whether a child with a learning disability or an emotional problem qualifies for special education.

As you go through this chapter keep in mind the following:
- **Carefully read the definition of the "disabling condition" that applies to your child (these conditions are explained in the IDEA regulations at 34 C.F.R. § 300.8).** What is required for your child to qualify? For example, most definitions require that the condition cause

an "adverse effect," but the definitions for "deaf-blindness" and "specific learning disability" do not.

- **The terms "adversely affect" and "education" are not defined.** Is an education merely grades or test scores, or is it more, such as learning how to make friends, develop independent living skills, and gain greater control over anger or anxiety? Over the years, courts have provided some guidelines: While the law doesn't require the school to maximize a child's potential, the child is entitled to a full educational opportunity, and one that allows the child to develop self-sufficiency and academic advancement. Whether a program provides a meaningful benefit should be evaluated in relation to the child's potential. (More on this below.)

- **Focus on key portions of each definition.** Pay attention to words such as "severe" or "significant." These are clues that a minor disability may not qualify your child for special education. A child who doesn't fall under one of the delineated conditions may fit into the catchall category, "other health impairment." If your child's strength, vitality, or alertness is limited because of a chronic or acute health problem, he or she may qualify under this category.

Disabling Condition

IDEA provides a list of disabling conditions that qualify a child between the ages of three and 22 for special education. The list includes:

- hearing impairments, including deafness
- speech or language impairments, such as stuttering or other speech production difficulties
- visual impairments, including blindness
- deaf-blindness
- orthopedic impairments caused by congenital anomalies, such as a club foot
- orthopedic impairments caused by diseases, such as polio
- orthopedic impairments caused by other conditions, such as cerebral palsy
- specific learning disabilities

- emotional disturbance (see "Emotional Disturbance as a Disabling Condition," below)
- autism
- traumatic brain injury
- intellectual disabilities, and
- other health impairments that affect a child's strength, vitality, or alertness, such as a heart condition, rheumatic fever, nephritis, asthma, sickle cell anemia, hemophilia, epilepsy, lead poisoning, leukemia, diabetes, and Attention Deficit Disorder (ADD)/Attention Deficit Hyperactivity Disorder (ADHD).

Traumatic Brain Injury

Children who have had a "traumatic brain injury" (TBI) may be eligible for special education (34 C.F.R. § 300.8(c)(12)). The regulations define a TBI as an "acquired injury to the brain caused by an external force, resulting in total or partial functional disability or psychosocial impairment" and "adversely [affecting] a child's educational performance." TBI applies to injuries that impair at least one of the following: memory; attention; reasoning; abstract thinking; judgment; problem-solving; sensory, perceptual, and motor abilities; psychosocial behavior; physical functions; information processing; and speech.

The regulation states that a TBI does *not* apply to brain injuries that are "congenital or degenerative or to brain injuries caused by birth trauma." This exclusion seems odd. First, the IDEA generally is concerned with the consequences, not the cause, of the disability. Second, why these three injuries are excluded, when they too can result in the impairments listed, is not clear and suggests a rigid distinction not fully related to the reality of a child's disability and the conditions that affect the child's ability to learn.

RESOURCE

You can find the legal definition of each of the above disabilities at 20 U.S.C. § 1401(3) and 34 C.F.R. § 300.8.

Age Limits on Developmental Delay

The IDEA does not generally require that a disability occur at a specific age. However, the IDEA does limit "developmental delay" to years three through nine. This means that children younger than three or older than nine cannot be found to need special education and related services on the basis of developmental delay. (34 C.F.R. § 300.8(b).)

RESOURCE

If your child has learning disabilities, see *Nolo's IEP Guide: Learning Disabilities*, by Lawrence Siegel, which explains in detail the eligibility requirements for children with learning disabilities.

Fitting your child's condition into a disability covered by the IDEA and finding data to prove that your child's disability is causing academic problems can be tough—and emotionally trying. But it's a necessary part of qualifying for special education. If you find yourself in a muddle, remember these tips:

- **Take it slowly.** Some of the qualifying conditions have multilayered definitions. Don't try to take it in all at once. Breaking down a definition into manageable parts will help you figure out what evidence you need to show that your child meets all of the eligibility requirements.

- **You're not a doctor and you don't have to become one.** Don't be put off by some of the complicated terminology. For now, you need a basic understanding of your child's condition and how it affects his or her educational experience. Ask your pediatrician, the school nurse, or the evaluator for help. Contact other parents and local or national support or advocacy organizations. (Chapter 15 discusses parent organizations, and Appendix C on this book's Companion Page on Nolo.com lists useful resources. See Chapter 16 for the link.)

- **The IEP team has flexibility in finding eligibility.** The list of qualifying disabilities is long, but not exhaustive. If your child exhibits the characteristics of any of the disability categories, he or she may very well be deemed eligible for special education, even if there hasn't been a formal diagnosis. In addition, the IEP team has some discretion in determining eligibility. If your child has been diagnosed with a mild condition, it's up to the IEP team to decide whether it's serious enough to justify a finding of eligibility.

- **Your input is important.** The IEP team must draw upon information from a variety of sources, including parental input, when determining eligibility. (20 U.S.C. § 1414(d)(3)(A).) You can, and should, use this opportunity to make sure that the IEP team understands and considers every aspect of your child's disability, not just test scores.

- **Keep up with legal changes.** To stay on top of current interpretations of the rules, you'll want to stay in touch with advocacy groups for updates on how the eligibility process is evolving. (See Appendix C on this book's Companion Page on Nolo.com for a list of organizations. See Chapter 16 for the link.) You'll also want to make sure you have access to the text of the law. You can find key selections of the IDEA and its regulations in Appendix A on this book's Companion Page on Nolo.com. See Chapter 14 for ways to access the law on paper and online.

Adverse Effect

It is not enough to show that your child has a disabling condition; you must also demonstrate that your child's disability has an adverse effect on his or her educational performance.

The IDEA does not say how "adverse effect" is measured, but your child's grades, test scores, and classroom or other behavior will provide important evidence of adverse effect. While grades can most directly show whether a disabling condition is adversely affecting educational performance or achievement, they don't tell the whole eligibility story. A parent can (and should) argue that a child who receives As, Bs, or Cs but cannot read at age level, follow instructions, or relate to peers is not benefiting from his or her education, and therefore that his or her disability is directly affecting educational performance, regardless of grades.

Autism

Autism is a condition, some call it a neurological disorder, that affects a child's ability to communicate and socialize appropriately. It may also lead to behavioral challenges.

Autism can be quite severe or mild and the ways in which it is reflected in a child can vary greatly. Some children may rock or flap their arms. Others will simply be less responsive to social cues. People often think that autistic people are not as emotional as others. It is crucial, of course, that you have your child assessed as early as possible and by medical and educational professionals who are trained in autism.

Autistic children are fully capable of learning and growing. There are a variety of strategies for dealing positively with an autistic child, including Applied Behavior Analysis (ABA). Like with so many people with "disabilities," stereotypes and misunderstanding can affect how people (mis)judge autistic people. Temple Grandin, perhaps one of the most well-known autistic adults, has written that she prefers being who she is.

With the significant increase in the diagnosis of autism, the term Asperger's Syndrome is often used interchangeably with autism. Asperger's Syndrome is a developmental disorder often characterized by unusual interests and significant difficulties in interacting socially. Children with Asperger's are often high functioning and, unlike many children with autism, often do not have cognitive delays or low IQs.

The National Institute of Mental Health has published a parent's guide to Autism Spectrum Disorders.

If your child is getting passing grades, you will need to make the connection between your child's disability and school performance in some other way. Factors to consider (other than grades) include:

- limited progress—for example, little or no improvement in reading, math, or spelling even though the teacher does not fail your child; high school students might have significant difficulty in social studies, geometry, or English

- difficulties in cognitive areas, such as mastering basic concepts, memory, or language skills—forgetting to turn in homework, trouble with reading comprehension, or difficulty grasping abstract concepts might demonstrate these problems
- discrepancy between performance and ability—for example, the child is developmentally and chronologically ten years old, but reads at a six-year-old's level; an eighth-grader has an above average IQ but is performing at the sixth-grade level on math and spelling tests
- evidence of emotional, behavioral, or social difficulties, or
- physical difficulties, such as handwriting, hearing, or coordination problems.

The IEP team has a lot of discretion in determining whether your child is eligible for special education. If your child has passing grades, the team may need to exercise that discretion to find that his or her disability has adversely affected educational performance in other ways.

Children's disabilities often adversely affect their education in nontraditional, nonacademic, or nonscholastic ways. For example, a disability may impact your child's ability to develop language, make friends, and deal with anxiety and other emotional challenges. The child may receive good grades but may have no friends and cannot communicate with peers or staff. That child has a disability that is "adversely" impacting her education.

TIP

Pay attention to state law if you're dealing with a discrepancy between performance and ability. As we have noted, each state has its own special education statutes. They generally parallel federal law, but often have some additional language. For example, California requires that there be a "severe" discrepancy, whereas another state may refer to a "significant variance."

What's Not in the Law

Almost as telling as what IDEA requires is what it doesn't. Contrary to what school district representatives may tell you, none of the following is required by the IDEA.

Requirement of Numeric Proof

The IDEA does not require that your child score at a certain level on specific tests to qualify for special education. Numeric information is important and may prove a key element in determining eligibility, but a test score is not the end of the story.

Emotional Disturbance as a Disabling Condition

A child who has an "emotional disturbance" (this is the term now used by the IDEA) qualifies for special education. Although this term can conjure up images of bizarre behavior and institutionalization, children with a wide range of emotional difficulties can qualify for special education in this category. When you look at the actual defining language in the IDEA, you'll see that it encompasses issues that might affect most human beings at some point in their lives, and certainly could arise for children who have a disability.

The IDEA defines an emotional disturbance as a condition that has existed over a long period of time to a marked degree and adversely affects your child's educational performance (20 U.S.C. § 1401(3)(A), 34 C.F.R. § 300.8(c)(4)). The regulations don't specify how long "over a long period of time" must be. Nor do they define "to a marked degree," or what is needed to show that the disturbance "adversely affects" a child's educational performance. The first two requirements are not part of the eligibility requirements for other disabling conditions. The emotional disturbance is a disabling condition if it results in:

- an inability to learn that is not explained by intellectual, sensory, or health factors
- an inability to build or maintain satisfactory interpersonal relationships with peers and teachers
- inappropriate behaviors or feelings under normal circumstances (for example, extreme frustration, anger, or aggression over minor setbacks or disagreements)
- a general pervasive mood of unhappiness or depression, or
- a tendency to develop physical symptoms or fears associated with personal or school problems (for example, a child might get a stomachache before tests or oral reports).

Emotional Disturbance as a Disabling Condition (continued)

A child who is only socially maladjusted will not qualify for special
education, although a child who is emotionally disturbed under the IDEA
can, of course, be socially maladjusted. Like any other disability, emotional
disturbance must adversely affect your child's educational performance in
order to make him or her eligible for special education. If your child qualifies
for special education in another disability category but also shows some
signs of emotional disturbance, the IEP team can (and should) address those
emotional difficulties in the IEP by developing goals and providing services
to meet those emotional needs. Rather than label the behaviors as an
"emotional disturbance," simply have the IEP team address them as one of
many aspects of your child's disability. For example, the IEP might describe
how the teacher, teacher's aide, school counselor, and written goals could
address how your child might deal in a concrete and helpful way with peers
who make fun of his or her disability.

One Test as Sole Determinant

Eligibility cannot be determined based on the results of one test. The IDEA
specifically requires that any evaluation to determine eligibility include
information provided by the parents of the child. Furthermore, the IDEA
requires that the school district draw upon information from a variety of
sources, including aptitude and achievement tests, teacher recommendations,
and the child's physical condition, social or cultural background, and
adaptive behavior.

Not All Disadvantages Make a Child Eligible for Special Education

The IDEA specifically states that a child cannot be eligible for special
education solely because of limited English proficiency or lack of
appropriate instruction in reading or math. (34 C.F.R. § 300.306(b)
(1).) Further, a child will not be eligible under the "specific learning
disability" category if his or her problems are primarily the result of
visual, hearing, or motor difficulties, of mental retardation, of emotional

disturbance, or of environmental, cultural, or economic disadvantage. (34 C.F.R. § 300.8(c)(10)(ii).) Of course, a child with these difficulties might qualify separately under other eligibility categories.

A Word About Labels

This list of disability categories asks you to define your child as "this" or "that." Labeling is one of the difficult and unpleasant parts of the IEP process. Many people feel that labels are unnecessary, even harmful—and from a psychological perspective, they may be right. From a legal perspective, however, your child will be eligible for special education only if he or she fits into one of these categories. If you can, focus on the specifics of your child's condition rather than the label. Remember, your goal is to secure an appropriate education for your child; proving that your child qualifies for special education under one of the eligibility categories is part of the process.

It is important, however, to acknowledge the label for the purpose of meeting the eligibility criteria while making sure your child does not become defined by that label. For example, Brent has dyslexia, which causes him some significant problems in school and qualifies him for special education. But Brent is also a terrific center on the basketball team, he hates to clean up his room, at times he frustrates and worries his parents, he has a good heart, and, most importantly, he is determined to make his way in the world. These are the qualities that define him.

Preparing for the IEP Eligibility Meeting

After your child is evaluated, the school district will schedule an IEP meeting to discuss your child's eligibility for special education. Depending on the circumstances of your case, your school district may hold off scheduling the IEP program meeting until after your child is found eligible. But if eligibility seems likely, the school district may be prepared to hold the IEP program meeting immediately after the eligibility meeting; otherwise, it must do so within 30 days of determining that your child is eligible for special education.

RELATED TOPIC

The strategies for a successful IEP eligibility meeting are the same as for a successful IEP program meeting. In preparing for the IEP eligibility meeting—or the possibility of a joint IEP eligibility and program meeting—review Chapters 10 and 11.

To prepare for the eligibility meeting, follow these tips:

- **Get a copy of your child's school file.** If you don't already have a copy, see Chapter 3.
- **Get copies of all school evaluations.** Evaluations are covered in Chapter 6, including a sample letter requesting the report.
- **Know the school district's position in advance.** If the evaluation report recommends eligibility, call the special education administrator and ask if the district will agree with that recommendation. If the answer is yes, ask if the IEP eligibility meeting will go right into an IEP program meeting. If the evaluation report is not clear about eligibility, call the administrator and ask what the district's position is on your child's eligibility. If the evaluation recommends against eligibility, be prepared to show that your child is eligible. Here are a few suggestions:
  - *Review the school file and evaluation report.* Cull out test results and other information that support your child's eligibility.
  - *Organize all other reports and written material that support your position on eligibility.* Observations from teachers and teacher's aides are especially important. Ask anyone who has observed your child and who agrees that he or she should be in special education to attend the IEP eligibility meeting. If a key person cannot attend, ask for a letter or written observation report.
- **Consider having your child evaluated by an independent evaluator.** An independent evaluator may be necessary if the school district's report concludes that your child is not eligible for special education. Even if your child is found eligible, you may disagree with the school's recommendations regarding services and programs—many times these are spelled out in the school district's report.

- **Get organized.** Get your documents together before the eligibility meeting so you can immediately find what you need.

RELATED TOPIC

Chapter 8 provides tips on how to best organize existing material—and develop new information—to make your case at an IEP eligibility or program meeting. Chapter 8 also discusses how to use an independent evaluator.

Attending the Eligibility Meeting

Many of the procedures and strategies used at the IEP eligibility meeting are similar to those used at an IEP program meeting. Chapters 10 and 11 explain how to prepare for, and participate in, an IEP meeting. This section highlights some issues that are particularly important for eligibility meetings.

Who Should Attend?

Who should attend the eligibility IEP meeting depends a great deal on whether you anticipate a debate about eligibility. If your school district appears ready to find your child eligible for special education, then you may not need anyone at the meeting other than you and your child's other parent. If the school district does not agree that your child is eligible, or you don't know the district's position, you may want to ask people who can support your position to attend the meeting. Such people might include:

- an independent evaluator
- your child's current teacher, and
- other professionals who know your child.

Whether you ask any of these people to attend the IEP eligibility meeting may depend on their availability, the strength of their point of view, and cost. Sometimes, a letter from your pediatrician or another professional might be just as effective—and is certainly less expensive—than paying the expert to attend in person. As a general rule, do not pay someone to attend the IEP eligibility meeting unless you are certain that there will be a disagreement and that you will need that person to support your position. In most cases, an independent evaluator is your most effective advocate.

Preparing Your Participants

Make sure your participants are prepared to:

- describe who they are, their training, and how they know your child
- discuss their conclusions about your child's eligibility for special education and the basis for those conclusions—observation, long-term relationship with your child, or testing, and
- contradict any material concluding that your child is not eligible for special education.

Submitting Your Eligibility Material

As you prepare for the IEP eligibility meeting and accumulate material (such as an independent evaluation supporting your child's eligibility), you will have to decide whether to show the material to the school district before the meeting.

The IDEA does not require you to do so, but consider the kind of relationship you want to establish with the school district. If you ask for the school district's evaluation in advance, it is only fair to offer the district a copy of yours. Granted, you will give the school a chance to prepare a rebuttal. On the other hand, if you submit an independent evaluation or other material at the IEP meeting, the school may ask to reschedule the meeting in order to review your material. In the long run, your best bet is to treat the school district as you want to be treated. If you have favorable material not in the school district's possession, submit it in advance, or at least call the administrator and ask if he or she wants your information ahead of time.

Remember that the material the IEP team considers can be drawn from a "variety of sources" including aptitude and achievement tests, parental input, and teacher recommendations. (34 C.F.R. § 300.306(c) (1)(i).) Moreover, there is no prohibition of materials not listed in the law. For example, if you have a letter from a doctor, a report from a private school or tutor, or any useful observation from anyone, you can and should include them for the eligibility team to consider.

Meeting Procedures

An IEP eligibility meeting generally proceeds as follows:
- general introductions
- review of school material
- review of any material you want to introduce, and
- discussion of whether your child qualifies for special education and, if so, on what basis.

Outcome of Meeting

If the school district determines that your child is eligible for special education, then it will proceed to the IEP program meeting—either immediately after the eligibility meeting or on another date. If the school district finds that your child is not eligible for special education, read "If Your Child Is Not Found Eligible for Special Education," below.

Joint IEP Eligibility/Program Meeting

The school district may combine the IEP eligibility and program meetings into one. In such a situation, your child would be found eligible for special education, and then the IEP team would shift gears and immediately begin developing the IEP program—goals, program, placement, services, and the like. Holding one meeting may save you time and scheduling headaches, but it also requires that you do a lot of preparation up front. If you're not ready to discuss the IEP program at the IEP eligibility meeting, ask for another meeting to give yourself time to prepare.

On the other hand, if you'd like to combine the meetings (assuming your child is found eligible), ask the school district to do so. Make your request well before the scheduled eligibility meeting so everyone will have enough time to prepare.

FORM

A sample Request for Joint IEP Eligibility/Program Meeting is below; a blank, downloadable copy is available on this book's Companion Page on www.nolo.com. See Chapter 16 for the link.

If Your Child Is Not Found Eligible for Special Education

You may attend the IEP eligibility meeting, point out significant information supporting your child's eligibility, and argue your point in a manner worthy of Clarence Darrow—all to no avail. What then? You have two options.

Exercise Your Due Process Rights

"Due process" is your right to take any dispute you have with your child's district—whether a disagreement about an evaluation, eligibility, or any part of the IEP—to a neutral third party to help you resolve your dispute. Due process is covered in Chapter 12.

Seek Eligibility Under Section 504 of the Rehabilitation Act

Section 504 of the federal Rehabilitation Act (29 U.S.C. § 794) is a disability rights law entirely separate from the IDEA. It requires all agencies that receive federal financial assistance to provide "access" to individuals with disabilities. Historically, Section 504 has been used to require public agencies to install wheelchair-accessible ramps, accessible restrooms, and other building features, and to provide interpreters at meetings. Section 504 also requires school districts to ensure that children with disabilities are provided access to educational programs and services through physical modifications (such as ramps, widened doorways, and accessible restrooms and other school facilities) and assistance from interpreters, note takers, readers, and the like.

Your child may be entitled to assistance under Section 504 even if he or she is not eligible under the IDEA. The first step in the process is to refer your child for Section 504 services—this simply means asking the school to consider your child's eligibility under Section 504. Some school districts automatically consider children who are found ineligible under the IDEA for Section 504 services; if yours does not, request—in writing—that it do so.

Request for Joint IEP Eligibility/Program Meeting

Date: <u>march 10, 20xx</u>

To: <u>Valerie Sheridan</u>

<u>mcKinley Unified School District</u>

<u>1345 South Drive</u>

<u>Topeka, KS 00078</u>

Re: <u>Grace Lee, student in fourth-grade,</u>

<u>Eisenhower School</u>

I believe there is sufficient information for us to discuss both my child's eligibility for special education and the specifics of my child's IEP at the same meeting. I would appreciate it if you would plan enough time to discuss both of those important items at the <u>April 14, 20xx</u> IEP meeting. I would also like to see any and all reports and other written material that you will be introducing at the IEP meeting, at least two weeks before the meeting.

Thanks in advance for your help. I look forward to hearing from you soon.

Sincerely,

Albert Lee

<u>Albert Lee</u>

<u>78 Elm Drive</u>

<u>Topeka, KS 00078</u>

<u>Phones: 555-1111 (home); 555-2222 (work)</u>

Once a child has been referred, the school will evaluate eligibility. It will look at:

- whether the child has a physical or mental impairment
- whether the child's impairment substantially limits the child's "major life activities," including learning, and
- what types of accommodations the child needs in order to receive a free appropriate public education.

If your child is found eligible for help under Section 504, the school must develop a written plan describing the modifications, accommodations, and services your child will receive. Like an IEP, the Section 504 plan must be individually tailored to meet your child's needs. Many schools have developed a standard form for Section 504 plans; ask your school if it has one.

Because Section 504 tries to achieve the same result as the IDEA—to give children the help necessary for academic success—many of the tips and strategies described in this book will be useful to you as you develop a Section 504 plan for your child. The eligibility, procedural, and other requirements of Section 504 are different from IDEA's requirements, however. Because this book focuses on the IEP process, you'll need to get more information on Section 504 if you decide to proceed.

TIP

Need more information on Section 504? Contact the U.S. Department of Education, Office for Civil Rights (www.ed.gov/about/offices/list/ocr/index.html), your school district, your local community advisory committee, or one of the disability groups listed in Appendix B. You can find a copy of the Section 504 regulations in Appendix A. You can find the appendixes on this book's Companion Page on Nolo.com. See Chapter 16 for the link.

Exploring Your Options and Making Your Case

O nce your child is found eligible for special education, the IEP team must decide what type of instruction and assistance your child will receive. This chapter will help you develop material supporting your child's special education needs. By now, you should have a copy of your child's school file and the school district's evaluation report. You should also have developed a rudimentary IEP blueprint for your child. In addition, you may have spoken to other parents, your child's teacher and classroom aide, your child's pediatrician, and others who have recently observed your child. In other words, you may have a mountain of information available—and you may not know exactly how to put it to use.

The key to a successful IEP meeting is developing and using information that supports your position regarding your child's educational needs. This chapter will explain how to:

- review your child's school file and the school district's evaluation report
- keep tabs on your child's current progress in school
- look into available special education programs and services— both in and out of the school district—that may be appropriate for your child
- figure out whether available programs and services fit your child's education needs and whether you need additional information to make your case, and
- make a list of other materials you might generate to support your position, such as an independent evaluation, a statement from your child's teacher, or a statement from your child's pediatrician or other professional.

RELATED TOPIC

Chapter 10 provides a system for organizing all of your materials— positive and negative—to best make your case at your child's IEP meeting.

Key Elements for Child's Program

Child: Jasmine Perez

Date: June 1, 20xx

Desired IEP Components	District Material	District Position
Placement in regular class	4-4-xx Evaluation	Agrees, p. 14
1:1 aide for regular class	4-4-xx Evaluation	No position
	3-12-xx Biweekly Teacher Report	Teacher agrees
Adaptive Physical Ed	5-2-xx Adaptive P.E. Evaluation	Disagrees (but see comment on p. 5)

Review the School District's Information

Your first step in preparing for the IEP program meeting is to figure out what position the school will probably take, and whether you can use any of the school district's own documents and statements to show that your child needs a particular program. Start by reviewing all of the information you've received from the school district. As you look over your child's school file, evaluation report, and other school district items, there are several issues to consider.

Read Between the Lines

Can you figure out what position the school district will take, simply by reading your child's file and evaluation report? Sometimes it's easy—for example, if the report says "Matteo qualifies for special education as a student with specific learning disabilities," or "Lila needs speech therapy twice a week," you'll know exactly where the school district stands. Sometimes it's not so clear. For example, the report might say, "Lila has difficulty in producing the 'th' and 's' sounds," but not mention needed services. Don't be surprised to find more vague statements than definitive ones.

Where to Look for the School District's Position

You can find the school district's position in a variety of materials. It is most likely to come up in an evaluation report, but you may also find the school district's position in a letter, teacher report or memo, your child's report cards, or another written item in your child's file. Your child's teacher, the school evaluator, or another district employee may even have stated the school district's position in a conversation.

 RELATED TOPIC

If the school district employee's statement supports your position, be sure to send a confirming letter (see Chapter 4).

Sources of the School District's Data

It's important to figure out who is saying what in the school district's material. These speakers are the district's experts, and their opinions will greatly influence the IEP process. Specifically, you'll want to know each person's:

- name and position—for example, a teacher, teacher's aide, or evaluator
- training and expertise, and
- firsthand experience with your child.

Keeping Track of the School District's Statements

Once you've reviewed all of the information available from the school district, make a chart like the one shown above to highlight key elements of your child's program (see your blueprint for ideas), whether the school district agrees or disagrees with your position, and where in the school district's materials the issue is addressed. Note where the school district's data supports or opposes your position, and where you have gaps to be filled—little or no information to show that a particular program or service is necessary for your child to receive an appropriate education. Finally, note the source of the information—was it in writing, or did someone say it to you?

Changing a Report or Evaluation

If there is something in your child's school file or the evaluation report that is inaccurate and harmful to your child, find out whether the school district is willing to change the statement. Start with a phone call. For example:

> "Hello, Ms. Wong, I'm Aida Henry's father. I read your evaluation, and I appreciate your help in evaluating Aida's needs. I did want to ask you a question. You say on page 4 that Aida does not need help with her reading comprehension. Did you see the teacher's report, which says that she needs one-on-one reading help?"

To make a formal request for a change, see "Amending Your Child's File" in Chapter 3 (to change something in a school file) and "Reviewing the Report" in Chapter 6 (to change a draft evaluation report).

Keep Tabs on Your Child's Progress

As you prepare for an IEP program meeting, take some time to learn how your child is currently doing in school—in regular or special education. If your child is doing poorly in school and you're preparing for an IEP eligibility meeting, you'll want to describe at the IEP meeting exactly how your child is floundering. If you are preparing for an IEP program meeting, be ready to explain why the current program is right for your child or why it needs changing.

Here are a few suggestions for getting current information about your child:

- Ask the teacher, teacher's aide, and service provider for periodic reports focusing on key areas of need for your child—reading, behavior, language development, social interaction, physical mobility, and the like.
- Ask the teacher for samples and reports of your child's work.
- Visit your child's class.
- Set up periodic meetings with your child's teacher. If your child already has an IEP, ask the teacher whether the current IEP goals are being met. If your child has not met his previous goals, find out how far off he is.

EXAMPLE: One of your child's current IEP goals is to read a three-paragraph story and demonstrate 80% comprehension by answering questions. Ask the teacher if your child can read a three-paragraph story. Then ask about your child's reading comprehension level. If it's not up to 80%, where is it—60%, 40%, 20%?

It's always best to have information about your child's progress before the next IEP meeting so you can double-check what is written in the IEP for each goal. Pay attention to whether the written conclusions match what you were told.

When securing this information from the teacher or aide or resource specialist, you don't want to ask too far in advance of the IEP meeting. Ask a week or two before the meeting so that the information given to you is fresh when the IEP meeting is held and goals are discussed.

To organize this material, you can create a chart for your child's teacher to complete on a regular (such as monthly) basis, updating your child's progress in key areas such as math, reading, behavior, and motor development, as well as emotional and psychological issues and self-help skills.

Progress Chart

Student: _micah Jacobs_

Class: _ms. Frank's 3rd Grade_

Date: _February 23, 20xx_

Key Goals	Current status	Comments
Math	Progressing appropriately? ☒ yes ☐ no	On schedule to complete goals.
Reading	Progressing appropriately? ☒ yes ☐ no	On schedule to complete goals. Needs to improve reading fluidity.
Writing	Progressing appropriately? ☒ yes ☐ no	On schedule to complete goals.
Spelling	Progressing appropriately? ☐ yes ☒ no	Reversals continue to be problem.
Social-Behavior	Progressing appropriately? ☐ yes ☒ no	Still problems with focus; hard time not teasing others.
Language development	Progressing appropriately? ☒ yes ☐ no	On schedule, but some problems going from specific to general.
Motor development	Progressing appropriately? ☐ yes ☒ no	Small motor problems affecting handwriting.
Other	Progressing appropriately? ☒ yes ☐ no	When struggling with spelling and handwriting, seems to feel high level of stress.

FORM

A sample Progress Chart is above; a blank, downloadable copy is available on this book's Companion Page on www.nolo.com. See Chapter 16 for the link. You can tailor this chart to your child's particular goals. This form will help you track your child's general progress, as well as whether your child is meeting the IEP goals. (See Chapter 9 for more details on developing goals.)

Explore Available School Programs

To prepare for the IEP program meeting, you will want to gather information about your child's existing program and other possible programs that may be appropriate for your child.

Program possibilities include:

- placement in a regular classroom, perhaps with support services—ask about local options, including your child's neighborhood school
- placement in a classroom designed specifically for children with learning disabilities, difficulties with communication, or other disabling conditions—ask about special day classes at your neighborhood school, nearby schools, or other schools in the area, or
- placement in a specialized program, such as a private school or residential program—ask about the existence and location of any such programs.

Ask About Available Programs

Contact your child's teacher, the school evaluator, the district special education administrator, other parents, your PTA, and your local community advisory committee. Ask about programs used for children with similar needs.

The school administrator (or even the classroom teacher) may be reluctant to tell you about programs. You may hear, for example, "It is way too early to be looking at programs for next year, Mr. and Mrs. Williams.

We've just started this year." Or "We don't think it is appropriate to discuss programs until the IEP team meets and drafts goals. Then we can talk about programs."

Although school personnel may have reasons for making assertions like these, you have every right to find out about available program options. Emphasize that you are not looking to change programs or force an early IEP decision—you are merely trying to gather information. You might respond, "I appreciate what you are saying, Ms. Casey, but it will really be helpful to me and my child to begin as early as possible, so we can plan ahead. I am not looking for a change in programs or for a commitment on your part. Is there some reason why I shouldn't gather information about programs in the district?"

Visit Programs

The best way to find out what a particular school or program has to offer is to spend some time there. However, while school administrators may provide you with some information about existing programs, they may be reluctant for you to actually visit a program before the IEP meeting. Although the IEP team may not know which program will meet your child's needs until after you have the IEP meeting, nothing in the IDEA prevents you from visiting potential programs before the meeting, as long as your requests are reasonable.

If the administrator refuses to let you visit programs, put your concerns in writing.

FORM

A sample Program Visitation Request Letter is below; a blank, downloadable copy is available on this book's Companion Page on www.nolo.com. See Chapter 16 for the link.

If the administrator still refuses your request, don't give up. Indicate that you understand his or her concerns, but feel that you could not possibly make a decision in the IEP about placement without some basic

Program Visitation Request Letter

Date: _November 6, 20xx_

To: _Mr. Carlos Avila, Special Education_

Administrator

Carlson Unified School District

8709 Fourth Street

Helena, MT 00087

Re: _Elizabeth Moore_

I am writing to request permission to visit programs in the District that might be appropriate future placements for my daughter, Elizabeth.

I appreciate the concerns you have, and I realize that you can't know for sure which programs are appropriate until after the IEP meeting. Nonetheless, I think it would be very helpful for me to see existing programs so I can be a more effective member of the IEP team. I do not feel I can make an informed IEP decision without seeing, firsthand, all possible options. I want to assure you that I understand that by giving me the names of existing programs, you are not stating an opinion as to their appropriateness for my child.

I assure you that I will abide by all rules and regulations for parental visits. If those rules and regulations are in writing, please send me a copy.

Thanks in advance for your help. I hope to hear from you soon.

Sincerely,

Arnette Moore

Arnette Moore

87 Mission Road

Helena, MT 00087

Phones: 555-3334 (home); 555-4455 (work)

information about available programs. Make it clear that you are more than willing to visit programs again after the IEP meeting.

If you get nowhere, contact the administrator's superior. If that fails, you can file a complaint with your state department of education or other appropriate educational agency, as discussed in Chapter 13. The complaint might not be processed until after the IEP meeting. If this happens, you'll have to decide whether to postpone the IEP or ask (at the IEP meeting) to see the programs after the meeting. In that case, you may not be ready to sign the IEP at the meeting. (See Chapter 11 for information on signing the IEP.)

You don't need a school administrator's permission to visit private programs in the area. Simply call and schedule your own appointments.

When to Visit Programs

Ideally, you will want to visit programs in the fall of the school year. While it may seem logical to visit right before the IEP meeting, checking out possible program options earlier offers these advantages:

- The sooner you see a particular program, the sooner you'll have a sense of whether or not it is appropriate for your child.
- If you can't judge whether a particular program is a good fit for your child, there will be time for others, such as an independent evaluator, to take a look and give you an opinion.
- You'll have time to visit a program more than once, if necessary.

Visitation Guidelines

The purpose of your visits is to gather information. As you plan your visits, keep in mind these points:

- Ask to visit *all* program options.
- Follow the policies and rules established by the school district, school site administrator, and teacher.
- If an independent evaluator or other professional will attend the IEP meeting, it is a good idea to have him or her visit with you. Be sure to inform the school district ahead of time.

- Do not ask for any personal information about the students, such as names of individual children. A teacher should *not* give you this information. You can (and should) talk with any parents you know who have children in the programs.
- Secure as much detail as possible about each program or class. Include the same categories of information you use in your blueprint (see Chapter 5):
  - student description (number of students in the program; students' disabilities, age, cognitive range, and language range)
  - staff description (details on teachers and aides)
  - teacher-student instruction (teacher-to-class, small group, or individual)
  - curricula, methodology, and other teaching strategies used
  - classroom environment (behavior problems, noise level, number of teachers and teacher aides, and how much time teacher aides spend in class)
  - related services (how many children leave the class to go to another program and how often; how many children receive related services in the class), and
  - any other comments you have on the program.

The IDEA does not require that the teacher provide you with this information, so you should ask in a pleasant, matter-of-fact way. If the teacher balks, indicate that the information you seek is important and noncontroversial, and should be made available.

Write down your observations and the answers to your questions. You can write as you watch the class and talk to the teacher. If you "interview" the teacher with notebook in hand and pencil poised, however, the teacher may be intimidated. By saying, "I have a poor memory; do you mind if I take notes while we talk?" you may put the teacher at ease. If not, try to take notes in an unobtrusive way, or wait until you're outside and write down what you remember as soon as possible.

Class Visitation Checklist

Date: _9/11/xx_   Time: _9:00–10:15 a.m._

School: _Jefferson School, Chicago_

Class: _3rd Grade Special Day Class for Learning Disabled (Teacher: Sue Avery)_

Student Description:

Total students: _17_   Gender range: _12 boys; 5 girls_

Age range: _7 – 10 (ten kids are nine or younger; seven ten-year-olds)_

Cognitive range: _"Wide range; probably from pre-K through 5th grade skills," says S. Avery (teacher)._

Language/communication range: _Two students with hearing impairment; two other students with delayed communication skills (1st grade level)._

Disability range: _12 students have specific learning disability, three have borderline intellectual disability, one has emotional disturbance, and one autistic-like behavior._

Behavioral range: _Five students acting out throughout class, four other students constantly demanding of teacher. Two students sent to principal because of behavior. Rest of class generally cooperative, quiet._

Other observations: _Overall impression was of a class of children with varied needs and behavior, which made it difficult for the teacher to focus on any one group of children for very long._

Staff Descriptions:

Teachers: _Sue Avery has four years' experience working with learning disabled children. She was generally very patient with students (less so with the behaviorally troubled children), but she seemed easily distracted._

Class Visitation Checklist, continued

Aides: In class two hours per day; worked with all children, no one child more than few minutes. Seemed mostly to superficially check in with students, but not provide any sustained 1:1 help. Aide has no specific training working with learning disabled children.

Other observations: Neither teacher nor aide seemed fully comfortable with curriculum, particularly given varied needs of students. Both were very nice to students.

Curricula/Classroom Strategies:

Curricula: "Using mathematics" (Book 2) for math, teacher-developed materials for spelling, and "Project Explore" for science lessons.

Strategies: Teacher/aide when working 1:1 in reading divided words into simple sounds using much repetition; no overall strategy or specific curriculum designed for learning disabled children.

Classroom Environment:

Description: Classroom had tiled floor so sound echoed. Quite loud; no other apparent acoustical treatment to reduce noise; all added to a noisy room. Various work stations and cubicles set up so students can work 1:1 or by themselves. Somewhat effective, but noise was distracting to all students. Classroom situated near playground, so much visual stimulation outside classroom window and noise from outside.

Related Services:

At least four students received their related services in class, one had speech therapy, another had a special aide that worked with her in the corner.

Class Visitation Checklist, continued

Other Comments:

School site principal (Lee Parsons) is interested in special education, but
has no training or expertise in the field. She did express reservations about
excessive mainstreaming of children with disabilities into regular classrooms.
Visited one mainstreamed class, teacher seemed interested, but expressed
concern that the school had not provided any support or training for dealing
with special education students in her regular class.

How This Program Relates to IEP Blueprint:

Program does not meet Tara's blueprint:
- Cognitive and behavioral range of students too wide
- Teacher unable to provide individual attention
- Aide not trained for working with L-D kids
- Question about curriculum

FORM

A sample Class Visitation Checklist is above; a blank, downloadable copy is available on this book's Companion Page on www.nolo.com. See Chapter 16 for the link. Be sure to keep copies of this important form in your IEP binder.

Find Out About Related Services

Classroom programs are only one component of your child's IEP program. Related services, such as occupational, physical, or speech therapy, are also very important (see Chapter 2).

Gathering information about related services will be a little different from gathering information about programs. You'll still want to talk to your child's teacher, the school evaluator, the district special education administrator, other parents, your PTA, and local parent groups for disabled children to find out about related services for children with similar needs. But the similarities end there.

Service providers, such as physical therapists, usually work one-on-one with individual children or in small groups. So visiting these specialists in action may not be possible. Instead, when you talk to people about the services available, ask about the background, training, and experience of the specialists. Candid conversations with other parents should be most helpful.

Keep detailed notes of your conversations and include them in your IEP binder.

Compare Your Blueprint With the Existing Programs and Services

Once you have information about your school district's programs and services, compare what's available to what you believe your child needs. Obviously, if the school provides programs and services you feel will meet your child's needs (as described in your blueprint), the IEP process will go more smoothly. On the other hand, if there is a gap between what your child needs and what is available, you face the task of convincing the IEP team that the school options are inappropriate.

You'll need to detail the shortcomings of the programs and services offered by the school district. Be as specific as possible: Is the problem the frequency or location of a service, the pupil-teacher ratio, the qualifications of the teacher or service provider, the class make-up, the teacher methodology, the curriculum, or other important features?

Make a comprehensive, side-by-side comparison of your blueprint and what you know about the school's options, and put the details on the bottom of the class visitation checklist.

Generate Additional Supporting Information

Once you've reviewed your child's school file, developed your blueprint, reviewed the school evaluation, evaluated your child's progress, and gathered information about program and service options, you may need further data to support your goals. This material will be invaluable in preparing for the IEP meeting.

Help From School Personnel

Contact any teachers, evaluators, or service providers who are likely to support your position. You can do this by phone or in person. Explain what programs and services you want for your child (your blueprint), and why you feel they are appropriate. Note any discrepancy between what you want and what you believe the school district has available. Explain why you want what you want for your child and ask for their ideas and opinions.

Ask if the teacher, evaluator, or service provider would be willing to either write a statement supporting what you want for your child or state this position at the IEP meeting.

If you talk to someone who supports your point of view but doesn't want to put anything in writing, follow up the conversation with a confirming letter (see Chapter 4), such as, "Thank you for the chance to chat today. I appreciate your frankness and was glad to hear that you agree that Max needs an aide in order to function effectively in the regular class."

Be aware that a confirming letter can put the teacher in an awkward position. If the teacher says one thing to you (and you confirm it in a letter) and then says another thing at the IEP meeting, the letter may be important proof of what was originally said—but this may lead to some friction between you and the teacher. If the teacher will not speak frankly at the IEP meeting, however, the confirming letter will be valuable proof of what was said earlier—and might discourage the teacher from changing his or her tune.

No matter what, be sure to keep notes of what was said, including the date, time, and place of the conversation, in as much detail as possible. This is your record in case the school representative gives a different story later.

Help From People Outside the School

Anyone who knows your child or has some expertise in special education or your child's disability may be of value. This includes your child's doctor, tutor, therapist, or other specialist.

Ask each person to write a letter to the IEP team stating:
- how he or she knows your child
- his or her expertise
- any specific comments on your child's condition and educational experience, and
- recommendations for your child in terms of programs, services, or other IEP components.

EXAMPLE: "Teresa needs extensive help with small and large motor skills, and should work with an occupational and physical therapist at least three times a week."

Independent Evaluations

An independent evaluation may be the most important document supporting what you want for your child. An independent evaluation, like the school district's evaluation, can be as comprehensive or as narrow as your child's needs dictate. In most cases, an independent evaluation will use a variety of tests to evaluate your child's needs.

> **RELATED TOPIC**
> Chapter 6 discusses evaluations in general, and Chapter 11 covers how to present an independent evaluation at the IEP meeting.

Under the IDEA, you have an absolute right to have an independent evaluation of your child. Moreover, your school district is required to provide you with information on where you can get an independent evaluation.

While the IDEA requires the school district to consider the results of the independent evaluation in making any decision regarding your child's education, it does not require that your school district agree with the results. While an independent evaluation may include persuasive information, your child's school district can reject the conclusions. (You do have the right to go to due process to prove the district is wrong. See Chapter 12.)

When to Use an Independent Evaluation

You may want an independent evaluation because you need more information about your child or because the school district's evaluation does not support what you want. If the district's position is clear—and you disagree with it—an outside evaluation may very well be needed.

Finding Independent Evaluators

Independent evaluators generally work in private practice or are affiliated with hospitals, universities, or other large institutions. How do you find a qualified independent evaluator?

Your school district is required to provide you information about local independent evaluators, although its list may not be complete. The reality is that sometimes districts do not want to include the names of independent evaluators who may have in the past been too supportive of expensive placements for the student.

Here are a few tips for finding more independent evaluators:

- Ask parents of children with similar disabilities. Check with the PTA or your school district's advisory committee of parents with children in special education.
- Get recommendations from the school. A trusted teacher, aide, service provider, or other school employee may be able to give you some names.
- Talk to your child's pediatrician.
- Call a local hospital, particularly a university medical hospital. A department that employs experts in your child's disability may be able to do the evaluation or refer you to someone who can.
- Contact an organization that specializes in your child's particular disability. (See Appendix B on this book's Companion Page on nolo.com. See Chapter 16 for the link.)
- Call local private schools for disabled children. Private schools often work with credible independent evaluators.

How Not to Find an Independent Evaluator

Evaluators are often psychologists. If you look in the phone book, you will see a long list of psychologists. But choosing randomly from the phone book is a poor method for selecting a reputable and knowledgeable evaluator. The only thing you really know about these people is that they could afford to pay for a listing.

Selecting the Right Evaluator

Speak to various independent evaluators, and ask the following questions for each person:

- Does the evaluator have significant expertise, training, and experience in dealing with your child's disability?
- Is the evaluator affiliated with a well-respected institution?
- Were you referred by someone who actually worked with the evaluator?
- Do you trust the person (or institution) who recommended the evaluator?
- Will the evaluator give you references?
- Did the evaluator's references like the results of the evaluator's work and find the evaluator easy to work with?
- Is the evaluator impartial? (An evaluator who has previously done work for—and been paid by—your child's school district may not be truly independent.)
- Can the evaluator complete the evaluation and written report well in advance of the IEP meeting?
- Can the evaluator attend the IEP meeting, if necessary?

The answers to these questions, your own impressions, and recommendations from others are key factors in making your decision. It is also important that the independent evaluator be able to clearly articulate his or her position, professionally and vigorously.

Getting an Independent Evaluator on Your Side

The reason you are hiring an independent evaluator is to support your educational goals for your child. Be very clear on your plans and perspectives.

EXAMPLES:

- You have very specific desires (your blueprint) concerning the program you believe is appropriate for your child—you know what you want in terms of type, amount, and duration of service; type of service provider; and teacher-pupil setting. Be sure the evaluator makes recommendations that support the program and services you want for your child: "Given Michelle's need to develop expressive speech, she requires speech therapy four times a week, with each session lasting 50 minutes. She also needs one-on-one work with a qualified speech therapist experienced in working with children who have an expressive language delay."
- You want your son placed in a school for children with emotional disturbances. Ideally, the evaluator will write, "Philip requires placement in a program with no more than ten children, a full-time aide, a teacher qualified to work with emotionally troubled children, and a class where there are no behavioral problems. The Woodson School in Boston is the only program in this area that can meet Philip's needs."

If the evaluator can't or won't name a specific school or program, then make sure he or she will name the specific components of an appropriate program. Continuing the example above, if the independent assessor won't say Philip needs to be placed in the Woodson School, he or she should say that Philip needs placement in a program that has the characteristics of the Woodson School.

It is of course possible that your goals may not be supported by the data. Good evaluators will not write something they disagree with or make a recommendation they do not believe in. They will tell you when the evidence—the testing data—does not support what you want.

You want an evaluator who will:

- show you a draft evaluation report
- consider your concerns about the draft report
- make specific recommendations about your child's educational status and appropriate programs and related services to meet your child's needs, and
- provide a written rationale for these recommendations.

How an Independent Evaluation Proceeds

Most independent evaluators will meet with you and review your child's school file, the school district's report, and other district material. The evaluator will then explain what testing will be done, secure your approval, do the testing, and prepare a report. Depending on your child's characteristics and needs, the evaluator may also want to observe the child in class.

When to Submit the Independent Evaluation

Just as you want to review the school district's evaluations before the IEP meeting, the school district will likely want to see your independent evaluation before the IEP meeting. Of course, the more time the school has to review the independent evaluation, the more time the administration will have to find data to counter its conclusions. Does this mean you should delay giving the school district your evaluation? While such a strategy has its attractions, the bottom line is that the school district is entitled to the same courtesy that you are.

Holding off on giving the district a copy of your evaluation could ultimately prove counterproductive. The district may distrust you and your evaluation. The delay may be grounds for postponing the IEP meeting. And your relationship with the district may be affected. Because you will likely be working together for many years, you should maintain a positive relationship, if possible. If one party will be nasty, unfair, or untrustworthy, let it be someone other than you. While there is no hard-and-fast rule here, providing the independent evaluation (and other key material) a week before the IEP meeting is usually appropriate.

Cost of an Independent Evaluation

Independent evaluations can be quite costly, anywhere from several hundred dollars to several thousand dollars.

But you may not have to pay for the evaluation. Under the IDEA, you have the right to an independent educational evaluation of your child (by someone of your choosing) at public expense if you disagree with an evaluation obtained by the school district. The IDEA requires that, after you request an independent evaluation to be paid for by the school district, the district must, "without unnecessary delay," either arrange to pay for the evaluation or file for due process and prove at the hearing that the district's evaluation was appropriate.

Assuming the district has already assessed your child and you ask for an independent evaluation, the district may in fact agree to pay for one. Much will depend on your child's needs and complexities and, in some cases, whether the district feels it has an evaluator on staff who has the expertise to evaluate your child's conditions.

If the district does not agree to pay for an independent evaluation, it will likely give you what is called a "prior written notice." The district has to give you this notice when it refuses to agree to an independent evaluation (see 20 U.S.C. §§ 1415(b)(3)(4) and (c)(1); 34 C.F.R. § 300.503).

One practical problem is that you might need to have the evaluation done while you are waiting for the district to either pay or go to due process. In this case, you might need to pay the evaluator yourself. This certainly underscores the importance of requesting an independent evaluation early—so that if district ends up paying for the evaluation, you won't have to put any resources out for it. If you must have the evaluation completed prior to the district's action (to pay or go to hearing), you might discuss with the evaluator whether you can delay payment or pay over a period of time.

Finally, you have the right to only one independent evaluation at the district's expense each time the district does its own evaluation and you disagree with it. (34 C.F.R. § 300.502(b)(5).) No matter who pays for the evaluation, you have the right to present the evaluation at the IEP meeting. (34 C.F.R. § 300.502(c).)

What If the District Hasn't Done an Evaluation?

Your child is entitled to an independent evaluation at school district expense if you disagree with an evaluation completed by your school district. You can request an independent evaluation even if the school district hasn't done an evaluation, but it's unlikely the district will agree to an independent assessment before it does its own.

If a disagreement over this issue goes to a hearing, your not waiting for the district to evaluate first might result in the district's not being ordered to pay for your independent assessment. It's wise to let the district assess first.

If there is a more urgent matter, however—say your child is self-destructive and you need to secure a residential placement—you may have to proceed immediately (with the understanding that you may not be reimbursed).

For the full requirements regarding independent evaluations, see 20 U.S.C. § 1415 and 34 C.F.R. § 300.502.

Requesting that the District Pay for an Evaluation

It is important that you formally request in writing that the district provide and pay for your independent evaluation. In this letter, you should also state who you want to do the evaluation and what the evaluation will encompass. Use this formal statement in your written request: "We are formally requesting an independent evaluation to be paid by the district, pursuant to 34 C.F.R. § 300.502."

Send the letter certified mail, return receipt requested, so that you have proof it was received.

When you request the independent evaluation, the district has the right to ask you why you object to the district's evaluation. You are not required to respond. If you do respond, do so in general terms—for example, "We felt the evaluation done by Ms. Harkins on behalf of the district was not thorough, we have some concerns about whether the administered tests were the right ones, and we're not sure whether she supported her conclusions with evidence." When in doubt, don't explain. If you choose not to respond to the district's request for explanation, simply say that you understand it is your right not to respond. If you choose not to respond, the district cannot delay either paying for the independent evaluation or going to due process. (34 C.F.R. § 300.502(b)(4).)

Writing Goals

G oals are the nuts and bolts of your child's education: the academic, cognitive, linguistic, social, and vocational aims you have for your child.

Objectives Are No More

Special education law used to use the term "goals and objectives" to describe the accomplishments a child would aim for during the school year. In 1997, Congress changed the term "objectives" to "benchmarks," but the meaning remained the same: short-term accomplishments that would help a child achieve a larger goal and measure progress toward that goal.

In 2004, Congress eliminated both terms. The statute now refers to "measurable annual goals, including academic and functional goals, designed to meet the child's needs." (20 U.S.C. § 1414(d)(1)(A)(i)(II).) The definition is broad enough to give the IEP team latitude to develop whatever aims are appropriate for your child. This chapter includes examples of broad goals, as well as more detailed, short-term goals.

EXAMPLES OF IEP GOALS:

- Tim will improve his reading comprehension.
- Tim will read a four-paragraph story and demonstrate 75% comprehension using objective classroom tests.
- Ellen will improve her peer relationships.
- Ellen will initiate three positive peer interactions each day, per teacher observation.
- Juan will master all third-grade math skills.
- Juan will identify sets of ones and tens with 90% accuracy, using appropriate textbook tests.
- Jane will improve her writing skills.
- Jane will write a three-sentence paragraph with subject and predicate sentences, per teacher evaluation.
- Mark will improve short-term auditory memory.

- Mark will be able to listen to a set of ten related items and list them with 75% accuracy.

The IDEA requires that an IEP program include a statement of measurable annual goals (20 U.S.C. § 1414(d)(1)(A)) for two reasons:

- to ensure that the child is involved and progressing in the general curriculum, and
- to meet other educational needs that result from the child's disability.

Because the IDEA requires the school district to provide an appropriate education for your child, the question underlying many IEP decisions is, "Can this child's goals be achieved in a specific program or with a particular related service?" Your child's progress in meeting the goals helps determine whether the school district is providing an appropriate education.

What Goals Are Not

- Goals are not used for students who are in regular education. They are written for special education students—even special education students who are mainstreamed into regular classes.
- Goals are not part of a contract between you and the school district—that is, the school is not legally liable if your child does not meet the goals. Goals are a way to measure your child's progress.
- Goals are not the totality of your child's instructional plan. They are important aims to be accomplished during the school year.

Skill Areas Covered by Goals

Goals can cover a wide variety of skill or need areas. If your child is not having difficulties in certain areas, however, the IEP team typically will not develop goals in those areas.

The areas that goals can cover include:

- academic skills, such as math computation, reading comprehension, spelling, and writing

- cognitive skills, such as abstract thinking and memory
- emotional and psychological issues, such as overcoming fears or improving self-esteem
- social-behavioral skills, such as relating to peers
- linguistic and communication skills, such as expressing oneself effectively
- self-help and independent living skills, such as using money, dressing, using transportation, or using the toilet
- physical and recreational skills, such as improving fine and large motor skills
- vocational skills, such as work skill development, and
- transition skills, such as exploring work or college options.

Developing Goals

IDEA does not specify how to write goals, what subjects to cover, how many goals to include, or how to implement or measure them. The details are up to the IEP team. This flexibility allows you to develop goals that will be useful in conjunction with the programs and services you want for your child.

This section describes the typical elements of goals.

FORM
A sample Goals Chart appears later in this chapter. Also, see the section on goals in the sample IEP available on this book's Companion Page on www.nolo.com. See Chapter 16 for the link.

Child's Present Level of Performance

The written IEP must include a statement of your child's present levels of "academic achievement and functional performance," including how the child's disability affects his or her involvement and progress in the general curriculum. (20 U.S.C. § 1414(d)(1)(A).) This information will demonstrate how your child is doing and where your child needs to improve, which will in turn help the IEP team develop appropriate goals in each subject and behavioral area.

The IEP program should spell out your child's current level of skill in each particular goal area. For example, for a reading comprehension goal, a child's present level of performance may state, "Beth's current reading comprehension is at the mid–fourth-grade level. She enjoys reading but requires help in maintaining focus."

Who Implements Goals

Your child's classroom teacher is usually responsible for implementing your child's goals. Depending on the goal, however, an aide or support professional may also be involved. For example:

- A child's language goals may be the responsibility of a speech therapist.
- Physical education or motor goals, such as handwriting improvement, may be the responsibility of an occupational or physical therapist.
- Emotional goals may be addressed by a school counselor or therapist.

Completion Dates

Goals are normally written for a one-year period, but this is not set in stone. Some goals may be reached in less than a year—and it may be a good idea to set a shorter time frame in the written IEP.

EXAMPLE: Lily is in a special day class with no mainstreaming in a regular classroom. Her IEP reading goal has a completion time of one year. Lily's parents feel that she could reach her reading goal more quickly if she were in a regular classroom. Establishing a shorter period may help her parents convince the school that Lily should be mainstreamed.

Measuring Goals

The IDEA requires a child's goals to be "measurable." The IEP must describe how your child's progress toward the annual goals will be measured and when "periodic reports" on that progress will be given to you. (20 U.S.C. § 1414(d)(1)(A).)

There are a number of ways to measure goals, including objective testing, teacher or other staff observation, assessment of work samples, or any other method agreed to by the IEP team. Many IEP goals include a quantifiable accomplishment level, such as "Mia will read a four-paragraph story with 90% reading comprehension as measured by the Woodcock Reading Mastery Test."

Don't Set Your Sights Too Low

Be wary if an IEP team member from the school district suggests setting your child's goals fairly low. The district may want to set low standards so your child can achieve them without too much help from the school. If the school wants to eliminate a particular support service (such as a one-on-one aide) or keep your child in a special day class rather than mainstreaming him or her in a regular class, it might propose goals that your child can meet without this extra help.

The IDEA does not require goals to be quantifiable—that is, capable of being measured in numbers. Although numbers can be of value, not everything of value can be reduced to numbers. For example, how does one measure numerically whether goals were met in areas relating to emotions, psychology, self-help, or vocational skills?

> EXAMPLE: As a part of Serena's IEP program, Serena will explore whether she wants to go to college or begin work right after high school. As goals, these are stated as follows:
> - Serena will explore at least five areas of vocational interest.
> - Serena will read about five areas of vocational interest, write a brief explanation of each, and visit local examples of each.
> The best ways to "measure" Serena's achievement may be teacher observation or Serena's completion of a personal diary.

When to Draft Goals

While specific goals are approved at the IEP meeting and included in the IEP program, it makes sense to draft them ahead of time.

In fact, it is not uncommon for school representatives to write goals in advance. Under the IDEA, the school cannot simply present its goals at the IEP meeting, insist that you accept them, and refuse to discuss alternatives. That would violate a basic tenet of the IDEA—that the IEP team makes all IEP decisions as a group, at the meeting. Still, you should anticipate that the school district might draft goals in advance. Prepare for the IEP meeting by asking the school district (in writing) to give you a copy of any predrafted goals at least two weeks in advance.

You, too, should draft goals before the IEP meeting. You do not have to give a copy to the school district ahead of time; however, you can choose to do so. Some advocates might argue against doing this because it gives the district time to counter your goals. Others argue that if you present your goals for the first time at the IEP meeting, the school district might need time to review them—and may have to postpone the meeting.

In general, it is best to be open and provide the school district information in advance, unless the element of surprise is necessary in your particular situation.

Writing Effective Goals

Writing goals for the first time may seem as foreign to you as writing a medical prescription or nuclear physics equation. But don't worry— you'll get the hang of it. Like much of the IEP process, writing goals requires information gathering, asking questions, and a little practice.

Get Your School's IEP Form

Every school district has its own form on which the IEP program is written. You should get a copy and any guidelines that accompany it. As you begin to draft your child's goals, refer to the school's current IEP form for guidance.

Gather Your Information

Your dining room table or desk may be overrun with special education papers. If they are not already organized in a binder (as recommended in Chapter 4), take some time to gather them together. Make sure you have:

- your child's school file
- all evaluation reports
- written reports from professionals, and
- your blueprint.

Start with your blueprint—your desires for your child's education. The goals should support what's in your blueprint. While the blueprint won't show you how to write specific goals, it will help you think about what you ultimately want for your child. The goals you create will be the stepping stones your child uses to achieve these ultimate ends.

Talk to Professionals

Talk with your child's teacher, other support staff, your independent evaluator, service providers, and others who know your child. They might be willing to suggest specific goals, or at least to review yours.

If this is your child's first IEP, ask the professionals what areas your goals should cover and how to make them as specific as possible. Be sure to explore with them all the areas that you feel require goals.

If this is not your child's first IEP, ask professionals the following questions:

- What previous goals should be retained?
- If previous goals are carried over, why were they not accomplished before? What can be done to better ensure completion this year? Using the Progress Chart in Chapter 8 will help you monitor goals throughout the year.
- What new goals should be developed?

By talking with your child's teacher and other staff members about goals, you may learn their opinions about your child's placement and services. You may also develop an informal agreement on goals before the IEP meeting.

Talk to Other Parents

If you know other special education families, ask to see their IEPs, particularly if their child's needs are similar to your child's. Even if the needs are not the same, other parents may have very valuable information about how to draft goals; many are probably old pros at writing them.

Also, check with the PTA or school district's local advisory committee on special education for written material on goals, advice, and the names of any local individuals or organizations that provide help to special education parents. (Chapter 15 discusses parent organizations.)

Finally, check Appendix B on this book's Companion Page on Nolo. com for support organizations you can contact for help. (See Chapter 16 for the link.)

List Your Goal Areas

Your job is to develop goals for each skill area that relates directly to your child's needs. Eight such areas are listed at the beginning of this chapter. Be as precise as possible. For example, don't simply state "academic achievement." Specify reading, writing, math, cognitive, spelling, and the rest. Under social-behavioral, you might specify peer goals as well as self-control goals.

FORM
A sample Goals Chart is below; a blank, downloadable copy is available on this book's Companion Page on www.nolo.com. See Chapter 16 for the link. This chart is intended to give you a feel for what goals look like and provide you with language often used for different types of goals. Also, be sure to see the sample IEP form available on this book's Companion Page on www. nolo.com. See Chapter 16 for the link.

Goals Chart

Skill Area	Reading	Math	Emotional and psychological
Annual Goal	Josh, in his sophomore English class, will improve reading comprehension. He will demonstrate 90% comprehension of the assigned novel in his 10th grade English class	Alex, in his main-streamed class, will master 4th-grade math skills. He will subtract a one-digit number from a two-digit number with 90% accuracy	Leah, in a class of no more than 12 students in a small and protected educational environment, will reduce her outward anger
Present Performance Level	Josh demonstrates 50% comprehension of the assigned novel	Alex subtracts a one-digit number from a two-digit number with 25% accuracy	Leah averages five daily angry outbursts as observed
How Progress Measured	Essays assigned for homework, tests, and teacher observation	Teacher material	Teacher and therapist observation and recording
Date of Completion	June 20xx	June 20xx	June 20xx

Goals Chart, continued

Skill Area	Social-behavioral	Linguistic and communication	Self-help and independent living skills (transition services)
Annual Goal	Sarah will improve her peer relationships with the support of her aide and in a class of no more than ten students. Sara will initiate three positive peer interactions per day.	Adam, in his tri-weekly, 45-minute one-on-one speech therapy sessions, will improve articulation.	Nina will meet with the school guidance counselor each month, identify three fields of work that interest her, and arrange, with the counselor's help, to visit a workplace in each field by the end of the year.
Present Performance Level	Sara is unable to initiate positive peer interactions.	Adam produces the s, sh, and c sounds irregularly.	Nina doesn't know what she wants to do when she graduates from high school.
How Progress Measured	Teacher-aide observation and recording	Speech therapist observation and recording	Parent and guidance counselor observation
Date of Completion	June 20xx	June 20xx	June 20xx

Connect Goals to a Specific Program and Services

The best goals don't only state your immediate expectations for your child's performance, but also provide support for the program and services you want for your child. In fact, the goals in our sample form do just this. In the case of Leah, the sample is very descriptive—a "small and protected educational environment." While not all goals are written this way—schools often argue that goals are not the place to mention programs or services—the IDEA does not prevent such added language. You should argue for it and, at a minimum, include it in your draft goals.

The key is to write the goals so that an objective person will conclude that your child will need the particular program or service you seek to meet these goals. Write a variety of goals for each skill area, incorporating specific language and referring to the desired program and services. Then write a second set, omitting references to the program and services, but describing the programs and services you want. For example, assume you want your child in a regular classroom with a one-on-one aide in order to improve her reading comprehension. The ideal goal would be, "Mary, in Ms. Jones's regular third-grade class at Spencer School, will improve her reading comprehension, using her full-time one-on-one aide." The alternative would be, "With the assistance of her one-on-one aide, and by modeling her regular peers, Mary will improve her reading comprehension."

Preparing for the IEP Meeting

Now that you've gathered information and figured out what kinds of help your child will need, it's time to get ready for the IEP meeting, where you and the school district will hammer out the details of your child's special education program. Preparing for the IEP meeting will make you a better advocate for your child, allow you to influence the IEP meeting agenda effectively, and reduce your own anxieties. In short, preparation increases your chances of success.

If you are attending your first IEP meeting, be sure to read this entire chapter. If you've done IEPs before, you'll want to at least skim this chapter. You might find some new ideas that you can put to use.

While this chapter will help you prepare for the IEP meeting, everything that you've done to this point—gathering your child's school records, having your child evaluated, drafting a blueprint, and so on— will be crucial to the success of the meeting. If you've skipped any earlier chapters, you should go back and read them before reading this chapter.

Schedule the IEP Meeting

The IDEA sets out rules about scheduling the IEP meeting. (20 U.S.C. § 1414(d).)

- It must be held at a time and location convenient for all parties, especially the parents. The school district cannot simply schedule a meeting on a morning when you must be at work or pick a time without your input. (34 C.F.R. § 300.322(a).)
- It must be held at least once a year.
- It must be long enough to cover all issues.

Do You Need an Interpreter?

The school district must take necessary steps to ensure that you understand the IEP proceedings, including hiring an interpreter if you are deaf or hard of hearing, or if your first language is not English. (34 C.F.R. § 300.322(e).) Be sure to let the school district know in advance if you need an interpreter at the IEP meeting.

Date of the IEP Meeting

As discussed in Chapter 4, the best time for the IEP meeting is in the spring preceding the school year for which you are developing the IEP plan. Before you choose a date, you may have to make several calls to the district administrator and your attendees to make sure everyone can attend. Make sure to give yourself at least a month to prepare for the meeting.

Length of the IEP Meeting

The IDEA does not require that the IEP meeting last for a specific length of time. Before the meeting, ask the school administrator to find out how much time has been put aside. Two or three hours is common. If the administrator has allotted less time than you think is necessary, explain why you think a longer meeting is needed, particularly if it may eliminate the need for a second meeting. If the administrator insists that the time allotted is enough, put your concerns in writing and send a copy to the superintendent of schools. If you're really concerned, you can file a complaint (see Chapter 13), but there is no legal rule setting a minimum length for the IEP meeting.

Forgoing the IEP Meeting

Once you have your child's yearly IEP meeting, you and the school district can agree to make changes to the IEP without having another meeting. Instead, you can agree on a written document that changes the IEP. (20 U.S.C. § 1414(d)(3)(D).) Both you and the school district must consent to make changes this way.

IEP meetings can be taxing and often require parents to take time off work, so this can be a good alternative—unless you feel that you need the kind of discussion that typically takes place in an IEP meeting. If you choose to skip the meeting, be sure that your written agreement to change the IEP is clear and precise. You should also ask the school district to give you a new IEP document showing the changes, as required by 20 U.S.C. § 1414(d)(3)(F).

Sample Letter Requesting More Time for IEP Meeting

Date: February 28, 20xx

To: Ms. Julia Warner
    Director of Special Education
    Monroe School District
    892 South 4th Street
    Salem, OR 97307

Re: Karen Jamison, student in first-grade class of Drew Bergman

You indicated that we had one hour for my daughter Karen's March 14th IEP meeting. As I mentioned on February 27, I believe the issues we have to discuss will require at least two hours. It would be a hardship on our family to attend two meetings.

I will be calling you within the next few days to discuss this. I appreciate your understanding in this matter.

Sincerely,

Denise Jamison

Denise Jamison
909 Hanson St.
Salem, OR 97307
Phones: 555-3090 (home); 555-5000 (work)

cc: School Superintendent Maria Bander

Meeting by Conference Call or Video Conference

The IEP meeting can be held via phone or video conference. (20 U.S.C. § 1414(f).) (If you are deaf or hard of hearing, the school district will need to set up the meeting so you can use a relay system or TTY.) Both you and the school district must agree to use one of these alternate procedures; the school district cannot set this up without your approval.

While these options offer some advantages, especially if your schedule makes it difficult to leave your home or work to attend a meeting, there are also some potential drawbacks. In a phone conference, it can be difficult to identify who is talking and to clearly hear what is being said. These procedures can also inhibit the kind of free-wheeling discussion that can be very important in an IEP meeting.

When a Child With an IEP Transfers to Another School District

The IDEA has very specific rules about children who transfer from one school district to another. If a child transfers within the same state, then the new school district must provide, in consultation with the parents, a free appropriate public education with services "comparable" to that in the child's existing IEP. This comparable program will be in effect until a new IEP is developed. (20 U.S.C. § 1414(d)(2)(C)(i)(I).) If a child transfers to a different state, the same rules apply, except the comparable program will remain in effect until the new school district conducts an evaluation of the child, if the district thinks this is necessary, and a new IEP is developed. (20 U.S.C. § 1414(d)(2)(C)(i)(II).)

The term "comparable" doesn't necessarily mean "identical," but it certainly suggests something close. While you can't insist that your child be provided exactly the same program in all of its particulars, you shouldn't settle for a less effective alternative. For example, if your child had a placement in a regular classroom with a one-on-one aide two hours a week, a placement with comparable services would be a regular classroom with the same aide time, although the new aide may come only twice a week, rather than three times a week.

The new school district must also take reasonable steps to "promptly" obtain your child's records, including the written IEP and supporting documents, from the previous school district. The previous school district must take reasonable steps to respond to the request promptly. (20 U.S.C. § 1414(d)(2)(C)(ii).)

The IEP Meeting Agenda

Knowing the IEP meeting agenda in advance will help you tremendously as you prepare for the meetings. Although the IDEA does not require the district to provide you with an agenda, it does require that you be given the opportunity to participate in and understand the proceedings. (34 C.F.R. § 300.322.) It would not be unreasonable, therefore, to know what issues will be discussed.

Most IEP meetings cover the following issues:

- your child's current status—how he or she is doing, whether or not previous goals were met, and what the current evaluations state
- specific goals
- specific support or related services, and
- a specific program, including the type, makeup, and location of the class.

At least two weeks before the IEP meeting, ask the school district special education administrator for a written agenda or a description of the specific issues that will be discussed at the meeting. After you receive it, check it against your blueprint to make sure that the issues you've flagged will be covered at the meeting. If a crucial item is not on the agenda, let the administrator know, preferably in writing.

Organize Your Materials

Having access to key material is vitally important in an IEP meeting. You don't want to be fumbling about, looking for that one report or quote that could really help. Following these steps will help you organize the mountain of material.

Securing Documents Before the IEP Meeting

Before the IEP meeting, request from your district in writing, the following:

- all new assessments
- other new or recent reports, and
- if drafted, the IEP document itself.

Many districts do pre-print the IEP document before the meeting; reviewing this is especially important to see whether previous goals were met (or not), whether the new goals are the same or different, and whether the details of the program are already printed.

This last issue is crucially important because the key IEP components —program detail, goals, and related services—should be determined at the meeting, not before. Such a pre-printed document may be proof of "predetermination" (see Chapter 2, "The Importance of 'Process'").

In your written request, be sure to ask for the material at least two to three days in advance of the IEP meeting. Use simple language in your request. Here's an example: "in order to make the best use of IEP time and help to have a positive meeting, it will help us as parents a great deal to see the reports and the IEP document before the meeting. This will also more likely eliminate the need for a part two meeting."

Review Your Blueprint and All Written Material

Your starting point in getting organized is your blueprint. You should also gather all written material, such as evaluations, previous IEPs, notes and reports from your child's teacher and other staff members, work samples, and letters to and from your child's school district. These should be in your IEP binder, clearly labeled and organized for easy reference.

Review each document. Bring everything that supports your blueprint to the meeting. Also bring any materials that counter the negative points school district representatives might raise.

Highlight Supportive Material

Go through your binder and highlight or underline every important positive and negative statement. You may want to tab certain key statements for easy reference. How do you know what statements to highlight? Focus on the following:

- Test results, staff observations, reports, and other information on your child's current educational status. Highlight descriptive statements, such as "Tom scored at the first-grade level on the Brigance Test, Counting Subtest" or "Sheila has difficulty staying focused in class; any activity beyond three to five minutes can be quite taxing for her."

- Recommendations regarding program placement, related services, goals, and methodology. Look for statements such as "Carla would benefit from 30 minutes of speech therapy a week" or "Jason needs to be in a small classroom in which there are minimal disturbances or acting out behavior."

- The consequences of providing or not providing specific placements, services, methodologies, or other program components—for example, "Teri has significant fears about large groups and open space; placing her in a large class on a big campus will increase those fears and put her at risk for serious emotional difficulties."

As you go through all of your materials, you will probably highlight a lot of what you read, making the task of organizing seem overwhelming. To make it manageable, use different colored highlighters or tabs to differentiate the important from the less important statements or items— such as yellow for very important, green for somewhat important, and blue for less important. You can also make second copies of all significant items and keep them in a separate section in your IEP binder.

Use an IEP Material Organizer Form

Once your material is highlighted, you should take the time to create an additional document that will help you organize and access important information. I call it, for want of a more creative term, an IEP Material Organizer Form.

FORM

A sample IEP Material Organizer Form is below; a blank, downloadable copy is available on this book's Companion Page on www.nolo.com. See Chapter 16 for the link. Use one page for each major issue.

An IEP material organizer divides your written information, notes, and reports into important topics (such as related services or methodologies), keyed to your blueprint. As you can see from the sample, the IEP Material Organizer Form allows you to find specific information—such as an evaluation report, a pediatrician letter, or key statements made by a teacher or other potential witnesses—that support or dispute your blueprint items.

You can divide the IEP material organizer into subtopics that track your child's specific needs. For example, under "placement," you might have subtopics like class size, peer needs, type of class, location of class, and the like. Under the related service of a one-on-one aide, you might add the length and number of sessions, the qualifications of the aide, and what the aide will do. Under a curricula/methodology issue such as a reading program, you might include when the reading work is done or at what pace.

Feel free to use the IEP Material Organizer Form to subdivide issues in whatever way works for you.

Identify Negative Material and Prepare Rebuttals

Keeping in mind your blueprint and goals for your child, what materials hurt your position? Do test results, staff observations, or evaluator recommendations state that your child doesn't need what you want for him or her? Do statements such as "Ben does not need any special education services now" or "Leo should be provided one hour of aide time a week" (when you believe he needs one hour per day) or "Nicole cannot function in a regular classroom at this time" (when you're in favor of mainstreaming) appear in the written materials?

Some negative material is less direct. For example, a test result may not reflect the difficulties your child is actually experiencing. If an evaluation concludes that "Sandy is at age level for reading," you might face an uphill climb in convincing the school district she needs additional help. Or, a teacher's observation may undermine a placement or service you want. A teacher's statement that "Steven frequently acts out and disrupts classroom activities" may make it very hard for you to have Steven mainstreamed.

IEP Material Organizer Form

Issue: Related Service: 1:1 Aide

Use this form to track documents and people that provided support for or opposition to your goals.

Document Witness* Name(s)	Binder Location (if applicable)	Helps You	Hurts You	Key Supportive or Opposition Information	Rebuttal Document or Witness Name(s) (if hurts) (If none, what will you say at meeting?)
Lee Portaro (District) 2/1/xx evaluation	1C		✓	Recomm. #s 3, 6, 8, 10 (p. 8)	Brown Evaluation
Suzanne Brown 3/4/xx evaluation (independent)	1B	✓		Narrative (p. 3, ¶s 4, 5). Recomm. #s 1-7, p. 12	
Weekly Teacher Reports	1F	✓	✓	9/6/xx, 10/4/xx, 1/17/xx Support 10/14/xx, 11/5/xx, 2/2/xx Against	Portaro Report: No IEP Agreement on aide
5/2/xx IEP	1A	✓	✓	Narrative (¶s 7, 8) Against Narrative (¶s 2, 5) Support	Portaro p. 3 (¶2)
Dr. Baker (pediatrician) 1/22/xx letter	1G	✓		P. 2, Concerns for psychological impact if no aide	
Phil Anderson (tutor) 2/6/xx letter	1H	✓		Reports positive results with direct work, 1:1 work	
Karla Gamper (District psychologist)	1M		✓	Sees Scott once/month Reports no adverse psych. impact	
Student Work	1P	✓		Scott on 10/5 assignment writes "Don't understand, who cares."	

* A "witness" is someone (teacher, doctor, evaluator, tutor, psychologist) who gives an oral or written opinion regarding your child's needs at the IEP meeting.

Here are some ways to counter negative material:
- Look for anything that directly or indirectly contradicts a troublesome statement or report. For example, an aide's statement that "Steven's behavior is erratic, but with help he can control his behavior and focus effectively and quietly on his work" might help you convince the school that Steven can be mainstreamed.
- Look for professional opinions contrary to the school's position. Usually, statements in an independent evaluation can counter school data.
- Are the qualifications of the person who wrote the unfavorable statement appropriate? If a psychologist completed the school evaluation, find out if he or she has expertise in the specific areas to which the negative comments refer.
- Is the negative statement crystal clear? For example, what exactly does this observation mean: "While Jane does not need a small class, there is some indication that she has a difficult time in a large school environment"? The reference to a large school environment may indirectly support a small class placement.
- Is the unfavorable statement supported by data, testing results, or anecdotal information? If not, be prepared to point that out.

Use the IEP Material Organizer Form to identify negative statements and rebuttal information. While you should be prepared to address or rebut a troublesome statement, conclusion, or recommendation, this may not be possible. As a general rule, don't bring up negative statements unless the school district raises them first.

Provide Documents Before the IEP Meeting

In preparation for the IEP meeting, have everything in your binder marked, tabbed, highlighted, and referenced in your IEP material organizer. Also, make copies of material you want to show to school district representatives at the IEP meeting. This includes anything that supports your blueprint or rebuts negative information. The material can be in any form—a letter, report, independent evaluation, teacher's report, or work sample. You may want to make a copy for each person who will attend the meeting.

Provide the school district with a copy of all material you've generated, such as an independent evaluation. Give these to the district a week before the meeting. This way, school representatives can't argue that they need more time to review your material and must postpone the meeting.

As mentioned earlier, there may be a reason to surprise the district at the IEP meeting by introducing a particular item for the first time. As a general rule, however, it is best to play it straight and provide material ahead of time.

Draft Your Child's IEP Program

The IDEA requires you and the school district to develop the IEP program together. This does not mean, however, that you cannot—or should not—draft key portions of what you want to see in the IEP program beforehand. Drafting some language ahead of time can help you organize your arguments and recognize any potential roadblocks to getting what you want for your child.

Can Your School District Write the IEP Before the Meeting?

All IEP members, including you, must have a full opportunity to discuss all aspects of your child's IEP. This means that the district can't just present you with a completed IEP at the start of the IEP meeting and tell you to take it or leave it. Like you, however, the district can prepare draft statements ahead of time. School district representatives will probably have discussed the IEP agenda and their thoughts on your child's needs before the meeting—and they have every right to do so.

The key portions of the IEP program are:
- goals
- specific programs and placement
- related services, and

- other items, including curricula, methodology, and a description of the placement.

Writing out your IEP program will not only help you learn your material, but it will also force you to think again about how to make your case for the key issues. When you prepare your program you can either fill out a blank school district IEP form—you should get a copy early in the process—or write out your statements so you're ready to discuss them at the IEP meeting. As the IEP team proceeds, bring up the specific components you want in the IEP program.

Your blueprint and IEP Material Organizer Form will help you draft an IEP and participate effectively in the IEP meeting. Chapter 11 explains how the IEP form and blueprint work together and how to get as much of your blueprint as possible included on the IEP form.

Goals

Goals refer to the things you want your child to achieve—usually involving reading, math, and language skills, social development, motor skills, behavioral issues, and other cognitive areas of need. Chapter 9 covers goals in detail.

Specific Programs and Placement

Program and placement refer to the exact school, class, and classroom characteristics you want for your child.

EXAMPLES:
- Placement in the special day class for learning disabled students at Hawthorne School.
- Placement in a special day class for children with developmental delays, no more than 12 students, and a qualified teacher; SDC at Laurel or Martin schools is appropriate.
- Placement in Tina's home school, the regular third-grade class.

Child Profile

The school district might balk if you present them with a fully drafted IEP program or blueprint. As an alternative, you might prepare a statement for the IEP meeting that incorporates important information without necessarily triggering school district opposition. Instead of emphasizing goals, placement, and services, emphasize your child's personality and needs.

> EXAMPLE: Kira has a learning disability with specific difficulties with auditory memory, spelling, and reading comprehension. She has some emotional difficulties because of her learning disability, which appear in the forms of anxiety, fear of other children, and concern with safety. She has on a few occasions run off campus. When placed in a large classroom her fears can be increased.
>
> Kira needs a program in which the environment is not overly active, with no behavioral problems; she should not be on a large campus, which might overwhelm her. She needs to be in a classroom of no more than 15 children; she benefits from the Slingerland method and requires instruction in simple, small steps. She needs one-on-one help with reading for at least two hours a day, and does best when this help is provided in continuous segments that are at least 30 minutes long.

This child profile combines parts of the blueprint with a description of your child and her needs. It is not unlike a school district's evaluation, which normally includes a narrative section describing your child. Although you will want to draft the child profile for the meeting, do not give it to the school district in advance. Focus on:

- describing your child (quiet, kind, determined, afraid)
- your child's areas of need, including academic, social, and environmental, and
- weaving in references to specific service and placement needs.

Related Services

Related services are developmental, corrective, and other supportive services (such as transportation) that your child needs to benefit from special education or to be placed in a regular class.

> EXAMPLES:
> - Jade needs three speech therapy sessions per week, each session for 30 minutes, one-on-one with a qualified speech therapist.
> - Maria needs a full-time one-on-one aide in order to be mainstreamed in a regular fifth-grade class, the aide to be qualified to assist Maria specifically in the areas of reading comprehension, spelling, fifth-grade math, and developing positive peer relationships.

The IDEA requires the provision of related services to be based on peer-reviewed research, "to the extent practicable." This means that the IEP team should decide which services are appropriate based on well-established data, gathered according to prevailing methods in the field—not simply on what you or the school district "feel" might work or on what the school district has to offer. Of course, there may not be peer-reviewed research on every potential related service, and there doesn't have to be. If your child needs a related service to benefit from his or her education, that service is required by the IDEA—the "to the extent practicable" language protects your right to a necessary related service even if there isn't peer-reviewed research to back it up.

Other Components

Other components of the IEP program include:
- curricula, including how your child will be involved and progress in the general curriculum found in the regular classroom, and whether specific related services or special education are needed to ensure your child's involvement and progress
- teacher methodology

- program modifications or supports required for your child;
  a program modification might be allowing your child to sit
  at the front of the classroom or providing a classroom that is
  acoustically designed to minimize distracting noise
- transition plans, including vocational needs, and
- extracurricular activities such as after-school clubs, lunchtime
  activities, and sports.

RELATED TOPIC
Chapter 2 provides details on each of these components of the IEP.

Establish Who Will Attend the IEP Meeting

Under the IDEA, any person with knowledge or expertise about your child may attend the IEP meeting. This includes the following people:

- you and your child's other parent
- your child, if appropriate (see "Representing the Parents," below)
- a representative of the school district who is qualified to provide or supervise your child's special education and is knowledgeable about the general curriculum
- your child's special education teacher
- your child's regular classroom teacher if your child is, or may be, in a regular class
- a person who can interpret the evaluations and their impact on instructional strategies
- at your discretion or the discretion of the school district, other people who have knowledge or expertise regarding your child or her needs
- if your child is 16 or older, someone who knows about transitional services, and
- if your child received early childhood services (called Part C services in the IDEA), a representative of those Part C services can be invited to the meeting at your request. (20 U.S.C. § 1414(d)(1)(B) and (D).)

Rules on Meeting Attendance

Certain IEP members can be excused from the IEP meeting. If the member's area of curriculum or related services will not be modified or discussed, that person does not have to attend—but only if you and the school district both agree, in writing, to excuse that person. For example, if your child receives physical therapy and that service is not going to be discussed or changed, then the physical therapist need not attend. (20 U.S.C. § 1414(d)(1)(C)(i).) Of course, if you think the service should be discussed or changed, you should insist that the member attend.

Even if someone's area of curriculum or services will be discussed or modified, that person may still be excused, but only if you and the school district consent and the absentee submits written "input into the development of the IEP" to the team before the meeting. (20 U.S.C. § 1414(d)(1)(C)(ii).) In this situation, you should be very sure that the written report is sufficient before you agree to excuse that person. Because IEP meetings are fluid, you cannot always know which issues may come up, what direction the discussion will take, or when a response or comment from a particular team member might be helpful. Proceed with caution when considering excusing an IEP attendee.

Representing the School District

Knowing who will attend the IEP meeting on behalf of the school district will help you prepare. The school district should give you a written list of attendees, but if you are not told at least two weeks before the meeting, write the district and ask for the following information for each person who will attend:

- name
- reasons for attending
- qualifications and specific title, and
- whether he or she knows your child and, if so, in what capacity.

Prepare a list of all participants, including the positions they are likely to take on your child's needs.

FORM

A sample IEP Meeting Participants form is below; a blank, downloadable copy is available on this book's Companion Page on www.nolo.com. See Chapter 16 for the link.

Your Child's Teacher(s)

If your child is in a regular class, then his or her current teacher must attend the IEP meeting. Your child's teacher has the most information about your child's education and the most experience with your child. The teacher may write reports about your child's progress, help write goals, be responsible for seeing that these goals are met, and make recommendations for the next school year.

The teacher can be your best ally or your worst enemy in the IEP process. Either way, the teacher is often the most convincing team member. If the teacher supports your position, you have a better chance of success. If the teacher does not, the school district may feel it would win any due process dispute and, therefore, may decide to stand its ground at the IEP meeting.

Making sure the teacher understands your concerns and is prepared to speak frankly about them is crucial, but not always easy to achieve. Teachers work for their school districts, and may face subtle or not-so-subtle pressure to make recommendations that fit within the school's budgetary or other constraints. A teacher who speaks frankly regardless of what a school administrator thinks is invaluable—but not always easy to find. It is therefore vital that you keep in contact with the teacher, ask his or her opinion, and indicate your concerns. Be specific, direct, fair, and always conscious of the teacher's time.

RELATED TOPIC

Chapter 8 discusses the importance of keeping in regular contact with your child's teacher and talking with teachers and other school personnel before the IEP meeting.

IEP Meeting Participants

Name	Position/Employer	Purpose for Attending	Point of View
Fred Gomez	Third grade teacher, Kensington School District	Gene's teacher	Supports Gene's placement in regular class; does not think Gene needs aide
Diana Hunt	Psychologist, Kensington School District	Did evaluation	Recommends placement in special day class
Violet King	Psychologist, Independent evaluator	Did Independent evaluation	Supports regular class and aide
Jane Lim	Speech therapist, Kensington School District	Representative of school district	Agrees with need for speech therapy, but not on amount
Phil Chase	Administrator, Kensington School District	Representative of school district	No stated position

Which Teacher Must Attend the IEP Meeting

The IDEA says the IEP team must include "not less than one regular education teacher of the child if the child is or may be participating in the regular education environment." (34 C.F.R. § 300.321(a)(2).) Here a key question is whether the required regular education teacher has to be the child's current regular teacher or simply any teacher. Some districts have interrupted "of the child" to mean a teacher who could be but is not currently the regular education teacher. This makes sense if the child is not currently in the regular education environment, but it doesn't make sense if the child is currently in regular education. In this case, "of the child" should be read to be the child's actual regular education teacher. If that regular education teacher does not attend the meeting, that is a procedural violation and may very well be significant (see our discussion of significant procedural violations, "The Importance of 'Process'" in Chapter 2).

School Administrator

In most cases, someone representing the school district will attend the IEP meeting. This may be the district special education coordinator, student services director, county or regional office of education administrator, or school principal. There are all kinds of administrators, just like there are all kinds of parents. The administrator may be kind, cooperative, and a terrific advocate for your child—or may be burned-out, unpleasant, and remarkably bureaucratic.

Before the meeting, you will be working with the administrator a good deal and may want to ask what his or her position is regarding the key issues for your child's IEP. Is it a good idea to do so? Many a wise administrator will let you know when he or she agrees with you, but will not let you know in advance about disagreements. That doesn't mean you can't ask, but it does mean you should consider the pros and cons of asking the administrator's position prior to the IEP meeting.

Pros

- You will find out if the administrator agrees with you.
- If you get an honest answer, you'll know what the administrator thinks and how strong his or her feelings are.
- If you disagree with the answer, you may convince the administrator to change his or her mind, or you will better know how to prepare for the IEP meeting.
- You may learn about options you like.

Cons

- The administrator will learn your goals and be able to counter them.
- You may put the administrator on guard, making it difficult for you to communicate with staff, visit programs, and the like.

If you decide to ask and the administrator opposes your goals for your child, consider the following:

- If the administrator will not support you on a particular item, he or she may have violated the IDEA—that is, made a decision before the IEP meeting. This may be the basis of a formal complaint against the school district (see Chapter 13). This doesn't mean you should trap the administrator into making a decision outside of the IEP meeting. But if it happens, be aware of your rights.
- If the administrator has not made a decision, you may want to share the materials you have that support your position. You might give the administrator some ideas as to why the district can agree with you. On the other hand, this may help the administrator rebut you at the IEP meeting. You'll have to judge the chances of making the administrator into an ally versus a well-prepared adversary.

School Psychologist and Other Specialists

Depending on your child's condition and needs, other professionals may be involved in the IEP meeting, such as a school psychologist, speech therapist, occupational therapist, physical therapist, adaptive physical education specialist, or resource specialist. They may provide evaluation reports and other information regarding your child, and are likely to have opinions about goals, services, and placement. Like your child's teacher, these specialists may be great allies or formidable foes.

As with the teacher or administrator, speak with the specialists ahead of time to find out their positions on key issues.

Representatives From Noneducational Public Agencies

Sometimes, representatives from other public agencies may attend an IEP meeting, particularly if responsibility for certain IEP services is entrusted to an agency other than the school district. In California, for example, mental health services are provided by the county mental health department, and therefore a representative from that agency will often be present. In Vermont, a representative of an agency other than the school district will attend to discuss transition services. If the child has been involved with the juvenile authorities, a probation officer may attend, depending on the laws in your state.

Prior to the IEP meeting, talk with any of these additional folks and find out why they are attending the meeting, what they will do there (such as report on your child), and what position (if any) they plan to take on your child's needs.

Limits on School Representatives

Are there limits to who can attend the meeting? Federal policy states that a school may not invite so many people as to make the IEP meeting intimidating. State laws and policies may also cover who may attend IEP meetings. California, for example, requires that the IEP meeting be "nonadversarial"—and having ten district employees may make the IEP meeting feel very adversarial indeed.

The IDEA requires that people who attend the IEP meeting at the invitation of a parent or the school district have knowledge or special expertise about the child. If it seems inappropriate for a particular person to attend based on this standard, notify the school in writing of your concern. State why the individual is not qualified to attend, or why his or her attendance is not necessary or helpful. If the school insists that the person attend, see Chapter 13 on filing a complaint. And at the IEP meeting, state for the record, without being personal, that you feel so-and-so should not be there. When it's time to sign the IEP plan, reiterate your objection.

FORM

A sample letter objecting to a particular person attending the IEP meeting is below; a blank, downloadable copy is available on this book's Companion Page on www.nolo.com. See Chapter 16 for the link.

One Teacher Too Many

I once represented a child at an IEP meeting where there were a dozen school representatives, including several administrators, the school nurse, and Bruce, the "teacher of the day." I asked Bruce if he knew my client, Laura. The answer was no—he had neither met her nor knew anything about her. I asked him why he was there. Without hesitation he said he was there to "represent the teachers of the area." The involvement of someone like Bruce—or anybody else with no knowledge of your child or the relevant educational issues—would be contrary to federal policy and the underlying purpose of the IEP meeting.

Representing the Parents

While some of the people representing the school district may support your goals for your child, you may want some or all of the following people to attend the IEP meeting on your behalf:

- your spouse or partner
- your child

- others who know your child, such as a relative or close family friend
- independent evaluators or other professionals who have worked with your child, and
- an attorney.

Contact these people well in advance to let them know the date, time, location, and likely duration of the meeting. Make sure they understand the key topics that will arise during the IEP meeting, and the issues and solutions they are there to discuss. Let them know the positions of the various school representatives on the key issues, and be sure to show them copies of materials that both support and are contrary to your goals.

Remind your attendees that the IEP meeting is informal and that points of view should be stated in a positive but firm way. Disagreements can be spirited, but should remain professional and respectful.

Some of the people you ask to attend—such as an independent evaluator, a pediatrician, another specialist, or a lawyer—might charge you a fee. Find out the cost ahead of time. If you can't afford to have the person stay for the entire meeting, let the school administrator know in advance that you will have someone attending who needs to make a statement and leave. Before the meeting, ask the administrator to set aside a specific time for that person to speak.

Some people you want to attend might not be able to, or you might not be able to afford to pay them to attend. In either situation, ask the person to prepare a written statement for you to read at the meeting. Some people's testimony may actually be better in writing than it would be in person—for example, someone who is timid or reluctant to strongly state a position in person might come across better in writing.

RELATED TOPIC
Chapter 8 discusses items to include in a written statement from your child's doctor or other people from outside the school.

IEP Meeting Attendance Objection Letter

Date: _May 15, 20xx_

To: _Dr. Sean Gough_

Hamilton School District

1456 Howard Avenue

8709 Fourth Street

Little Rock, AR 72212

Re: _Amy Crane, student in 3rd grade class of Carol Silberg_

I understand that _Joan Green, the district's psychologist_ will be at _Amy's_ IEP meeting. _Joan Green_ knows nothing about _Amy_ and appears to have no knowledge that might be of use to the IEP team. I am formally requesting that _Ms. Green_ not attend, unless there is some clear reason that makes _Ms. Green's_ attendance appropriate and necessary for the development of _Amy's_ IEP plan. As you know, IEP meetings can be particularly difficult for parents. We are already anxious about ours and would prefer that you not take action that will heighten our stress level.

If you insist on _Ms. Green_ attending without a good reason, then we will file a complaint with the state and federal departments of education.

I will call you in a few days to find out your decision on this issue. Thank you for considering my request.

Sincerely,

Eva Crane

Eva Crane

88 2nd Street

Little Rock, AR 72212

Phones: 555-1998 (home); 555-8876 (work)

Parents

While work schedules or living arrangements may make attending the IEP meeting difficult, it is generally best if both parents attend, even if they are divorced or separated. If you have differences of opinion, resolve them before the IEP meeting. If you argue with each other during the IEP meeting, you could damage your credibility and chances of success.

If one of you cannot attend, prepare a strong and emotional statement for the other to read.

Can an IEP Meeting Be Held Without You?

Your school district has a duty to ensure that you are present at the IEP meeting. It can hold an IEP meeting without your involvement only in unusual situations, and only after following very specific procedures, including:

- notifying you early enough of the meeting to ensure you have the opportunity to attend
- scheduling the meeting at a mutually convenient time and place, and
- finding ways of including you—including individual or conference telephone calls—if you cannot attend.

The district can proceed without you only if it can prove that it took specific steps to convince the parent to attend, by showing records of attempts to arrange a mutually agreeable time and place, detailed phone records, correspondence, and even visits to your home or workplace. (34 C.F.R. § 300.322(d).)

Your Child

A student may attend the IEP meeting if it is appropriate or if the IEP team is considering transition services for a child. (20 U.S.C. § 1414(d)(1).)

When is it considered appropriate for a child to attend? A child who can speak about his or her hopes and needs may be a compelling self-advocate. But be careful—if your child is unpredictable or unsure of the importance of the meeting, you may not want to risk the possibility of a "wrong" answer. For example, you want your son to remain in his mainstreamed program. A school district representative says, "Tell me, Tommy, do you want to stay in your class?" You're not going to be happy if Tommy responds, "Nope."

If your child does attend, focus on his or her feelings and hopes. You probably want to avoid referring to the written materials, unless your child is older—perhaps a teenager. In that case, you can ask something like, "Chris, the school evaluator says you had a hard time in Ms. Shaver's class, particularly with other students. Why do you think that was so?" Be sure you know what his answer will be.

Sample Statement to IEP Team

To: Morgan Haversham's IEP Team

From: Claudine Haversham (Morgan's mom)

Date: March 1, 20xx

I cannot attend the March 15th IEP meeting, but I wanted you to know that I am very concerned that Morgan might be removed from her regular program. She is such a happy child now that she is mainstreamed. As her mother, I see the joy in her eyes when she gets up in the morning to get ready for school. A placement in a more restrictive environment would be devastating to my daughter. I must be frank and tell you that we will vigorously oppose any efforts to remove Morgan from her current program.

I greatly appreciate your sensitivity to Morgan's needs and your past assistance in making her educational experience a positive one.

Sincerely,

Claudine Haversham

Claudine Haversham

Relatives, Friends, and Child Care Workers

It is important to limit the number of people who attend the IEP meetings—the more people in attendance, the longer the meeting can drag on. Therefore, you'd normally not bring a relative, friend, or child care worker to the meeting. But if someone can present a view of your child that wouldn't otherwise be told, you might want that person to come. For example, if your daughter's regular babysitter can describe how your otherwise shy and reserved child talks for the first 30 minutes after she gets home about how she loves being in a regular class, it may be powerful testimony.

Generally, a sibling or peer of your child, particularly a young one, should not attend unless he or she is the only person who can speak to an issue or has a really powerful presence. Preparing young attendees will be very important, with focus on the sibling or peer's "feelings" about your child, rather than more formal information.

Bring Someone to Take Notes

Ask a friend or relative to attend the IEP meeting and take notes for you —paying careful attention to who says what regarding important items. A notetaker can be invaluable, particularly if you anticipate a controversial meeting.

Independent Evaluators and Other Professionals

Because the conclusions reached by any independent evaluator who tested your child will probably be instrumental in helping you secure the right services and placement, it is crucial that the evaluator attend the IEP meeting. The evaluator must be able to clearly articulate his or her professional opinion on the key blueprint items and on all evaluation data. The evaluator must also be prepared to rebut contradictory information presented by the school district.

Other professionals, such as a pediatrician, private tutor, therapist, or psychological counselor, can be important witnesses on your behalf if they know your child and can speak to key issues affecting the IEP plan. Prepare these individuals as you would prepare an independent evaluator.

See "Independent Evaluations" in Chapter 8 for a detailed discussion of your right to, and the usefulness of, an independent evaluation.

An Attorney

If you hire or consult an attorney during the IEP process, that person can attend the IEP meeting. You can also hire a lawyer just for the IEP meeting. (See Chapter 14 for information on working with lawyers.) As a general rule, you may want an attorney at the IEP meeting if your relationship with the school district has deteriorated and you anticipate a complicated and difficult IEP meeting.

If you bring an attorney to the IEP meeting, school representatives are more likely to be on guard and less likely to speak frankly. On the other hand, if the school administrators haven't been cooperative and you feel the plan that will emerge from the IEP meeting will be harmful to your child, bringing an attorney shows you mean business. You're much better off not using an attorney—it does change the entire experience—but if you must, then find one who is reasonable and cooperative.

If you plan to have an attorney at the IEP meeting, you should notify the school district reasonably in advance. Except in unusual situations, you will be responsible for paying your attorney, with little chance of reimbursement. (See "How Attorneys Are Paid" in Chapter 14 for information on when you might be reimbursed for lawyer's expenses.)

Final Preparation

As you finish your IEP preparation, consider these additional recommendations.

Taping the IEP Meeting

You (and the school district) have the right to tape-record the meeting. While a tape recording may be the best proof of what was said, it may have an inhibiting effect. People don't always want to make a particular statement "on the record." In addition, tape recordings are not always of great quality; participants are not always audible, and it can be hard to discern what was said and who said it.

If you decide to tape-record, bring a good quality recorder. Bring extra tapes and batteries in case an outlet is not accessible. The school district can tape-record even if you object—just as you can tape over the objections of school representatives. If the school district tapes the meeting, you are entitled to a copy of the tape, and it becomes part of your child's file—just as the district can ask for a copy of your tape.

You should notify the district in advance that you want to tape-record the meeting.

School Resistance to Tape-Recording

The U.S. Department of Education, Office of Special Education Programs, has issued several statements reinforcing the right of parents to tape-record IEP meetings. If, once you get to the meeting, the special education administrator says you cannot tape-record, ask to reschedule the meeting. You can also state that this affects your ability to function at the IEP meeting, that it is against the law, and that you will file a complaint. (After the meeting, follow up with a letter to the school administrator; see Chapter 13 for advice on filing a complaint.)

Reducing Your Anxiety

It is a given that you will be nervous at the meeting, so don't worry about being anxious. But do give some thought to what you might do before the IEP meeting to relax. It may be taking a walk or jogging, going out for breakfast, or any other activity that helps you settle your nerves. If you need to get a babysitter or take time off from work, set it up well in advance, so you're not scrambling the day before the meeting.

By preparing—knowing your material, completing your IEP blueprint, drafting your IEP plan, and talking to your IEP participants ahead of time—you will do much to reduce your anxiety.

IEP Preparation Checklist

Things to do before the IEP meeting:
- Find out the date, time, and location.
- Get a copy of the school's agenda.
- Make your own agenda.
- Prepare your IEP material organizer.
- Draft an IEP plan.
- Find out who is attending on behalf of the school district.
- Invite and prepare your own IEP meeting participants form.
- Give the school a copy of the following:
  - independent evaluations
  - documents such as formal reports and work samples
  - names and titles of people attending the IEP meeting, and
  - notice of intent to tape-record IEP meeting (if applicable).
- Create meeting reminder list of items you want to be sure to remember:
  - "Make sure we read statements of Dr. Wilson and Rona (babysitter), who can't attend."
  - "Make sure Dr. Ramirez covers Lydia's physical therapy needs."
  - "We don't have to sign all of the IEP—we can object."

FORM

An IEP Preparation Checklist is available on this book's Companion Page on www.nolo.com. See Chapter 16 for the link.

Attending the IEP Meeting

Your IEP meeting is soon. You'll enter the room, sit down, put your binder on the table, take a deep breath, and do just fine. You'll do fine because being nervous is natural, the school administrator probably feels the same way and, most important, you are prepared for this meeting. You've developed your child's blueprint and drafted an ideal IEP, supported by various documents. You're familiar with the school's IEP form, policies, programs, and services. You know who will attend the meeting and where each person stands on key issues. You have people with you who are prepared to help you make your case.

RELATED TOPIC

Chapter 10 provides valuable advice on preparing for the IEP meeting. Chapter 7 provides tips on preparing for and attending an IEP eligibility meeting.

TIP

IEP meetings are not always required. Once the annual IEP meeting takes place, you and the school district may agree to make written changes to the IEP without holding another meeting. This can save time, but there may be some risks to proceeding without a meeting. See Chapter 10 for more information on how having an IEP meeting may be the best way to advocate for your child.

Getting Started

IEP meetings can take a lot of time, so it's very important that you be punctual. In fact, you'll want to be at least ten to 15 minutes early so you can get the lay of the land, see the meeting room, and perhaps say a few words to the teacher or school administrator. Also, being early will give you the chance to talk to your participants and make sure they are clear about their roles at the meeting.

What to Bring

Bring your IEP binder and the written material you've gathered, including evaluations, letters, reports, and your IEP Material Organizer

Form. Make sure you have extra copies of key documents, such as an independent evaluation.

Get the Notetaker Organized

It's a good idea to bring someone to take notes, particularly if you anticipate a controversial meeting. Make sure you provide your notetaker with paper and pens (or a laptop computer). Remind your notetaker to take detailed notes regarding important items, particularly those that relate to your blueprint—what was said and who said it are especially important. These notes, particularly for items that you and the school district dispute, will be extremely important should you end up filing for due process (see Chapter 12) or making a formal complaint (see Chapter 13). If you do not have a notetaker, make sure you give yourself time to jot down important statements.

Set Up the Recorder

If you're planning to record the meeting, set up the equipment and check that it's working.

RELATED TOPIC
"Final Preparation" in Chapter 10 explains how to notify the school district in advance of your intent to record the IEP meeting and how to deal with any dispute that arises about recording the meeting.

How the Meeting Will Begin

The IEP meeting is typically led by the school administrator responsible for special education programs, although it may be led by the school site principal, the school district evaluator, or even a teacher.

Most IEP meetings begin with introductions. School representatives will explain their roles at the meeting. You should do the same with your participants. If, for example, a friend will take notes or an outside evaluator will present a report, make that clear.

After introductions, the administrator will probably discuss the agenda and then explain how the meeting will run and how decisions will be made.

 RELATED TOPIC

Obtaining the agenda in advance is discussed in Chapter 10.

IEP Meeting Basic Dos and Don'ts

Is there an etiquette to the IEP meeting? There should be. As in any potentially difficult encounter, try to proceed in a positive way.

Dos

- Do respect other opinions.
- Do try to include all IEP team members in the process.
- Do ask questions in a fair and direct way.
- Do state your position firmly, but fairly.
- Do explore ways of reaching consensus.

Don'ts

- Don't interrupt.
- Don't accuse.
- Don't make personal attacks.
- Don't raise your voice.
- Don't question another's motives.

You might begin by saying that you appreciate everyone's attendance, the time and energy they're giving to your child, and their professional dedication. Emphasize that you are determined to discuss all issues in a fair and thorough way, and that you are looking forward to a challenging but ultimately positive meeting in which everyone's point of view is respected.

If the agenda is different from what you anticipated or omits issues you want to cover, bring up your concerns at the beginning of the meeting. You have the right to raise any issue you want at the IEP meeting. Also, if the agenda appears too long for the allotted time, explain that you don't think there will be enough time to cover everything, and ask that certain items be discussed first. If your request is denied, do your best to keep the meeting moving forward.

While most IEP meetings follow a certain pattern (discussed in "Writing the IEP Plan," below), don't be surprised if yours seems to have a life of its own, going in directions you did not anticipate. Just make sure your key issues are covered before the meeting ends.

Simple Rules for a Successful IEP Meeting

Several simple rules can help you get the most out of the IEP meeting.

Know Your Rights

The IDEA was created for your child and provides for:

- a free appropriate public education (FAPE) in the
- least restrictive environment (LRE), based on an
- individualized education program (IEP).

Parents are coequal decision makers—just as important as everyone else at the IEP meeting.

RELATED TOPIC
Chapter 2 explains your child's legal rights under the IDEA.

Don't Be Intimidated

You have special knowledge of your child's needs. School personnel are not the only experts. If you have documents to support each item you want in the IEP plan, you may be even better prepared than school representatives.

At the same time, don't automatically assume that teachers or other school officials are wrong. There are many dedicated teachers and school administrators who want to provide the best education for your child, have expertise in educating children with disabilities, and have been through this process numerous times before. This doesn't mean you won't encounter opposing opinions or perhaps even run up against someone who is incorrect or just plain nasty. But as a general rule, most folks are in special education because they want to help.

Focus on Your Child's Needs—Not Cost or Administrative Constraints

The IDEA recognizes that each child's needs are unique and, therefore, that each individual program will be different. If you can show that your child needs a specific service, such as a one-on-one aide or two hours of occupational therapy each week, then the law requires it.

If the school district does not have the staff to provide the related service your child needs, such as a speech therapist, then the school should pay for a private therapist.

A child's needs—not cost—should dictate all IEP decisions. For example, the school administrator cannot refuse to discuss or provide a service or placement because it "costs too much." An administrator may try to get the point across indirectly, by saying something like "If we provide that service for your child, another child will not get services she needs." Don't argue the issue; simply respond with something like this:

> *Mr. Keystone, it is wrong for you to make my child responsible for your budgetary difficulties. I won't be put in the position of making a choice between my child's needs and the needs of other children. The law is clear that we should be discussing an appropriate education for my child, not the cost.*

If you can't reach agreement, and the school district representatives continue to admit that there is an administrative or budget problem, be sure you (or your notetaker) has written this down in case you end up in due process.

This is not to say that cost is never an issue. Let's say you want your child in Program X and the school offers to put your child in Program Y, which is less costly for the district. You're unable to reach an agreement and decide to resolve the matter through due process. If the district can prove Program Y is appropriate for your child, it will likely prevail at the due process hearing.

Remember: The IDEA does not require the best education for your child, but an appropriate one. You won't win a fight for the ideal program when an appropriate one is available.

> **TIP**
> **Don't describe the program you want as "the best," "optimum," or "maximum."** The school district might use these descriptions as evidence that you want more than the "appropriate" education to which your child is entitled under the IDEA. If you feel that a program or service offered by the school isn't right, characterize it as "inappropriate"—this will signal that you don't think the school district is meeting its legal obligations.

Know When to Fight—and When Not To

Understanding the IEP process and having a clear step-by-step strategy does not mean that all problems will be resolved in a manner you think best. It is important to realize when you don't have a case. You may be fully prepared, do a superb job in the IEP meeting, and still not have enough evidence to support your position. Knowing the strength of your case will help you know when to fight and when to concede.

Fight for the crucial issues and be more flexible on others. For instance, goals and test protocol may be important, but, ultimately, the related services, placement, and methodology are what matter in your child's education. Fighting for half an hour over the wording of one goal is probably a waste of time; spending half of the meeting on a major issue like placement is probably worth it.

Ask Questions

You should always feel comfortable asking questions—and there will undoubtedly be times during the IEP meeting when you need more information or clarification. There are several very good reasons to ask questions: to obtain basic information, to persuade someone of your position, or to question a blanket assertion.

How to Deal With Intimidating or Nasty Comments

For many parents, dealing with teachers and school administrators in an IEP meeting can be intimidating. You don't want to (but may) hear:

- *I'm sorry, Mr. Walker, but you're wrong.*
- *I'm sorry, Ms. Richards, the law doesn't say that.*
- *Your evaluation report is incorrect.*
- *Our policy precludes that.*
- *Maybe they do that in another school district, but we don't.*
- *I will not agree to that!*
- *That's enough on that subject!*

In most cases, you can ignore these kinds of comments or make a simple response. (In "Ask Questions," above, we discuss how to challenge blanket assertions.) Try to determine whether the comment is anything more than just an impolite or negative remark. If it is unimportant, say your piece and move on.

"I don't appreciate your tone of voice, Ms. Hanson. I have treated you with respect and expect the same from you. Even if we disagree, we can do it in a civil way. More important, your statement is not correct (or reasonable or productive or conducive to a positive IEP meeting)."

If the comment seems important, you may need to be more assertive.

"Ms. Hanson, I resent your comment and believe you are undermining this IEP meeting. Please understand, I will do what is necessary to ensure that my child receives the program she needs and will bring your behavior to the attention of the appropriate individuals."

If you don't feel calm and your voice is shaky, that's okay, too. Just don't yell or get overly aggressive. If necessary, you may want to raise the possibility of filing a formal complaint regarding something that seems illegal—for example, if the district won't allow you to discuss your independent evaluation. (Chapter 13 covers complaints.) But don't make a threat without first thinking it through. Do you really have grounds to file a formal complaint? Is there any validity to the school representative's comment? Is it worth alienating the school district and changing the atmosphere of the IEP meeting? In most cases, you can make your point without threatening to file a formal complaint.

Obtain Basic Information

During the IEP meeting, many technical terms will be used. If you don't understand something, ask what it means. It's better to ask—even for the tenth time—than to proceed without understanding.

Most important, find out what these terms mean for your child. Knowing that your child scores at the 42nd percentile on the Wechsler is useless unless it tells you something about your child's abilities and opportunities to improve.

Persuade

Asking questions can be an effective way of persuading others that your position is right and theirs may be wrong. State your questions positively, such as "Do you [IEP team members] agree with the recommendations on page eight of Dr. Calderon's report?" or "Ms. Porter, do you agree that Amy should be placed in a regular eighth-grade class with a one-on-one aide?"

Sometimes you may need to establish agreement on preliminary matters before asking these kinds of big questions.

EXAMPLE: You want a particular IEP member to agree with you on placement. You realize that you must first establish agreement on the evaluation supporting that placement. You first ask, "You read Dr. Harper's report. She states that Carolyn needs, and I am quoting, 'a quiet environment in which there are no behavioral problems or acting out by other students.' Do you agree with Dr. Harper?" The IEP member agrees and you follow up by asking, "Given Dr. Harper's report and our desire that Carolyn be placed in the special day class at the Manning School, do you agree with that placement?"

Someone may chafe at being asked such a pointed question and may feel cross-examined. One good way to respond would be to say, "I certainly don't mean to cross-examine you and appreciate your reminding me of that. Please understand that I am not a lawyer but a parent. What is important to Carolyn is not the nature of the question but the answer. I will certainly try not to be too formal; would you like me to try to put it another way?"

Challenge Blanket Assertions

Nothing is more frustrating for a parent than hearing lines like these:
- *"Unfortunately, we are not allowed to discuss that issue."*
- *"We don't provide that service."*
- *"That's not our policy."*
- *"Sorry, but we can't do that."*
- *"That's not the law."*

If an assertion seems illegal or illogical, ask what it's based on. If the administrator says something vague like "It's our policy," "It's the law," "It's our best judgment," or "It's the way things are," keep asking why. Request a copy of the law or policy.

If possible, refer to your documentation. For example, the district administrator says that as a general rule, the district doesn't provide more than two hours of a related service per week. An evaluation states that your child needs three hours. Point that out and ask how the district's rule complies with the IDEA, which requires that the specifics of a service be determined by the IEP team.

The administrator may say something like "Mrs. Wasserman, that is just the way it is and I won't respond any further to that question." You'll want to follow up with something like "I'm sorry you won't answer my question; it is a fair question, and I plan to ask your superintendent or the school board to answer it." If the issue is key, you may want to file a complaint, as discussed in Chapter 13.

Or the school district may not agree with you on an important IEP component. For example, you feel there is clear support for a specific placement, but the administrator disagrees. Ask for a detailed explanation of the school district's reasoning, supported by appropriate materials.

Sample Responses to School District Statements

Here are some common statements made by school districts at IEP meetings and how you might respond.

Statement: "I don't have the authority to authorize that aide/service/material."

Response: The law requires that a person be at the IEP who has the authority to authorize a service that the IEP team agrees on. You might respond that "the IDEA requires that decisions about what services will be provided need to be made at the IEP meeting, and someone with authority needs to be at the IEP meeting."

Statement: "The district supervisor preapproved only one hour of speech therapy/occupational therapy/one-on-one aide per week."

Response: A predetermined IEP decision is an absolute violation of the IDEA (see Chapters 2 and 11). You might respond, "Are you saying even though my child needs two hours of speech therapy and we may agree on that, you are not going to provide it?" Make sure you keep detailed notes on who said this and when.

Statement: "You can't add your comments to the IEP form because it's a school document."

Response: This is absolutely contrary to the IEP process and the law that creates the IEP. You might say: "Please tell me where it says that in the law. As a parent, and to be a fully involved decision maker and participant in the IEP, I have a right to see that my thoughts, requests, comments are in the IEP. You don't have to agree with them and you can make it clear on the IEP form that these are only my thoughts."

Note any unresolved matter on your addendum. (See "Parent Addendum Page," below.)

Pay Attention to What's Written on the IEP Form

Make sure you know what statements are entered onto the IEP document, and voice any objections immediately—whether it's about a particular goal, or a general statement made on the narrative page of the IEP form. (We discuss the narrative page later in this chapter.)

Keep Your Eye on the Clock

Whether the school has allotted two hours or five hours for the IEP meeting, keep track of time. If you are 45 minutes into a 90-minute meeting and the IEP team is still talking in generalities, you should say, "We need to move on to a specific discussion of Cora's goals, placement, and related services."

A good school administrator will keep the meeting on schedule. If the administrator is not doing so, take the lead. Be ready to suggest moving on to the next issue when the discussion on a particular topic has gone on long enough.

Don't Limit Your Options to All or Nothing

At some point during the IEP meeting, you may realize that you will not reach agreement on all issues. For example, you feel your child needs at least two sessions of speech therapy a week, 30 minutes per session. The district offers one 30-minute session. You've done your best to persuade them, to no avail. What do you do?

The school district cannot present you with a "take-it-or-leave-it" position—for example, "We've offered speech therapy once a week. You want it twice a week. You can either agree with us and sign the IEP or disagree and go to a hearing." Furthermore, the school district cannot insist that you give up your right to due process—for instance, "We've offered speech therapy once a week and that's all we'll offer. We'd advise you to sign the IEP form and not make waves."

Your best bet is to make sure the IEP document specifically states that you agree that a specific service is needed—or that a particular placement is appropriate—and that your child will receive at least what the school district has offered. Then make sure your opinions are reflected on the parent addendum page.

You can agree to the lesser amount of a service such as speech therapy and indicate on the IEP form that you believe your child needs two sessions of speech therapy, but will accept the one session so he or she will have something while you pursue due process. Or you agree on placement and related services, but not certain goals (or vice versa).

Later in this chapter we discuss how to prepare and use a parent addendum page, which is a very important IEP tool for any disputed items.

Don't Be Rushed Into Making a Decision

If you're on the fence about a particular issue, don't be rushed into making a decision. Ask for a break and go outside for a few minutes to think about what the school has offered. If you are concerned that pausing on some issues may mean delay on others, ask for a day or two to make up your mind on a particular issue so that the IEP team can proceed with other items. This may require a second IEP meeting, unless you eventually agree with the rest of the IEP team on the issue. If an item is that important, however, then a second meeting is worth the time.

Become Familiar With Your School's IEP Form

You should get a copy of your school district's IEP form before the IEP meeting. While forms vary, they will almost always have sections on the following:

- present level of educational performance
- goals (and evaluation procedures)
- related services
- placement/program
- effective dates of the IEP
- attending summer school or an extended school year, and
- a narrative page or pages for recording various important statements, such as comments on evaluations, or keeping a running account of the meeting discussion. (This important part of the IEP is described in "Writing the IEP Plan," below.)

In addition, IEP forms typically include the following types of information:

- identifying information, such as your child's name, gender, date of birth, grade, school district, and parents' names and addresses
- the type of IEP (eligibility or annual review) and date of the IEP meeting
- your child's eligibility status and category of disability
- the amount of time your child will spend in a regular or mainstreamed program, if applicable
- your child's English proficiency, and
- signatures of IEP team members and parents.

The IEP team may include other important information in the IEP, such as a specific curricula or teaching methodology, a specific classroom setting, peer needs, or a child profile.

The IEP Form and Your IEP Blueprint

The IEP form and your blueprint (your list of desired program components) will have similar categories but will not be identical.

Most of your blueprint items, such as related services and placement, have a corresponding section in the IEP. But in some cases, you may find that the IEP form does not have space for all the details you included on your blueprint. For example, the IEP form will allow you to specify the kind of program or placement—such as a regular class or special day class— but might not provide space for the details of the placement—such as peer numbers and makeup, the classroom environment, and the school environment. Other blueprint items, such as methodology and curricula, may not have a corresponding section on the IEP form. And the school administrator may not be familiar with a blueprint like yours.

As you prepare for the IEP meeting, keep in mind that while the IEP form may not reference all of your blueprint items, the IDEA allows the IEP team to discuss and agree on any element it feels is necessary for your child. These types of details can go on the IEP narrative page or, if the school disagrees, a parent addendum page.

FORM
You can find a sample IEP form on this book's Companion Page on www.nolo.com. See Chapter 16 for the link.

Writing the IEP Plan

Usually, someone from the school district will write the IEP plan as the meeting progresses, by filling in specific sections, checking off boxes on the IEP, and completing the narrative or descriptive page.

You should ask frequently to see what has been written, to make sure it accurately reflects what was discussed or agreed upon. You may want to check every 30 minutes or so, with a simple "Excuse me, but can we break for just a few minutes? I want to see what the IEP looks like so far." If these breaks seem forced, ask to review the form each time you complete a section. Pay special attention to the narrative page—this will be more subjective than other parts of the IEP.

How does the IEP team make an actual decision on IEP components? The IDEA establishes no set method for reaching agreement. The school administrator may not even raise the question of how agreement is reached. You can request voting, but, in most IEP meetings, the team tries to reach consensus through discussion. No matter how the administrator proceeds, make sure your objections are heard and no one assumes consensus when there isn't any.

How items are recorded on the IEP plan is equally important. From the beginning to the end of the IEP meeting, you want to be sure that the IEP's narrative page, goals, placement, and related services reflect your point of view.

Under the IDEA, the written IEP must include:
- your child's current levels of academic and functional performance
- how your child's disability affects his or her involvement and progress in the general curriculum
- measurable annual goals, including academic and functional goals designed to meet your child's needs

- a statement of the special education, related services, and supplementary aids and services your child will receive, as well as program modifications necessary for your child to meet annual goals and be involved and progress in the general curriculum
- a description of how your child's progress toward those goals will be measured, and when and how that progress will be reported to you
- a statement of any accommodations your child will need when taking state or other system-wide assessments and tests
- if your child is 16 or older, a transition plan
- if your child will not be in a regular classroom or program, an explanation of the reasons for this placement, and
- a description of the program where your child will be placed.

Child's Current Educational Status

If your child is presently enrolled in school, the IEP team will review your child's current educational status, IEP goals, program, and related services. Your child's current status may be reflected in testing data, grades, and teacher reports or observations. If this is an eligibility IEP meeting, the team will review evaluation data; it will do the same every three years (or more frequently) when your child is reevaluated. Discussion of your child's current status may be broad or specific. It may occur at the beginning of the IEP meeting or as you review specific items, such as goals, for the upcoming year.

Watch what you—and others—say about your child's current situation. For example, if you are concerned about the current program, you won't want the IEP narrative page to state that "Sam's placement has been highly successful this past year." If such a statement is made and entered onto the IEP document—perhaps on the narrative page— be sure to object, with something like "I'm sorry, but I don't think that statement is accurate, and I certainly cannot agree with it. It should not be on the IEP form as reflecting our consensus."

Evaluations

A school district representative (most likely the evaluator) will either read or summarize the school district's evaluation. If the evaluator starts reading the report, ask him or her to synthesize the salient points, rather than spend precious time reading the report verbatim—especially if you reviewed a copy before the meeting.

This may be the time to use your IEP material organizer (see Chapter 10) to point to other documents—such as previous IEP plans, an independent evaluation, other reports, teacher notes, and the like—to support or contradict the school evaluation.

If you haven't already introduced the independent evaluation, you will do so once the district has finished presenting its evaluation. You or your evaluator should provide a synopsis of the report, focusing on:

- the evaluator's credentials
- the reason for the evaluation
- the tests used
- the key conclusions regarding the testing, and
- the specific recommendations.

Be sure to highlight the test results and recommendations not covered in the school evaluation. This is also the time to introduce any other supporting material, including letters, work samples, and other professional opinions.

On most IEP forms, the narrative page refers to the evaluations. The IEP plan might specify the sections, results, or statements in the reports on which you all agree. Even if there is only one statement you all agree on, be sure it gets into the IEP document if it is essential to your child's needs. If the person drafting the IEP plan includes something from an evaluation with which you disagree, make sure your objections are noted.

Sometimes, the evaluation reports are attached to the IEP document. This can work in your favor if you agree with the report.

If an evaluation is not attached, or there is some disagreement over the evaluation, the narrative page should specify what parts of the evaluation are included or excluded.

EXAMPLES:

- The IEP team agrees with Sections 1, 2, 4, 6, and 8 of the school evaluation and Sections 3, 5, 9, 10, and 12 of the independent evaluation, and incorporates them into the IEP.
- The IEP team disagrees with the rest of both evaluations and does not incorporate them into the IEP.

You can use the parent addendum page to state the reasons for your disagreement (see "Parent Addendum Page," below).

Goals

If this is not your child's first IEP, the IEP team will next review the previous year's goals. This discussion is likely to lead to one of four different outcomes:

- You and the school district agree that the goals were met.
- You and the school district agree that certain goals were met, but others were not.
- You and the school district agree that the goals were not met.
- You and the school district disagree on whether the goals were met.

Although you won't be working on placement and services during this part of the meeting, keep in mind that your child's success or failure in meeting the goals will likely affect whether the placement and services are changed. If your child met the goals, perhaps it means the placement is correct and should continue. Or maybe it means your child is ready to be mainstreamed. If the goals weren't met, your child may need a smaller class. Or maybe the placement is fine, but more tutoring (a related service) is necessary.

Once you finish reviewing the previous goals—or if this is your child's first time in special education—it's time to write goals for the coming year. Chapter 9 explains how to draft goals—and recommends that you do so in advance. The school representatives will probably have also prepared goals ahead of time.

Remember, you want the IEP team to agree on goals that support the placement and related services you want for your child.

What if you disagree with each other's goals?

- Do your best to convince school members of the IEP team that your goals are consistent with the recommendations made by others, such as the evaluator, the classroom teacher, or your child's aide.
- Ask school members what they specifically disagree with in your goals.
- If you can't agree on all goals, try to reach consensus on some— half a loaf is better than none.
- If attempts to compromise fail, suggest dropping all predrafted goals and coming up with something new.

If you and the school representatives disagree about past or future goals, be sure the IEP document clearly states that. At the very least, record your concerns on your parent addendum.

Common Core Standards and Special Education

Every state has laws and procedures for what may be called "common core" competencies or "standard-based" competencies; these represent required growth in specific academic and other areas. Each student is intended to meet those requirements. And while a child's IEP can include reasons why the child cannot meet those common core requirements, it is important, of course, that every special education child have the opportunity to do what every other child has the opportunity to do: have access to and succeed in the general curriculum and meet all state standards.

As a parent of a special education child, ask your school to provide you with a written and detailed explanation of the state's requirements surrounding common core. Talk to your child's teacher and all other professionals involved in your child's education and find out their thoughts on how your child can meet all or some of those standards. Finally, be prepared to discuss at the IEP meeting what support, related services, and accommodations are necessary for your child to meet these state requirements.

Transition Services

If your child is 16 or older, the IEP team must discuss transition services, including advanced courses and vocational classes.

The IEP team does have the authority to provide transition services before the child reaches 16 if the team determines that is appropriate. (34 C.F.R. § 300.320(b).) There's that vague word again—"appropriate." How do you prove that your child needs transition services earlier than 16? As with any desired service, you should secure support for that service, in writing or in person. You must show that your child requires assistance with his or her work or educational plans, and that he or she can't wait until age 16. For example, if you have evidence that your child will require significant help in developing independent living skills, you may be able to show that starting training at age 16 may be too late. Or, if your child appears to be heading toward a certain job or educational placement after high school, you may be able to show that he or she will need help as soon as possible to ensure those possibilities.

The IEP team should consider strategies to assist your child in assessing, securing information about, and taking steps regarding vocational, employment, independent living, and post-high-school educational plans. Your child can receive transition services in a variety of areas, including looking at potential jobs, learning how to function in the community, accessing other agencies that provide support for adults with disabilities, and researching college opportunities.

Once your child reaches the age of 16, the IEP must include a statement about his or her transition needs, as those needs relate to your child's courses of study. This means that the team must indicate what advanced placement or vocational courses or classes are necessary to meet your child's unique educational and career needs. Whether your child wants to go to college, do clerical work, or look into computer jobs, his or her studies must provide for ways to explore these possibilities.

The IEP must also include a statement about necessary transition services. This means that the IEP must provide for services that will help your child develop the skills necessary to meet his or her vocational, academic, or independent living plans for the future (after high school ends). Such transition services might include help in developing the skills to create a résumé, perform certain jobs, access and use community services (such as public transportation), and find out about job training or college programs.

The IEP must also indicate whether there are noneducational agencies that might provide additional support to your child (such as the department of health or job training agencies), and how your child can access the services these agencies provide. If one of these "outside" agencies fails to provide the transition services described in the IEP, the IEP must reconvene to "identify alternative strategies" to meet the transition objectives described in the IEP. (34 C.F.R. § 300.324(c).)

As you prepare for the IEP meeting, talk to your child's teacher and other professionals about his or her vocational, college, and independent living skill needs. If your child wants to go to college, what skills will that require, and what institutions or agencies might be available to help your child develop those skills? If your child plans to look for work after high school, what are his or her vocational interests, and how can your child get the training and experience necessary to get into those fields? If your child needs help developing independent living skills, such as using transportation, balancing a checkbook, or keeping house, what kinds of school activities will help?

Diploma or Certificate of Attendance

An important separate but related topic is whether your child should receive a diploma or certificate of attendance from high school (the title of this certificate may vary from state to state). A diploma is certainly preferred; receiving only a certificate of attendance may impact your child's future education or employment opportunities. Your state may have laws that allow your child to receive a diploma with waivers on certain subjects; for example in California, the algebra requirement may be waived for purposes of the issuance of a diploma. And be aware that, while many states have testing requirements for graduation, your child's IEP (or 504 plan) may include accommodations for those tests.

There is a wide variety of potential supports to consider for your child's transition plan, although of course it may be very different from another student's transition plan:

- Preemployment transition services such as job exploration, exploration of career interests, and job exploration counseling
- Work-based learning experiences, in-school or after school opportunities, or internships
- Help with enrollment in comprehensive transition or postsecondary educational programs at institutions of higher education
- Training for workplace readiness, social skills development, and independent living, and
- Help in developing self-advocacy skills.

Resources for Transition Services

There are many available resources on the subject of IDEA transition services. The U.S. Department of Education has published two helpful guides, which you can find by searching for "transition" on the Department of Education's website at www.ed.gov:

- "Students with Disabilities Preparing for Postsecondary Education: Know Your Rights and Responsibilities," and
- "A Transition Guide to Postsecondary Education and employment for Students and Youth with Disabilities" (The definitions of "student with a disability" and "youth with a disability" are listed in the Glossary of this guide.)

You can find these by searching online or going to the Department of Education's website at https://www.ed.gov.

In addition, the National Joint Committee on Learning Disabilities has published a guide called "Transition to School and Work: A blueprint for your child's success after high school." Find it by searching for "blueprint" on their website at www.ldonline.org.

In order for students and youth with disabilities to secure meaningful careers/employment, the IDEA funds can be used for transition programs on college campuses or in community-based settings as well as at your child's school, and Section 504 of the Rehabilitation Act authorizes a continuum of services, such as preemployment transition services, transition services, job placement services, other vocational rehabilitation (VR) services, and supported employment services for students and youth with disabilities.

When developing your child's transition program and goals, other agencies can be involved. For example, your state's vocational rehabilitation department may be able to provide services and assistance for your child and can be involved in the IEP and/or 504 process. You should check with your state's department of vocational rehabilitation regarding qualifying and applying for vocational programs.

The services available through VR programs include preemployment transition services that are available only to VR eligible or potentially eligible students with disabilities and transition and other VR services available to youth with disabilities under an approved Individualized Plan for Employment (IPE).

Related Services

Your discussions regarding related services (and placement, covered in the next section) are likely to generate the most debate. You and the school district may have very different notions of the type and amount of related services that are appropriate for your child.

Under the IDEA, related services are developmental, corrective, and other supportive services, including transportation, that a child with disabilities needs to benefit from special education. They also include the services your child needs to be educated in a regular classroom. Remember, the burden is on the school district to show that your child cannot achieve satisfactorily in a regular classroom, even with the use of some related services (see Chapter 2).

Independent evaluators and others supporting your position should be prepared to state their opinions in detail—for example, "Given

Gavin's severe difficulties in articulation, he needs a minimum of three 30-minute sessions each week, one-on-one with a speech therapist who has a lot of experience in articulation work." If someone is not there to make this statement, be prepared to point to written materials that show your child's need for the particular related service.

The related services section of the IEP document requires more detail than any other. It's not enough to say, "Gavin will receive speech therapy." The IEP team should specify how often (three sessions per week), how long (30-minute sessions), the ratio of pupils to related service provider (one-on-one), and the qualifications of the service provider.

The more vague the description, the more flexibility the school district has to give your child something less than (or different from) what he or she needs. Speech therapy two to three times a week is very different from speech therapy three times per week. Try to avoid terminology such as "or," "about," "to be determined," or "as needed." When in doubt, be specific; it's that simple.

The IDEA now requires the provision of related services to be based on peer-reviewed research "to the extent practicable." (34 C.F.R. § 300.320(a)(4).) Of course, most parents want their children to receive services that are based on sound research. On the other hand, the school district cannot refuse to provide a necessary service just because there is no such research available. The phrase "to the extent practicable" creates a way around the research requirement.

Some advocates worry that this language creates a rationale for school districts to avoid providing related services: "Sorry, we'd like to provide it, but there is no peer-based research." While this fear is real, the bottom line is that the IDEA requires the school district to provide a related service if your child needs it, whether there is peer-reviewed research available or not.

Some parents have argued that the "peer-reviewed research" requirement means that districts must provide related services that are heavily reviewed. For example, in several cases involving children with autism, parents have claimed that districts must use Applied Behavior Analysis (ABA) because it is strongly supported by peer review. (ABA focuses on systematically applying learning principles, particularly those focused on improving social behavior.) Hearing officers have ruled that there is no specific right to ABA, and that school districts can use other approaches. The mere presence of peer reviews does not require adoption of a certain approach, nor does the absence of such reviews necessarily mean that an approach is not appropriate. (*Joshua A. ex rel. Jorge A. v. Rocklin Unified School Dist.* (E.D. Cal. 2008).)

The bottom line about peer based research: IEP decisions should be based on well-reasoned research, but ultimately, as one court said, the student's IEP team retains flexibility to devise an appropriate program in light of the available research. (*Ridley Sch. District v. M. R.*, 680 F.3d 260 (3d Cir. 2012).)

Some Related Services May Be the Responsibility of Other Agencies

In some states, certain related services, such as mental health services or occupational or physical therapy, are the responsibility of a noneducational public agency. Still, these services should be discussed at the IEP meeting, and the school district is responsible for making sure representatives of those other agencies attend the meeting. Those noneducational agencies have the same responsibilities as the school district—and therefore the same role to play at the meeting—regarding the services they must provide.

Placement or Program

Placement or program refers to both the kind of class (such as a regular class, special day class, or residential placement) and the specific location of the program (such as a regular fifth-grade class at Abraham Lincoln School). Placement or program, sometimes referred to on the IEP form as the instructional setting, is central to a successful IEP and an effective educational experience. Placement or program is most often some kind of public program, but the IDEA requires placement in a private school if there is no appropriate public option. Placement or program is generally the last item discussed at the IEP meeting.

As explained in Chapter 2, the IDEA requires that your child be educated in the least restrictive environment. This means that to the maximum extent appropriate, children with disabilities are to be educated with children who are nondisabled. Special classes, separate schooling, or other removal of children with disabilities from a regular class should happen only if the nature or severity of the disability is such that your child cannot receive a satisfactory education in a regular class, even with the use of supplementary aids and services.

Despite the LRE guideline, there is no absolute rule that your child be mainstreamed. The IDEA prefers a mainstreamed placement, but many courts have ruled that a child's individual needs determine the appropriateness of a placement.

If you don't want your child mainstreamed, point out that although the law favors regular classroom placement, individual need determines whether a particular placement is appropriate for a particular child. Courts have clearly stated that there is no prohibition to placing a child in a nonregular class. In fact, if a child needs such a placement, it is by definition the least restrictive environment. (See *Geis v. Board of Education,* 774 F.2d 575 (3d Cir. 1985) and *Stockton by Stockton v. Barbour County Board of Education*, 25 IDELR 1076 (4th Cir. 1997).) (For more on court cases and legal research, see Chapter 14.)

If you want your child mainstreamed, emphasize your child's basic right to the least restrictive environment. You should also emphasize your child's right to be educated as close to home as possible, in the school the child would attend if not disabled. Ultimately, the burden is on the school district to prove that your child should be removed from a regular classroom.

School representatives may be prepared to discuss a specific program in a named school. Or, they may propose a kind of class, such as a special day class, but want to leave the specific location up to the school administration. If the school representatives suggest this latter option, object. The IEP team should decide both the kind of class (such as a special day class for language-delayed children) and the specific location (such as a regular class at King School).

Keeping an Open Mind at the IEP Meeting

Your school district should approach the IEP meeting with an open mind, willing to discuss and decide all parts of your child's education plan. When a school district has made up its mind in advance on critical aspects of the plan, such as the class your child will be placed in or the related services that will be provided, the school is hardly fulfilling its obligation. Under the IDEA, a school's premeeting, entrenched position is known as a "predetermination," and it's not allowed.

School districts certainly have the right, as do you, to investigate, consider, and even have opinions about a particular placement, service, or methodology. But when the district has fully made up its mind about what should be in the IEP, it has denied the child's family the opportunity for meaningful input in the IEP decision-making process. (*Doyle v. Arlington County Sch. Bd.*, 806 F.Supp. 1253 (E.D. Va. 1992).) For example, take the district administrator who said to a client of mine at the beginning of an IEP meeting, "We believe Mary should be placed in the Jefferson school program and we will not place her in the Wilson school program." Or, consider the school whose attitude at the meeting clearly conveys that the district views any discussion as a mere formality. Though less blatant, such an approach is also evidence of predetermination.

Proving predetermination can be difficult, particularly if the school district says or writes little or nothing before the IEP meeting, and nothing about the district's statements or attitude in the meeting itself is obvious. This is another reason why you should always keep a record of what is said to you, by whom and when, whether in or out of an IEP meeting. Put together, these tidbits may add up to impressive evidence of predetermination (see Chapter 8).

If you think your district has predetermined an IEP issue, you should file for due process. For example, if you think your child should be placed in a private school and a district employee remarks, before the IEP meeting, that the district does not place children privately, the nature, extent, and impact of those comments would be an issue for a due process mediation or hearing. If, on the other hand, your district has an official policy that clearly predetermines an IEP issue, you should file a complaint (see Chapter 13). If you are not sure which route to take, it is wise to do both.

You and the school administrator will probably know before the meeting where each of you stands on placement. Still, an open-minded IEP team should fully discuss your child's placement needs. The school administrator will probably state that the IEP team has reviewed your child's record, agreed on goals, resolved related services, and decided that a particular placement is called for.

If you disagree with the administrator's conclusion, state your preference and refer to supportive materials—particularly items that are very persuasive about placement. Then ask (or have your independent evaluator ask) pointed questions, such as:

> *Ms. Parton, you said Betsy should be placed at Johnson School in the special day class. We believe Betsy should be placed in the regular class at Thompson School with a one-on-one aide. The evaluation by Dr. Jang is specific about that, and Betsy's current teacher agrees. Can you explain why you disagree?*

If the school administrator is not persuaded or does not answer your question adequately, be direct and frank:

> *With all due respect, I think your answer is vague and does not address the specifics in Dr. Jang's report and your own teacher's comment about Betsy's readiness for a regular classroom. I feel very strongly about this, and we will go to due process on the issue of placement if we have to. I also think that with the documentation and the law on mainstreaming, we will be successful in a due process hearing. I really feel that going to hearing is a bad use of school resources and will only make the ultimate move more expensive for you. I just don't understand—given the evidence—why you want to put me and my wife, your district personnel, and, most important, our child through that.*

Narrative Page

The narrative page is the place to record information that can't be conveyed by checking a box or won't fit in the space provided on the form. The narrative page can include information on any other topic covered at the meeting, whether in the IEP document or not. Here are some examples of narrative page statements.

EXAMPLES:

- The IEP team agrees that the school district and outside evaluations are complete and appropriate, and are incorporated into the IEP.
- The IEP team incorporates the child profile provided by Steven's parents into the IEP.
- The IEP team agrees that Melissa needs a school environment in which there are no behavioral problems.
- The IEP team agrees that Henry is beginning to show signs of emotional distress; the classroom teacher will report on a weekly basis to the family about any signs of such distress. The district psychologist will observe Henry in class. The IEP team agrees to meet in three months to review this matter and to discuss the possible need for more formal evaluation or the need for additional related services.
- The IEP team agrees with the recommendations made by Dr. Jones on page 4 of her report.
- Ms. Brown, Destiny's teacher, is concerned about Destiny's lack of focus.
- The IEP team agrees with recommendations 1, 2, 5, 7, and 9 made by Dr. Valdez on page 4 of her report.
- Aiko's parents expressed concern about class size.

Include a Child Profile in the IEP Plan

Chapter 10 suggested that you create a child profile to give school officials a perspective on your child beyond numbers and test results. The school administrator may question whether law or policy allows a child profile to be included in the IEP document. The IDEA does not prohibit it, so nothing prevents the IEP team from discussing and including a child profile.

Emphasize that your statement about your child will help the school staff implement the goals, and for that reason it should be included in the IEP document. If the school administrator disagrees, ask why. Try to convince the team of the importance of the profile. If the administrator continues to refuse, use the parent addendum to include it.

Sometimes, the person recording the IEP document may write something that you and the school district don't agree on. Make sure the narrative is changed to reflect your disagreement or to indicate that the statement reflects only the point of view of the school personnel. Basically, you don't want the narrative to imply agreement when there is none.

Signing the IEP Document

At the end of the IEP meeting, the school administrator will ask you to sign the IEP document. School officials will be signing the form as well. You don't have to sign the IEP document on the spot. You may want to take it home and return it the next day. This will give you time to decide whether you agree or disagree with each aspect of the plan. It will also give you time to record your disagreements coherently on a parent addendum (discussed below).

Of course, if you agree with the school representatives on all issues and don't need time to mull anything over, then go ahead and sign. Read the document carefully, however, to make sure the statements and information are correct and reflect the IEP team's intentions. Also, make sure that everything on your agenda was covered and that all important issues have been resolved.

If you do take the IEP document home, be sure that all other participants have signed off on each item to which they agreed.

Every IEP form has a signature page with a variety of checkboxes, including:
- a box to indicate you attended
- a box to indicate that you were provided your legal rights
- a box to indicate your approval of the IEP document, and
- a box to indicate your disapproval.

There may also be boxes to indicate partial approval and whether or not you want to initiate due process.

Make sure to check the right boxes. If you partially agree, check the partial agreement box or, if there is no partial agreement box, check the approval box—but carefully and clearly write next to it: "Approval in part only; see parent addendum."

You must state your position clearly on the IEP. There are no legally required phrases to use—plain and direct English will do fine.

Full Agreement

Congratulations! Check the correct box and sign the form.

> **TIP**
> **If you have the slightest doubt, take the document home.** This rule really applies to all of the scenarios described here. It is highly unlikely the district will change its mind as to what it has agreed to provide if you don't sign right away, and giving yourself time to read the entire document at home is the safe way to go.

Nearly Full Agreement

It's possible that the IEP team will agree on all important items concerning related services, methodology, and program or placement, but disagree on some secondary issues, such as goals or statements in an evaluation. In this situation, you have two choices:

- You can check the box to indicate your approval and sign your name. This might make sense if the issues on which you disagree are minor and you want to foster a good relationship with the school district.
- You can check the box to indicate partial approval, list the items you dispute (on the signature page if there's room, or on the parent addendum), and sign your name.

Partial Approval Sample #1

Date: April 24, 20xx

Signature: *Lucinda Crenshaw*

I agree with all of the IEP except for:

- items 3, 4, and 6 on the district's evaluation, and
- goals 2 and 5.

You Don't Have to Accept "All or Nothing"

Remember that the school district cannot present you with an "all or nothing" choice. For example: "We're offering two sessions of occupational therapy. Either agree with the two sessions or there will be no occupational therapy for your child." You can agree to the two sessions without giving up your right to seek more.

Partial Agreement

In this situation, you agree on some, but not all, of the big issues (related services, methodology, and program or placement). You can check the box to indicate partial approval, state that your disagreements are on the parent addendum, spell out your disagreements on the parent addendum, and sign your name.

Partial Approval Sample #2

Date: April 24, 20xx

Signature: *Lucinda Crenshaw*

I agree with all of the IEP except for those items listed on the parent addendum page, designated as "Attachment A" and attached to the IEP.

Nearly Total Disagreement

In this case, you don't agree on any of the major items concerning related services, methodology, and program or placement, but do agree on certain goals, parts of the evaluation, and minor items. Again, you can check the box to indicate partial approval, state that your disagreements are on the parent addendum, spell out your disagreements on the parent addendum, and sign your name.

Total Disagreement

In some instances, there is total disagreement. If so, sign your name after checking both the box acknowledging that you attended the meeting and the disapproval box. You could also refer to the parent addendum page.

At this stage, your options are informal negotiations, mediation, or a due process hearing.

RELATED TOPIC

See Chapter 12 for information on due process, including your child's status when there is no IEP agreement.

Parent Addendum Page

When you disagree with the school personnel and cannot reach a compromise, make sure to state your position clearly. You or your notetaker should keep a list of all issues you dispute on a separate piece of paper.

A parent addendum page is an attachment to the IEP where you can record these disagreements and give your point of view. There is no IDEA requirement for an addendum page, although your district's IEP form may have one. The addendum page need not be a formal document—a blank piece of paper will do.

You will most likely complete the addendum page at or near the end of the meeting. The content of the addendum page is vastly more important than its format. Your statement should:

- relate to issues concerning your child's education—don't use the addendum to state general complaints
- be in plain English, and
- state your point of view on all key items of dispute.

You should indicate on the signature page that you disagree with part of the IEP document and refer to the attached addendum page for the detail of the disagreement.

Sample Addendum Page

Date: _____

Parent Signature*: _____

* See Addendum page (designated as "A") for a statement regarding what we are agreeing to and not agreeing to. My signature above is to be read only in conjunction with the statement on "A."

If your school's IEP form includes an addendum page, use it; otherwise, mark "Attachment A" at the top of a blank piece of paper and write something like the following:

Sample Attachment A

Parent Addendum Page of Cara and Marcus Stack

IEP for Beatrice Stack

March 12, 20xx

You have an absolute right to state your position, but if, for some reason, the school district does not allow you to attach an addendum, indicate on the signature page that you do not agree with everything in the IEP document, that you want to attach an addendum, and that the school administration will not let you. Mail your addendum to the school—certified mail if you can (keep copies)—with a cover letter stating that you asked to include this at the IEP meeting, were denied by the administrator, and are now sending it to be attached to the IEP. Then, file a complaint (see Chapter 13).

EXAMPLES OF ADDENDUM STATEMENTS:

- The district does not agree with the recommendations of Dr. Jordan's independent evaluation but has refused to state why. We believe that her evaluation is valid and should be fully incorporated into the IEP as representing useful and valid information about Tonya.

- We do not agree with recommendations 3, 6, 9, and 14 of Dr. Lee's evaluation of January 21, 20xx. We do agree with the rest of her report.

- The IEP team agrees with sections 3, 7, 8, and 9 of the school's report and all of Dr. Friedman's evaluation, but the school will not put this agreement into the IEP. We believe those agreed-to sections should be incorporated into the IEP.

- Dr. Pentan of the school district stated that we have no right to include a child profile in the IEP. The IDEA does not say that. If the IEP team agrees, the profile can be part of the IEP. We believe the profile provides valid and important information regarding Fernando.

- While the teacher reported that Drake increased his reading comprehension (this relates to goal #4 on page 2), we have observed at home, over a long period of time, that his reading comprehension seems substantially below the test results.

- We don't agree that Sandy's goals were met because the evaluation of the goals was inaccurate.

- The district offered speech therapy one time a week, 20 minutes per session. Moira needs three 40-minute sessions per week, each session to be conducted one-on-one with a licensed speech therapist. This is supported by the May 2, 20xx report of Dr. Shawn Waters. We accept the one session and give permission for that to begin, but this acceptance is not to be construed as agreement about the amount of the related services, only agreement as to the need.

- The IEP team agrees that Nick be placed in the regular fifth-grade class at Kennedy School. We agree with placement in the regular fifth-grade class at Kennedy School, but we believe Nick needs an aide to allow him to achieve satisfactorily in that regular class.

- We believe that regular seventh-grade classes at Roosevelt School are the only appropriate placement for Toni. We believe placement in the special day class at Roosevelt as offered by the school district is inappropriate. We agree to placement in regular classrooms at Roosevelt for three periods a day, although such agreement is not to be construed as agreement on partial mainstreaming. We will proceed to due process on the issue of full-time mainstreaming in regular seventh-grade classes at Roosevelt.

Less Frequent IEP Meetings: A New Model

As both parents and educators know, IEP meetings can be tiring, difficult, and sometimes contentious, and can involve a lot of paperwork. They take up a lot of time for teachers, administrators, and you. Congress received complaints about this and decided to establish a pilot program to find out what happened when IEP meetings were held less than once a year. The program called for participating districts to establish comprehensive, multiyear IEPs to last for up to three years.

Based on the lack of response from districts to the multiyear IEP pilot program, it does not appear that multiyear IEPs are the wave of the future. Most likely, districts will continue to hold annual IEP meetings for special education students.

Resolving IEP Disputes Through Due Process

The purpose of this book is to help you successfully develop an IEP plan for your child, and thereby make this chapter irrelevant. But by the nature of the IEP process, disagreements arise—and some cannot be resolved informally.

Under IDEA, you have the right to resolve disputes with your school district through "due process." (20 U.S.C. § 1415.) There are two ways to resolve disputes through due process: mediation and a hearing.

In mediation, you and representatives of the school district meet with a neutral third party who tries to help you reach a compromise. The mediator has no authority to impose a decision on you. You are not required to mediate, but it can be a very good way to resolve your dispute—and avoid the time, expense, and anxiety of a due process hearing.

If you cannot reach an agreement in mediation, or if you prefer to skip mediation altogether, you can request a due process hearing where you and school district personnel present written evidence and have witnesses testify about the disputed issues before a neutral third party, called a hearing officer. Much like a judge, the hearing officer considers the evidence, makes a decision, and issues a binding order. Either you or the school district can appeal the decision to a state or federal court.

Due process is available to resolve factual disputes—that is, when you and your child's school district cannot agree on eligibility or some part of the IEP plan. If the school district has ignored a legal rule—by failing to hold an IEP meeting, do an evaluation, meet a time limit, or provide an agreed-to part of the IEP—you must file a complaint rather than pursuing due process. (Complaints are covered in Chapter 13.)

Timeline for Requesting Due Process

The IDEA requires you to formally file for due process within two years after you knew or should have known of the dispute. (20 U.S.C. §§ 1415(b) and (f)(1)(C).) Time limits like these are known in the legal world as "statutes of limitations." If you don't file within the two-year limit, you lose your right to file for due process.

When does that two-year time limit begin to start (or "run")? The IDEA says it begins to run **within two years of the date you knew or had reason to know of the facts underlying the basis for the request.** (20 U.S.C. § 1415(f)(3)(C)). The bolded phrase above does create uncertainty; how do you prove when you knew something or did not know something? One federal court ruled that the two years began to run on the date the parents of a severely disabled child placed him in a residential program, not the date of the IEP disagreement. (*Moyer v. Long Beach Unified School District*, Case No. CV 09-04430 MMM (AJWx) (C.D. Cal. 2013).)

There are two exceptions to this two-year limit:

- If your state has a different statute of limitations, the state's statute will apply. Check with your school district, state department of education, and/or a parent support organization in your state to find out about time limits. (See the appendix for contact information.)
- If the school district misrepresents to you that it has resolved the dispute, or withholds information from you that is required by law, the two-year time limit will not apply. (20 U.S.C. § 1415(f) (3)(D).) For example, you ask for a specific related service and the school district tells you, at the IEP meeting, that its evaluator did not decide whether your child needed such a service. If the evaluator in fact recommended that your child receive the service but you didn't learn of the recommendation for a while, the two-year limit might not apply.

It would be fairly unusual to have a dispute with the school district that you weren't aware of for a lengthy period of time. After all, most due process matters involve a disagreement over services or placement, and these disputes are usually evident right from the start—and certainly by the IEP meeting. The school either agrees to mainstream your child, provide a one-on-one aide, and meet your child's other needs, or it doesn't.

It's generally a good idea to start considering a due process proceeding as soon as you know you have a disagreement that can't be resolved with another IEP meeting. I would, however, add a caveat; once you file, it happens fast, so you might not know whether you could have resolved the issue without a hearing. Let's say you met with the school district on March 1, 2020 and the district would not provide a regular class placement for your child. Once you file, you are generally on a fast track to the hearing—a hearing decision is required to be issued 45 days after you file. Holding off to see if you can resolve the disagreement without filing has its merits. And in this example (and most), you would have until February 28, 2022 to file.

When You Can Go Straight to Court Instead of Using the Due Process Hearing

As with many laws that have an administrative hearing process, the IDEA requires, in almost all cases, that a parent go through an administrative due process hearing before the conflict can be taken to a state or federal court. This is referred to as the "exhaustion" requirement—you must "exhaust," or use up, the due process hearing requirement before you can go to court. Almost all IEP disputes will involve a matter within the IDEA and therefore will need to go through an administrative hearing. To skip the administrative hearing requirement, you have to show that either the administrative process would be futile (pointless, because it would not be able to produce a useful result) or that there is an emergency that requires remedies (solutions) only available in a court of law.

Why is this "exhaustion of administrative remedies" required? Judges often say they do not have the expertise that school officials and hearing officers have. Therefore, they want to give school officials and hearing officers a chance to resolve the dispute first. That is why many laws, including the IDEA, establish a "lower" level hearing for possible resolution. This can also make sense from the point of view of the student's family. Litigation costs can be huge, and a matter that goes to court can take years, whereas a due process hearing is required to be held within 45 days of the hearing request.

Generally it makes sense to follow the administrative hearing process since going to court can be more time-consuming, costly, and complex. And by going straight to court you are eliminating one of only a few chances to win your case. You might be able to win at hearing, but if you go straight to court, you've lost the first chance to win. If anyone suggests you "take this thing to the court right now," be sure you carefully consider this and talk with a qualified attorney who understands special education and has a full understanding of the exhaustion requirements.

What are the arguments for forgoing the due process hearing and going straight to court? First, when there is an urgent matter that requires someone to issue an immediate order to protect the safety and health of a child, it can make sense to go straight to court.

Second, the due process system is not really equipped to deal with systemic problems. For example, there may be system-wide staffing problems or shortages that a due process hearing office is not able to address, whereas a court can order the state department of education to take specific steps (and spend money) to remedy the systemic problem. Such broad problems involve more than one child—and remember the IDEA is about the "individual" child. So the larger the group affected, the more likely the individual children in that larger group will not have to exhaust the administrative process and can go directly to court.

Exhaustion may also not be required when a party is seeking money damages. By this, I mean when parents are seeking a court judgment that requires a school district (local education agency) to pay a child for injuries. The IDEA does not provide for that remedy.

On the other hand, if the child needs something in his IEP that requires expenditure of monies, then it can be resolved squarely within the administrative hearing range. A hearing officer can order a school district to pay for a private therapist, bring in and pay for a tutor, or pay for placement in a non-public school.

What about the other laws that protect individuals with disabilities—Section 504 of the Rehabilitation Act of 1973 and/or the Americans with Disabilities Act (ADA)? A child in special education can assert rights from these laws in addition to the IDEA. This does not mean, for example, that a child would have to go through a hearing within the

IDEA before a separate 504 process, at least if the issues did not concern a free and appropriate public education.

> ## Supreme Court Case Addresses Exhaustion, the ADA, and Section 504
>
> In *Fry v. Napoleon Community Schools* (2017), a student (referred to as "E.F") who was born with cerebral palsy and had significant mobility challenges needed to bring her service dog to school to help her navigate throughout the day. The school barred the dog from school and so E.F.'s parents filed a lawsuit in federal district court, arguing that the school district violated two federal civil rights laws—the Americans with Disabilities Act and Section 504 of the Rehabilitation Act. The school argued that since E.F. had an IEP that provided for a human aide who could take care of her needs, E.F. would have to go through the IDEA process for any relief. The family argued that whether E.F. should have been able to bring the service dog to school was a separate issue from whether the school was providing a free and appropriate public education (since the dog helped with noneducational activities) and that a due process hearing under the IDEA would have been futile, since the IDEA does not provide for monetary damages for E.F.'s emotional harm.
>
> The U.S. Supreme Court unanimously ruled that E.F. did not have to exhaust the administrative hearing requirement under the IDEA because his right to have a service dog at school was not part of a "free appropriate public education" and therefore not subject to those administrative requirements.

Before Due Process: Informal Negotiations

Before invoking due process, you may want to try to resolve your dispute through informal discussions or negotiations with the school. While resolving some problems might require formal action, many issues can be settled informally.

In addition, some disputes may not even qualify for due process. (See "Typical Due Process Disputes," below.) For example, you and the school principal may disagree over when you can visit the classroom or why the evaluator had to reschedule your child's testing. Because you can't take these issues to due process, you'll have to hash them out informally or not at all.

The school district must set up a negotiating meeting after you file for due process. (See "Resolution Session," below, for more information.) Although this meeting occurs only after a hearing request is filed, you may still be able to resolve the dispute before moving on to mediation or a hearing.

Alternatives to Informal Negotiations and Formal Due Process

Informal discussions with the school district and formal due process aren't the only ways to resolve disputes. Other methods, such as building parent coalitions and becoming involved in the local political process, can also be effective. These options are discussed in Chapter 15.

In addition, the IDEA provides that a state or local school district can establish alternative dispute resolution (ADR) procedures for parents who choose not to use due process. (20 U.S.C. § 1415(e)(2)(B).)

In ADR, you and a district representative meet with a neutral third party who is under contract with a parent training center or community parent resource center, or who is from an appropriate alternative dispute resolution entity. The purpose of the meeting is for you to explore alternative ways to resolve your dispute and for the third party to explain the benefits of mediation. This ADR meeting is intended to be nonadversarial, while mediation is the first step in formal due process. Be aware, however, that using ADR may delay resolution of the dispute—so if you need immediate action or the time limit for pursuing due process is coming up, you might want to skip this step.

If you're interested in ADR, call your school district or state department of education to find out if ADR is available.

Pros and Cons of Informal Negotiation

Informal negotiation is useful for several reasons. Ultimately, it may save you stress, preparation time, and money. It will also help you maintain a more positive relationship with the school district, and will keep problems from escalating. Finally, informal negotiation is easier to pursue than due process.

Even if you eventually pursue your due process rights, it might be a good idea to start with informal negotiation. This will show that you are reasonable and fair-minded and don't immediately look to an adversarial method of settlement. Informal negotiations will also help you understand the school district's position, which will be valuable if you end up in mediation or at a due process hearing.

In limited situations, however, there may be reasons to go immediately to due process. For example, you should skip the informal negotiations if:

- You need an immediate resolution because the issue affects your child's well-being, safety, or health. For example, if you think that your child needs psychological counseling for depression, but the district disagrees, you may not have time for informal meetings.
- The school administrator is so unpleasant or inflexible that you just don't want to deal with him or her.
- The IEP meeting made it clear that it would be a waste of time to try to resolve things informally.

Basics of Informal Negotiation

To begin informal negotiations, call or write your child's teacher, school principal, or special education administrator and ask for a meeting to discuss your concerns. You can raise the issues in your phone conversation or letter, but ideally you'll want an appointment to discuss the problem face to face.

Before the meeting, prepare a brief and clear written description of the problem and a recommended solution. Also, find out if any school personnel support you. If so, ask them to attend the meeting or ask for permission to present their opinions at the meeting.

Here are some tips to keep in mind during the meeting:

- Emphasize problem solving, not winning.
- Try to structure the negotiation as a mutual attempt to solve a problem.
- Avoid personal attacks on school personnel.
- Respect the school's point of view even if you disagree.
- Acknowledge the school representatives' concerns. Even if you strongly disagree, you don't lose anything by saying, "I understand your concerns, but I think we can address those by doing …."

Finally, be respectful, but firm—for example, you can say, "It is clear we disagreed at the IEP meeting. I am open to trying to solve this informally, but I will not hesitate to pursue my due process rights if we cannot."

TIP

Some school districts play hardball. It has been my experience that there are school districts that simply won't begin any meaningful negotiations until a due process complaint has been filed. Each situation is fact-specific and individual-specific, but if you sense that informal negotiations won't work and you or your attorney feels that you have a strong case, it may be better to go ahead and file rather than waste further time informally.

Good Books on Negotiation

Getting to Yes: Negotiating Agreement Without Giving In, by Roger Fisher and William Ury (Penguin Books). This classic book offers a strategy for coming to mutually acceptable agreements in all kinds of situations.

Getting Past No: Negotiating in Difficult Situations, by William Ury (Bantam Books). This sequel to *Getting to Yes* suggests techniques for negotiating with difficult people.

Letter Confirming Informal Negotiation

Date: June 1, 20xx

To: Michael Chan, Principal

Truman High School

803 Dogwood Drive

8709 Fourth Street

Paterson, NJ 07506

Re: Tasha Kincaid, student in 2nd grade class of Marlene Walker

I appreciated the chance to meet on May 28 and discuss Tasha's placement I also appreciated your point of view and the manner in which we solved the problem.

I want to confirm our agreement that Tasha will be placed in the regular academic track at Truman High School with one hour per day of resource specialist help in math, English, and Social Studies for the upcoming school year. [If you have already requested due process, add: Once you have confirmed this in writing to me, I will formally withdraw my due process request.]

I greatly appreciate the manner in which you helped solve this problem. Please tell Tasha's teachers that I would be delighted to meet with them before school starts to discuss effective ways to work with Tasha.

Sincerely,

André Kincaid

André Kincaid

4500 Fair Street

Paterson, NJ 07506

Phones: 555-3889 (home); 555-2330 (work)

After Meeting Informally

If you do not resolve your dispute informally, send a letter briefly stating the problem, the solution you think makes sense, and what you are considering next, such as contacting an attorney, pursuing mediation or a due process hearing, or filing a complaint with your school board or the state department of education.

If you resolve your problem informally, it is very important to follow up the meeting with a confirming letter.

FORM
A sample letter confirming the results of your informal negotiation is above; a blank, downloadable copy is available on this book's Companion Page on www.nolo.com. See Chapter 16 for the link.

If the meeting does not resolve the problem to your satisfaction, then you may proceed to due process (either mediation or a hearing) or file a complaint.

Use the Law to Make Your Case
As you try to persuade your school district—in writing or in person— that you are correct, cite the legal authority for your position, if possible. Referring to a section in the IDEA or even a court decision may help you convince the school district. See Chapter 14 for tips on legal research.

Resolution Session

Once you or the school district files for due process, the school district must schedule a meeting, formally called a "resolution session," to try to resolve the dispute before mediation or a hearing. (20 U.S.C. § 1415(f), 34 C.F.R. § 300.510.) The rules for this session are as follows:

- You have the right to attend.
- Members of the IEP team who have knowledge about the dispute must attend.
- Someone who has the authority to make a decision on the school district's behalf must attend.
- The meeting must be held within 15 days after the school district receives notice of your due process request.
- The school district may not bring an attorney to the meeting unless you bring an attorney.
- If you resolve the dispute at the meeting, it must be put in writing and signed by both you and the school district representative. The written agreement can be enforced by any state or federal court.
- Either party can void the written agreement within three business days (weekends and holidays don't count) of signing it. The party who voids the agreement doesn't have to give a reason, and the other side doesn't have to approve the decision.
- You can waive the resolution meeting and go straight to mediation or a hearing, but only if the school district agrees. You cannot decide, on your own, to forgo the meeting.
- If you participate in the resolution meeting, but the district has not resolved the issue to your satisfaction within 30 days of filing your due process request, you can go on to a mediation or hearing. (34 C.F.R. § 300.510(b)(1).)
- If the district does not hold the resolution meeting within 15 days of receiving notice of your due process request, or if the district fails to participate in the resolution meeting, you can ask a hearing officer to begin the timeline (that requires a hearing decision within 45 days after the initial 30-day resolution period expires). (34 C.F.R. § 300.510(b)(5).)
- **Important:** If you decide not to go to the resolution meeting, you may have your case dismissed. If the school district is unable to obtain your participation in the resolution meeting—and it can document that it made "reasonable" efforts to do so—then after the 30-day period, the district may ask the due process hearing officer to dismiss your case. (34 C.F.R. § 300.510(b)(4).)

Typical Due Process Disputes

Remember, due process is used to resolve only factual disputes, not disagreements over what the law requires or allows. Here are some due process disputes:

- eligibility for special education
- results of an evaluation
- goals
- specific placement or program
- related services
- proposed changes to your child's current IEP program, and
- suspension or expulsion of your child.

Several kinds of disputes are *not* eligible for due process, including:

- requesting a specific teacher or service provider by name for your child
- hiring or firing school staff
- assigning a different school administrator to your case, or
- requesting a specific person to represent the school district in the IEP process.

These concerns may be addressed through non-IDEA activities, such as parent organizing (see Chapter 15) or informal negotiations with the school.

When to Pursue Due Process

Due process is hard; it takes time, energy, and sometimes money, and it can be quite stressful. When you consider whether to go forward, think about these factors:

- **The precise nature of the problem.** You will have to pinpoint exactly what your dispute is, and make sure it is a factual dispute. For example, if you feel your child's education is generally not working (and you have not yet gone to an IEP meeting), or you object to the attitude of the school administrator, your concern is not yet ready for due process. If, however, your child has fallen behind in a regular class, you feel he or she should be in a special class, and the IEP team did not agree, you have a problem that qualifies for due process resolution.

Don't File for Due Process Until After the IEP Meeting

Many parents make the mistake of requesting a due process hearing before the issue is considered at an IEP meeting. Unless there are very unusual circumstances—for example, your child's health or well-being is threatened—you must go to an IEP meeting and reach an impasse there before you can request due process. However, if your school district has been dragging its feet about holding the IEP meeting or otherwise failing to address your child's needs, filing for due process before the IEP meeting can get things moving.

- **The importance of the issue to your child.** Placement or related service disputes are often central to your child's educational well-being. On the other hand, a dispute over goals or evaluation conclusions may not be significant enough to go to due process, because it does not directly impact your child's placement and related services.
- **The strength of your case.** Can you win? What evidence do you have to support your position? What evidence exists against it? What are the qualifications of the people making supportive or contrary statements? Remember that the district is required to provide your child with an appropriate education, not the best possible one. After the IEP meeting, review and update your IEP Material Organizer Form (discussed in Chapter 10) to evaluate the evidence for and against you. If you want other opinions on the strength of your case, consider these sources:
  - Nonschool employees, your independent evaluator, an outside tutor, or an attorney. Describe the disputed issue, your evidence, and the evidence against you, and ask whether you have a good chance of winning.
  - Other parents, particularly those who have been through due process with your school district. How does the school district react? Is the school likely to take a hard-line position, or might it offer a compromise after you show you are determined to go forward?

- Local parent and disability organizations. (Chapter 15 discusses how to find and work with a parents group.) If you need help finding a local group, start by contacting a national organization (see the list in Appendix B on this book's Companion Page on Nolo.com). See Chapter 16 for the link.

- **The bottom-line concerns for the school district.** For any disputed issue, the school district will have some bottom-line concerns—notably the cost and administrative difficulty of providing what you want. For example, the school administrator may be willing to compromise on a dispute between two public school program options, rather than pay for costly private school placement. The school's bottom line may affect your bottom line.

- **The cost of going forward.** Due process witnesses (including independent evaluators) and attorneys will charge for their time. If you prevail at a due process hearing, you are likely to be reimbursed for attorney fees, but not if you lose. (See Chapter 14 for information on using an attorney and attorney's fees.) Even if you prevail, it's unlikely you'll be reimbursed for the cost of having an independent evaluator testify (see "The Cost of an Independent Evaluator Appearing in Due Process," later in this chapter).

- **Time considerations.** Remember, you must file for due process within two years of learning of the dispute or within your state's statute of limitations, if it has one. (See "Don't Delay Filing for Due Process—You May Lose Your Rights," above.) Don't take too long to weigh your decision or spend too much time trying to reach an informal resolution.

Who Can File?

While the great majority of due process requests are filed by families, districts also have the right to file. Generally, districts initiate due process when:

- a student is in a costly private program and the district wants to be excused from paying for that program
- a family refuses to consent to an initial evaluation or reevaluation, or
- the district feels a student's current program is wrong and needs a due process decision to change the program. The burden of (responsibility for) proving a due process case is on the party who files. When the district initiates due process it will have that burden; when you file, you have that burden.

Whether the district files for due process or you do, the timelines and procedures governing the hearing stay the same.

Your Child's Status During Due Process

While you are in dispute with the school district, your child is entitled to remain in the current placement until you reach an agreement with the school, settle the matter through mediation, receive a due process hearing decision that neither you nor the school district appeal, or get a final court decision. This is called the "stay put" provision. (20 U.S.C. § 1415(j).) "Stay put" can be a complicated legal right. If you are concerned about whether your particular situation involves a "stay put" issue, see an attorney at once or contact a nonprofit disability rights organization.

> EXAMPLE: Your child is in a regular sixth-grade class with a one-on-one aide, two hours a day. At the IEP meeting, the school district offers a special day class, not a regular class, for seventh grade. You want your child to continue in a regular class. You are unable to reach an agreement at the IEP meeting. You initiate due process, during which time your child is entitled to remain in a regular classroom with the same amount of help from the aide until the matter is resolved.

Exceptions to the Stay Put Rule

The IDEA entitles your child to remain in his or her current placement pending due process unless your child carries a weapon to school or a school function, or knowingly possesses, uses, sells, or solicits illegal drugs while at school or a school function. In these situations, the school district can change your child's placement to an appropriate interim alternative educational setting for up to 45 days, or suspend your child for up to ten school days. (20 U.S.C. § 1415(k).) See Chapter 2 for more information on discipline for students in special education.

Using a Lawyer During Due Process

Using an attorney in due process certainly escalates the adversarial nature of the dispute, but by the time you've reached due process, that is probably not your primary concern. Using an attorney may also speed things along and increase your chances of success.

In mediation, an attorney will present your case and counter the school district's arguments. In a due process hearing, an attorney should prepare witnesses, submit exhibits, make the opening statement, and direct the proceeding. An attorney can also play a less active role, such as providing advice and helping you organize your case material, without attending the proceeding. Your attorney will contact the district to let them know that he or she is involved in the case.

To prepare for and attend a one-day mediation session, an attorney will likely charge from $1,000 to $2,500; much depends on the complexity of the case (and therefore preparation time for the attorney) and how long the mediation takes. The cost for a two-to-three-day hearing may range from $5,000 to $10,000 or more. It is not unusual for an attorney to use ten to 25 hours to prepare for a three-day hearing. If you use an attorney for advice only—for example, to help organize your case—your legal costs will be lower.

RELATED TOPIC
See Chapter 14 for a thorough discussion of attorneys and legal fees.

Check Out Free or Low-Cost Legal Services

The school district must provide you with a list of free or low-cost legal services available in your area. See Chapter 14 for advice on finding and working with an attorney.

Attorneys' Fees in Mediation

During mediation, you should ask the school district, as part of your proposed settlement, to pay your attorneys' fees. Your legal fees are one of many bargaining chips you can use to negotiate a settlement in mediation. However, the school district doesn't have to pay your fees, just as it doesn't have to agree to any other particular settlement term. Because mediation (and any settlement you reach as a result of it) is voluntary, the school district may or may not agree to pay your fees. Remember, a mediation is usually a settlement in which neither party gets everything it wants; attorneys' fees may be one of those things you are willing to forgo in order to get something more important.

The school district's decision will depend largely on how strong your case is and how motivated the school district is to settle. The school district may try to avoid having to reimburse you by agreeing to provide the education you want, if you agree to drop your demand for attorney fees. You will have to assess the strength of your case to decide whether you are willing to forgo your legal fees. If your case is very strong, the school district may decide that they are better off paying your fees now rather than later, when they will be much higher. Your attorney can advise you of the pros and cons in this situation.

Attorneys' Fees in a Due Process Hearing

If your case goes to hearing and you win, you will be entitled to reimbursement of your attorneys' fees. If you lose the hearing, you're responsible for your own attorneys' fees, but you will not have to pay the school district's attorneys' fees, absent unusual circumstances (see below).

If you win on some issues but not on others, you will be reimbursed for the time your lawyer spent on the winning issues (but not on the losers).

Liability for the School District's Legal Fees

The 2004 amendments to the IDEA create a new risk for parents: You may have to pay the school district's legal fees if you file for due process for "any improper purpose," defined as an intent to harass, cause unnecessary delay, or needlessly increase the cost of litigation. In addition, your attorney may have to pay the district's fees if he or she filed for due process or filed a lawsuit and the action was "frivolous, unreasonable, or without foundation." (20 U.S.C. § 1415(i)(3)(B).)

These new rules are intended to discourage parents from filing unfounded or frivolous actions. Congress believed that some parents (and their lawyers) were filing actions even if they knew their claims weren't valid, in order to try to force a settlement. If the school district's potential legal costs to fight the claim were higher than the cost of giving in, the district might decide to settle rather than paying a lawyer to fight it out, even if the parents' claim was unfounded.

These provisions are controversial. Of course, parents should always think very carefully before filing for due process, and shouldn't file just to harass or delay. On the other hand, plenty of parents have had to fight their school districts at every turn just to get the services to which their children are legally entitled, and these parents shouldn't have to worry about having to foot the school district's legal bills.

Even with these new rules, however, there remains a big difference between filing a difficult or even losing case and filing one that is frivolous or unreasonable. I believe that courts will be very reluctant to dampen the rights of children and their families, and so will require compelling evidence of parental misconduct before ordering a family to pay the district's fees. This was the position taken by a judge who heard a case involving a family's request for reimbursement of private school tuition. The family had not given timely notice to the district that they were placing their child in the private school, which could have allowed the judge to reduce or deny their reimbursement request. The judge decided that they were not entitled to reimbursement because the district had offered an appropriate placement, but didn't saddle the family with having to pay the district's attorneys' fees because the family had some basis for believing that they could receive reimbursement (*Taylor P. ex rel. Chris P. v. Missouri Dept. of Elementary and Secondary Educ.*, 48 IDELR 242 (W.D. Mo. 2007).)

Of course, you don't want to have to respond to the school district's request for fees, defend your intentions to a judge, and possibly even face a separate hearing on the issue before you are vindicated. With that in mind, here are some examples of filings that may cross the line:

- **Harassment.** You request IEP meetings every two months, request reevaluations numerous times each year, come to the school daily to complain, and file for due process several times a year.
- **Unnecessary delay.** You stall IEP and/or due process procedures without any legitimate reason.
- **Increasing costs.** You and your lawyer file unnecessary motions and otherwise take steps that prolong the litigation, without any legitimate purpose.
- **Frivolous actions.** Your attorney files for violation of a right that doesn't exist under the IDEA or is patently beyond the scope of the law. Or, you ask that the teacher remain after school for an hour every day to help your child with homework.

- **Unreasonable actions.** You seek a placement or service that is not reasonable. For example, your child has a very mild speech impairment and all of the experts (including your own) recommend a regular classroom placement with two-hour pullout sessions with an aide once a week. You request that your child be placed in a private, residential program and refuse to budge from your position.
- **Actions without foundation.** You have no evidence or support for what you are seeking. For example, you want private counseling for your child, but there is no evidence that your child has any psychological difficulties.

While well-meaning parents who act in good faith should not run into trouble under these rules, you should proceed very carefully. Talk to a special education attorney to make sure you are nowhere near violating these provisions.

Reduced Attorneys' Fees

If you prevail and are entitled to have your attorney fees paid by the school district, a judge can order that you receive a reduced amount. The amount can be reduced if: your attorney unreasonably extended the controversy, your attorney's hourly rate exceeds the prevailing rate in your community (charged by attorneys with similar experience and expertise), your attorney spent excessive time and resources on the case, or your attorney did not properly inform the school district about the nature of the dispute.

These failings would typically be committed by your attorney (not you), so you should not be responsible for paying any amount the court disallows. You should discuss this possibility ahead of time, before you hire a lawyer. If the attorney doesn't know about this rule, it suggests a lack of knowledge about special education law in general. (See Chapter 14 for pointers on hiring an attorney.)

Other Legal Advocates

There are nonattorney advocates who can be quite skilled in due process. Their fees are usually lower than a lawyer's fees, but you are not entitled to reimbursement of an advocate's fees if you prevail in a hearing.

Special education attorneys, nonprofit law centers, and disability and parent support groups may know the names of special education advocates in your area.

How to Begin Due Process

You must formally request due process in order for a mediation or hearing to be scheduled. Due process requests are sometimes referred to as due process complaints, the term used in the IDEA. Note, however, that a due process complaint (filed when you and the school district have a factual dispute) is different from a complaint regarding a legal violation (covered in Chapter 13).

Filing a Written Request

You must provide specific written information about the dispute to initiate due process. There can be no hearing or mediation until you complete this first step. (20 U.S.C. § 1415(b)(7), 34 C.F.R. § 300.508(b).) You must provide this written notice to the school district *and* send a copy to the state department of education branch responsible for special education. (You can find the contact information through the federal Department of Education website at www.ed.gov.)

Your written request must include the following information:
- your name and address
- your child's name and address
- the name of your child's school
- a description of the disputed issues, including facts relating to the issues

- your desired resolution—not only what you want for your child's education, but also that you want to be reimbursed for your due process costs, such as attorneys' fees, witness fees, and independent evaluation costs, and
- whether you want to mediate or go directly to a hearing.

Most due process matters involve a disagreement between you and the school district over a particular disputed item—for example, you want a particular placement or service, but the school district won't provide it. You may also believe the school district has violated procedural rules under the IDEA. For example, if the school district does not hold a yearly IEP meeting, does not process your request for an initial evaluation, or does not allow you to bring anyone with you to the IEP meeting, you should raise those issues in your due process request.

When putting together the required information, it's best to be precise. You can use a short list to describe the existing problem and your proposed solution. The IDEA requires each state to develop a model form to assist parents in filing for due process. Ask your school district or state department of education for a copy.

Keep a copy of your due process request for your records. It's best to send this request via certified mail, return receipt requested, so you'll have proof of the date it was received.

FORM

A sample Letter Requesting Due Process is below; a blank, downloadable copy is available on this book's Companion Page on www.nolo.com. See Chapter 16 for the link.

Letter Requesting Due Process

Date: march 1, 20xx

To: Phillip Jones, Due Process Unit

Wisconsin Department of Education

8987 Franklin Avenue, La Crosse, WI 54601

**Sent via
Certified Mail**

Re: Steven Howard

Our son, Steven Howard, is a fourth grader at Clinton School in La Crosse.

His school district is the Central La Crosse Elementary School District, 562

5th Avenue, La Crosse, Wisconsin.

We are formally requesting due process, beginning with mediation. We believe

Steven requires a full-time, one-on-one aide in order to be fully

mainstreamed in next year's regular fifth grade class at Clinton School. The

school district has refused to provide that aide.

We believe an appropriate solution would include, but should not be limited to,

the following: • A qualified full-time academic aide, to work one-on-one with Steven

in the regular fifth grade class at Clinton School for the coming school year.

• Reimbursement for all attorneys' fees, witnesses, independent assessments,

and other costs accrued for the February 14, 20xx IEP meeting and subsequent

due process.

Please contact us at once to schedule the mediation.

Sincerely,

William Howard   Kate Howard

William and Kate Howard

1983 Smiley Lane

La Crosse, WI 54601

555-5569 (home); 555-2000 (work)

Sufficiency of the Written Request for Due Process

In my experience, at least in California, due process hearing officers often ask for very detailed written requests. Even when advocates, parents, and lawyers provide all the detail required by 34 C.F.R. § 300.508(b), it has not always been enough. I strongly urge you to carefully read 34 C.F.R. § 300.508(b) and cover all areas listed there. When in doubt, include more rather than less. If you run into a hearing officer who rejects your complaint for insufficiency and you think you provided more than enough detail per 34 C.F.R. § 300.508(b), remember this: 34 C.F.R. § 300.508(d) states that a complaint "must be deemed sufficient" unless, within 15 days of receipt of the complaint, the other party formally notifies the hearing officer that it believes the complaint is insufficient. In other words, the hearing officer should not make a determination about sufficiency unless the other side formally states that it believes the complaint is insufficient.

If the hearing officer finds your complaint does not meet the "sufficiency" requirement, he or she will often give you an opportunity to amend your complaint. The officer may even point out where the deficiencies are. You will also be allowed to amend your complaint if the other side agrees in writing to let you do so. (34 C.F.R. § 300.508(d).)

Other Notice Requirements

The party that receives a due process request (which may be you or the school district, depending on who files for due process) can object that the request does not meet the requirements discussed above. The objecting party has 15 days after receiving the request to send the other party and the hearing officer a written statement explaining why the request is insufficient.

Within five days of receiving this written statement, the hearing officer must decide whether the initial request is adequate. If it is not, the filing party can amend the request, but only if the other party agrees *and* has an opportunity to have a resolution session, or if the hearing officer consents. If the filing party needs time to file an amended request, the timeline for the due process decision will be extended as well.

Of course, you can avoid all of these rules by simply filing a clear, sufficient request in the first place. The IDEA requires your school district to provide you with written information about your due process rights, procedures, and requirements.

Preparing for Due Process

While a mediation session and a due process hearing are different, preparing for the former will help as you get ready for the latter. In addition, the preparation you did for the IEP meeting will be of enormous help as you go through due process. The recommendations in this section apply to both mediation and the due process hearing.

Organize Your Evidence

First, pull out your child's file, the reports, evaluations, and other documents in your IEP binder (see Chapter 4), your blueprint (see Chapter 5), and your IEP Material Organizer Form (see Chapter 10).

Make a list of the disputed issues. Using a blank IEP Material Organizer Form, write next to each disputed issue the witnesses, documents, or facts that support your point of view—and those that oppose it. You should make a separate list of your potential witnesses and people who might testify for the district.

Now find every piece of evidence you have to support your position. Review your binder, original material organizer forms, and notes from the IEP meeting. Focus not only on reports and evaluations, but also on comments made at the meeting. Gather all your supportive evidence together, or tab it in your binder and highlight key statements. Make photocopies of all written materials that support your point of view to have available during the mediation or hearing.

Now work on the school district's case—that is, figure out what evidence contradicts your point of view. Think about any evidence you can use to rebut the district's likely arguments.

Make a List of Expenses

Once you've gathered evidence, make a list of expenses you've incurred throughout the IEP process, such as the costs of:

- independent evaluations
- tutors
- lost wages for attending IEPs
- private school or private related service costs
- personal transportation costs, such as those incurred driving your child to a private school
- attorneys' fees
- costs for other professionals (such as a private speech therapist or counselor), and
- photocopying.

Note the date a payment was made or cost incurred, the name of the payee, and the purpose of the expense. Attach all receipts.

At the mediation or hearing, you will want to request payment for these expenses. If the district agrees to pay some or all of them, or if the hearing officer rules in your favor, the receipts are proof that you really spent this money.

Prepare an Opening Statement

At the beginning of a mediation session or hearing, you will need to make an opening statement explaining why you're there and what you want. Some people are comfortable making notes and then talking extemporaneously; others write out a complete statement and read it. Do what's easiest for you. The opening statement should include the following:

Description of your child. Briefly describe your child, including his or her age, current educational program, general areas of educational concern, and disabling conditions. Give a short explanation of your child's educational history.

Description of items in dispute. Briefly describe the specific items in dispute—for example, the amount of a related service or the placement.

Description of what you want and why. Summarize what your child needs—for example, speech therapy three times a week, in a one-on-one setting with a therapist qualified to work with students with language delays, placement in Sierra School, or the use of the Lindamood-Bell program or the Orton-Gillingham method.

Description of your evidence. Often, you'll close with a strong statement briefly summarizing the evidence you have for your position. In some mediations, however, you may decide not to reveal all of your evidence right away. You will have to judge the best approach given the situation, the personalities involved, and even your intuition. (See "How Much Evidence Do You Reveal in Mediation?" below.)

Mediation Specifics

Mediation is the first official step in due process. It is less confrontational than a hearing, and is intended to explore ways to compromise and settle your dispute.

The mediator is a neutral third party, usually hired by the state department of education, who is knowledgeable about the IDEA and special education matters. The mediator has no authority to force you to settle. If you reach a settlement, however, your agreement will be put into writing and will be binding on you and the district—you both must abide by and follow the written settlement.

While mediation is fairly similar from one place to another, the way sessions proceed will vary depending on the style of the mediator and the rules established by your state.

RELATED TOPIC

Contact your state department of education to find out the details of your state's laws on mediation. You can find the contact information through the federal Department of Education website at www.ed.gov.

Mediation must be made available to you at no cost. Mediation is completely voluntary. If you don't want to mediate, you don't have to. If you prefer, you can skip mediation and go straight to a hearing.

If mediation is not successful, any settlement offers and other comments made during the mediation cannot be used as evidence at the hearing or any subsequent legal proceedings. This rule allows you to discuss matters in a frank manner without fear that your statements will later be used against you.

Pros and Cons of Mediation

You may be asking yourself why you would try mediation, particularly because it ends in compromise, rather than a clear victory for one side or the other. There are some compelling reasons to go to mediation:

- **Know thine enemy.** Mediation gives you a chance to understand more fully the school district's arguments. Of course, the school district gets the same opportunity to hear about your case, but sharing information in this way may bring you closer to a solution.
- **The school district may be motivated to compromise.** Mediation takes the school district one step closer to a hearing and the possibility of a ruling against the school, with all the attendant costs, including possible attorney fees. The school administrator may be far more flexible in mediation than at the IEP meeting, feeling that a compromise now is better than an expensive loss later.
- **Mediation is constructive.** Mediation encourages the parties to work out disagreements. Thus, you may retain a more positive relationship with your school district by mediating the dispute. You also keep control over the outcome—you must agree with any mediated solution. When you go to a hearing, the decision-making power is out of your hands.
- **Mediation is cheap.** As a general rule, you will have few or even no costs at mediation; hearings can be expensive, particularly if you use an attorney.

- **Mediation can provide a reality check.** Even if you don't settle the case, mediation gives you a chance to have a neutral party assess your case and point out its strengths and weaknesses.
- **You get two bites of the apple.** By going to mediation, you give yourself two chances at success. If the mediation is unsuccessful, you can move on to a hearing.

There are also downsides to mediation:

- **Half a loaf can be disappointing.** Ideally, you can settle in mediation and get everything your child needs. In reality, however, mediation usually involves compromise, meaning you will probably settle for less than what you would have received if you had won at a hearing.
- **Mediation may delay resolution of your dispute.** The IDEA requires that a due process hearing decision be issued within 45 days after the 30-day resolution process period, whether you go through mediation or go straight to a hearing. In reality, however, extensions of that 45-day rule can be granted if you spend time in mediation. Unless you have a real time problem—your child must be placed in a specific program by a certain date or will suffer dire consequences—most cases can stand the delay.
- **You do things twice.** If you go to mediation and then a hearing, you will have been involved in two procedures, doubling the time, inconvenience, stress, and some costs, such as time off from your job.

TIP

Try mediation. Although there are some downsides to mediation, they are almost always outweighed by the benefits. Unless there is a compelling reason to go straight to a hearing—like a serious time crunch or a truly entrenched opponent—you should give mediation a try.

Mediators

The mediator's job is to help you and the school district reach a settlement. The mediator will not decide who is right and who is wrong. A good mediator will:

- put you and school representatives at ease
- try to establish an atmosphere in which compromise is possible
- be objective
- give you and the school district a frank assessment of the strengths and weaknesses of your positions, and
- go beyond your stated positions to explore possible settlements that may not be initially apparent.

Some mediators play a more limited role—they simply present everyone's positions and hope that the weight of the evidence and formality of the process will lead to a settlement.

Mediation Logistics

Mediation sessions must be held at a time and place convenient for you. They are often held at the school district's main office, but they can be held elsewhere. Some people are concerned that having the mediation at a school office gives the district an advantage, but I have found it usually does not matter.

The length of the mediation can vary, but sessions generally take several hours and often a full day. Expect the mediation session to take more time than you would think.

While districts vary, most will send the special education administrator and perhaps another person who has direct knowledge of your child to the mediation. While you can bring outside evaluators, aides, tutors, and any other individuals you want, including a lawyer, you will usually want to save them for the hearing. If you bring a lawyer to the mediation, the district will most likely bring one also.

Bringing in experts might make mediation more expensive and difficult to schedule. Whether you include experts will depend on:

- how forceful the experts can be
- whether there is any chance of changing the district's mind, and

- the risks of revealing some of your evidence prior to the fair hearing.

If you expect a hearing and don't want to put all your cards on the table at mediation, don't bring the experts. On the other hand, if you want to settle quickly and your experts can aid in that process, bring them along.

The Mediation Session

You, the mediator, and the school representatives will gather in a conference or meeting room. After brief introductions, the mediator will explain how the mediation process works, stressing that mediation is a voluntary attempt to resolve your disagreement.

Your Opening Statement

You begin by briefly explaining your side of the dispute. Do not hesitate to express your feelings. Your child has important needs, and his or her well-being is at stake. Say that. Express how worried you are. Explain why you feel the school district has not effectively served your child and how it has failed to provide an appropriate education. It's important to show the mediator how crucial the matter is to you and your child. This does not mean tirades or irrational monologues. Give your opinion, but don't question the honesty, professionalism, or decency of the school representatives.

Your opening statement should discuss every possible problem. It should be clear and succinct, and run from five to ten minutes.

If the school has committed any legal violations, you can raise these in your opening statement. While legal violations are subject to the complaint procedure (see Chapter 13), evidence of a legal violation may be a powerful addition to your case, showing the school district's disregard or lack of understanding of the law, and possibly the district's lack of reliability. Nothing in the IDEA prevents you from raising legal issues in the mediation. While the mediator cannot remedy legal violations, the mediator can say to district personnel, "You are in trouble because you clearly violated the law; you might want to think about settling this case now."

How Much Evidence Do You Reveal in Mediation?

I've suggested that you describe your evidence as part of your opening statement. But you may not want to reveal all your supporting evidence at mediation. By telling all, you may help the school prepare for the hearing. On the other hand, if your evidence is very strong, revealing it may lead to a settlement in your favor. If you're not sure what to do, ask the mediator's opinion in your private meeting. If the mediator feels that the school realizes its case is weak or for some other reason is close to settling, then it may be wise to share everything. Or if the mediator feels the school is rigid and unlikely to settle, then it may be better not to reveal all of your evidence.

In either case, you'll want to provide at least a synopsis of your evidence, noting where a professional (teacher, related service provider, administrator, doctor, outside evaluator, or private tutor) has made a clear statement about the disputed issue. Also note the credentials of the person, particularly if he or she is well known, and loaded with degrees and experience. Highlight all documents or statements by school district representatives that support your position.

School District's Opening Statement

After you make your opening statement, the school district's representative presents the district's point of view, perhaps responding to what you have said. Don't interrupt or respond, even though the school's version of the dispute may be very different from yours. Take notes of their main points.

After the school representative finishes, the mediator may invite you to respond to the school's statement to add anything you forgot. If you respond, make it brief and to the point, focusing on why you disagree with the school's position.

Private Sessions With the Mediator

After you and the school representatives make your opening state-ments, the mediator will meet privately with you, then with the school representatives, then back with you, then back with the school representatives, continuing back and forth as necessary. When you meet privately with the mediator, speak frankly. The mediator cannot disclose anything you say to the school representatives, unless you give the mediator permission. Be sure to clearly tell the mediator what you want conveyed to the school district and what you want kept between you and the mediator.

In your first meeting, the mediator may want to clarify issues and begin exploring whether you're willing to compromise.

As the mediator shuttles back and forth, specific evidence may come up related to a disputed issue. For example, you and the school district may have very different views on the validity of the district's evaluation versus your independent evaluation. You can say to the mediator something like "Please convey to Mr. Roberts that my evaluator is a recognized expert and is clear in her recommendations; the district's expert has limited knowledge of my child's disability."

After a few of these private sessions, the mediator should be able to tell you how far the school will go to settle the dispute. At this point, you will have to discuss your bottom line. You should start thinking about this before the meeting. Think about what is essential, what you can give up, how strong your case is, and how hard a line the school is taking.

At the mediation, you can make use of the mediator by asking direct questions, such as:

- What do you think the school will do on the placement issue?
- Do they understand that Dr. Parnell said Victor needs placement in the private school?
- What is their bottom line?
- Do you think we have a case if we go to a hearing?

The strength of the evidence and the work of the mediator will convince the district to settle (or not). If the district has moved from the position it held at the IEP meeting, but some issues remain unresolved, you'll have to decide what to do. You'll have to weigh the importance of the outstanding, nonresolved issues, your willingness to go to a hearing, and the likelihood of ultimate victory.

Wrapping Up the Mediation Session

After various private meetings with the mediator, there will be four possible outcomes:
- full settlement of all issues
- partial settlement—you agree on some issues and disagree on others
- no settlement, but you agree to try again with the mediator at a later date, or
- no settlement and no further mediation sessions scheduled.

Tips on Bargaining in Mediation

Bargaining is part of mediation. When presenting what you want, make your list as strong and inclusive as possible. Put in everything you could possibly want, including your expenses and even minor items. But know your priorities, including what you can live without and can therefore use as bargaining chips.

EXAMPLE: You feel your child should be in a private school, which costs $15,000 per year. You also want the school district to pay for your independent evaluation, which costs $1,000. You also have some reimbursement costs, including a tutor, totaling several hundred dollars. Your case is strong enough to go after all of these items. But to compromise, you may have to forgo the evaluation and other costs in order to get the district to agree to pay for the private school.

A mediation settlement can contain anything you and the school district agree to—including that the school will provide all or part of what you want for your child and pay your attorneys' fees.

Whatever the outcome, you will all return to the meeting room, and the mediator will complete a mediation form. The mediator will write down what the parties agreed to (if anything), what issues are unresolved (if any), and what the next steps will be if full agreement was not reached.

If you don't reach a settlement on all or some issues, there are three options for what happens next:

- you go to a hearing
- you drop the matter, or
- you go directly to court—this highly unusual approach requires you to prove that the problem is so serious you can't spend time at a hearing and need a judge to look at the matter immediately; you will need a lawyer's help (see Chapter 14).

Why Districts Are More Likely to Negotiate in Mediation: Money

If you do not use an attorney in mediation, it is more likely the school district will not as well. However, it might be useful to indicate that you will use an attorney at the due process hearing, which in most cases will mean the district will use one too. (If you win the due process hearing, you will be reimbursed for your legal fees, but if you lose, in almost all cases, you will not have to reimburse the school for its legal fees (see "Attorneys' Fees in a Due Process Hearing," above).) Because of the high cost of lawyers, the district has an incentive to settle before going to hearing.

For example, say you want the district to provide your child with a one-on-one aide for 15 hours per week with a cost of $1,500 per month or $18,000 per year. If the district loses at hearing, it will have that cost, plus your legal fees, plus their legal fees. And even if the district wins, It will still be paying its own attorney, which may well total the $18,000 it would cost for the aide. You can see that a simple cost analysis would strongly suggest the district settle before going to hearing, because the best case scenario will still cost them quite a bit and the worst scenario will cost them two to three times the cost of the aide. This kind of analysis does not always work—sometimes districts simply feel they must take a stand—but it is certainly worth keeping this in mind.

Be aware that it is within the district's rights to ask that you drop your request for a hearing in return for settling some of the issues between you. It is your right, of course, to agree to do so or not. The mediation agreement will spell out any agreement you reach on next steps.

Once you and the school district sign the mediation form, both of you are bound by whatever agreement you reached.

Due Process Hearing

A hearing is like a court trial, although it won't be held in a courtroom. You and the school district submit evidence in the form of written documents and sworn testimony from witnesses. A neutral third party, called a hearing officer, reviews the evidence and decides who is right and who is wrong. That decision is binding on you and the district. The hearing officer has the authority to act independently of you and the school district—in essence, as a judge. The hearing officer cannot be an employee of the school district or the state educational agency if either agency is involved in the education of your child. (20 U.S.C. § 1415(f)(3)(A).)

Although the IDEA establishes specific rules for hearings, states can vary some of the procedural details. For example, Ohio provides that attorneys will act as hearing officers; other states specify qualifications, rather than require that officers be members of a particular profession. In most states, the department of education provides a list of hearing officers or contracts with a qualified agency to do so. For instance, in California, the state department of education has contracted with another state agency, which in turn hires the hearing officers.

RELATED TOPIC

Contact your state department of education to find out the details of your state's laws on hearings. You can find the contact information through the federal Department of Education website at www.ed.gov.

Hearing Officer Qualifications

The IDEA imposes several rules on hearing officers. An officer may not be an employee of the state department of education or the school district, and may not have any personal or professional interest that might conflict with the officer's objectivity in the hearing. The officer must have the knowledge and ability to understand the IDEA, to conduct the hearing in accordance with appropriate legal standards, and to make and write a decision that complies with standard legal practice. (20 U.S.C. § 1415(f)(3)(A).)

A hearing is used to resolve factual disputes between you and your child's school district, including disagreements about placement, related services, curricula, or methodologies. See the list of typical IEP due process disputes at the beginning of this chapter.

Often, a factual dispute contains a legal dispute. For example, you want your child in a private school, and the school district offers a special day class in the public school. The factual dispute involves which placement is appropriate for your child. The legal issue is whether the IDEA allows a private school placement when supported by the facts (it does).

Or, the school district wants to place your child in a special school 15 miles from your home; you want your child placed in a regular class at the local school. Again, the factual dispute involves finding the appropriate placement. The legal issue is the IDEA's requirement that your child be placed in the least restrictive environment.

You may be thinking at this point, "I thought legal problems were subject only to the complaint process." Here's how it works: In a hearing, there may be legal issues that shape the factual analysis and outcome. In a complaint, you are only claiming that the school district broke the law—there is no factual dispute regarding an IEP issue.

TIP

You can do both. In some cases, you may simultaneously file a complaint and pursue due process, as discussed at the end of Chapter 13.

A witness may testify about a legal issue, or you or the school district may raise a legal issue in your opening statements. In most cases, however, legal issues are addressed in a posthearing brief (see "Posthearing Briefs," below). Discussing legal issues at the hearing or in a brief may seem quite daunting. If you anticipate major legal disputes, see Chapter 14 on lawyers and legal research, or contact an attorney for help with this part of the process.

Fear of Hearings

It's natural to be afraid of a due process hearing—after all, it's like a trial and can be difficult and complicated. So how do you get through one with your nerves intact?

- Be organized.
- Take some time to think through the issues and your evidence.
- Know that everybody else is nervous, too.

Never doubt that you can do it. Lots of parents have had these same fears—and done just fine. In preparing for the IEP meeting (and perhaps mediation), you already did a good deal of the hard work.

Your Due Process Hearing Rights and Responsibilities

The IDEA sets out many rights and responsibilities you and the school district have during the hearing process. (20 U.S.C. § 1415):

- You have the right to be advised and accompanied by an attorney or another person with special knowledge or training.
- At least five business days before the hearing, you and the school district are required to give each other all evaluations and any recommendations based on those evaluations. If you don't, the hearing officer can exclude all evidence about the evaluations. This five-day requirement is usually also applied to exchanging witness lists—the names, qualifications, and topics of testimony of everyone you and the school district will call to testify at the hearing.

- The party who requested due process cannot raise any issues at the hearing that were not included in the written request unless the other side agrees.
- Before the hearing, you can subpoena witnesses to ensure that they will attend. (Most state educational agencies have subpoena forms.)
- Before the hearing, you have the right to declare the hearing closed or open to the public. (34 C.F.R. § 300.512(c).) An open hearing gives access to the public, including the press, which you may want. But an open hearing may also increase the stress and invite district employees to come and go.
- At the hearing, you have the right to have your child present. (34 C.F.R. § 300.512(c).) This is usually not advisable. You want the hearing officer to base any decisions on the objective evidence presented, not on conclusions reached by observing your child. Also, you want to protect your child from any emotional harm that could result from hearing what the witnesses or district representatives say at the hearing. In rare circumstances, you may want your child to testify at the hearing. You should then simply call your child as a witness at the appropriate time. See "Your Child as a Witness," below.
- At the hearing, you can present written evidence in the form of exhibits and ask witnesses to answer questions.
- After the hearing, you are entitled to a verbatim record of the hearing (in a written or electronic format). This means that the hearing officer will tape the proceedings.
- After the hearing, you're entitled to a written decision, including findings of fact.
- You have the right to appeal a hearing decision to a state or federal court.

Check your state laws and regulations for any different or additional rules. For example, California requires each party to a hearing to submit a statement of issues and proposed resolutions at least ten days before the hearing. (Cal. Educ. Code § 56505(e)(6).)

Burden of Proof
In *Schaffer ex rel. Schaffer v. Weast*, 546 U.S. 49 (2005), the U.S. Supreme Court decided that the party initiating due process has the burden of proving its case at hearing. While the Court acknowledged that the term "burden of proof" is very difficult to define, this means that the party that files for due process must prove its case. For you, this means that if you file for due process, it's not up to the school district to show that it is providing an appropriate education for your child. Rather, it will be up to *you* to show that what the school district is offering is not appropriate.

Pros and Cons of a Due Process Hearing

There are several good reasons to request a hearing:

- If you win, your child will receive the education he or she needs.
- If you win, it's unlikely you will have to fight the battle again.
- If you win, your attorneys' fees will be reimbursed for every issue you prevail on.
- Whether or not you win, you buy time. If your child is currently in a placement you want to maintain, your child is entitled to remain there until the issue is finally resolved—either through the hearing decision or a final court decision, if you appeal.

There are also disadvantages to going to a hearing:

- Hearings are difficult, time consuming, emotionally draining, and contentious.
- You might lose.
- Your relationship with your school district will likely be strained and formal. Future IEP meetings may be hard. If you lose, the school district may feel invincible.
- If you lose, you won't be entitled to reimbursement for your costs and attorneys' fees.

Hearing Logistics

The due process hearing must be held at a time and place convenient for you. Normally, hearings are held at the school district office and last anywhere from one to several days.

Once you request a hearing, you will be sent a notice of the date and location of the hearing, as well as the name of the hearing officer. You will also be given the name, address, and phone number of the school district representative. This information is important—you must send your exhibits and witness lists to this representative, as well as to the hearing officer.

Preparing for the Hearing

If you go to mediation first, much of your preparation will be done by the time you go to a hearing. But you still have some very important and time-consuming work to do. Give yourself several weeks to prepare, more if you skip mediation and go straight to a hearing.

Know Your Case

Review your child's file (see Chapter 3), your binder (see Chapter 4), and your IEP blueprint (see Chapter 5). Be clear on the disputed issues—what you want, what the school district is offering, and how you disagree. Don't confuse personality conflicts with disputes over your child's needs.

Determine Your Strategy

At the hearing, you must clearly state your position on each disputed issue and offer evidence to support it, in the form of witnesses and documents.

> EXAMPLE: You want your daughter mainstreamed with a one-on-one aide, but your school district offers a special class. At the hearing, you will have to show that:
> - the school district failed to offer mainstreaming placement
> - an aide will help your daughter function in the classroom

- your daughter will benefit socially by being in regular class, and
- a special class will be detrimental to your daughter because it will not address her unique needs and is contrary to the IDEA's least restrictive environment requirement.

Prepare Exhibits of Written Material

An exhibit is any written document that contains supportive evidence or provides information that the hearing officer will need to make a decision. But be choosy about what you submit—you don't necessarily want to turn over your entire IEP binder. The issues in dispute will guide you. Review all of your documents, looking for everything that supports your position, such as an evaluation or teacher's report. Note the specific place in each document where the supportive statement is made—that is, the page number and paragraph. You have probably done much of this work with the material organizer form you developed for the IEP meeting.

CAUTION

Do not submit material that damages your case or reveals private information you don't want known. The school district may submit evidence that harms your case or points out the gaps in your evidence; obviously, you should not. Remember that the school district and hearing officer will get to examine the exhibits you submit—if they contain personal or confidential information that you don't want to reveal, you should try to find a different way to make your point.

Examples of exhibits typically presented at hearings include:
- IEP documents
- evaluations
- letters or reports from your child's teacher or physician
- articles about your child's disability, appropriate teaching methods, or any other issues in your case
- witnesses' résumés and articles they've written that relate to the issues in dispute, and
- your child's classroom work or artwork.

If in doubt, include the item. You never know when you might want to refer to something during the hearing. If you don't include the item when you prepare your exhibit exchange (at least five days before the hearing), you will probably be barred from using it at the hearing.

Arrange your exhibits in an order that makes sense to you, such as the order in which you think you'll introduce them or alphabetical order. Place them in a folder or binder with tabs and a table of contents. Be sure to page number each individual exhibit, too, so you can find specific statements easily.

You'll refer to these exhibits in your own testimony and when you question witnesses. At this stage, it is unlikely that you will have to develop new evidence. But if you do not yet have support for a disputed item, you may need new material—for example, a supportive letter or even an independent evaluation.

Choose and Prepare Witnesses

Witnesses are crucial to the outcome of the hearing. Choose and prepare your witnesses with care.

Choosing Witnesses

Double-check your list of all potential witnesses, both people who support you and people who might testify for the school district (including participants at the IEP meeting). Try to anticipate what each witness can testify about. One witness may be able to testify about several issues, while others may focus on only one disputed matter.

In choosing your witnesses, look for the following:
- the strength of the witness's testimony
- the witness's experience, training, education, and direct knowledge of your child, and
- the witness's willingness to testify under oath. You should consider whether a person is willing to testify at the hearing before you put him or her on your witness list. A favorable or supportive report won't help if the witness equivocates at the hearing. In that case, submit the person's written material and have other witnesses refer to that report.

In some cases, you may need to subpoena a reluctant witness to testify at the hearing. A subpoena is an order that requires the witness to appear. Ask your state's education agency where to get subpoena forms.

The Cost of an Independent Evaluator Appearing in Due Process

In the 2006 case of *Arlington Central School District Board of Education v. Murphy*, (548 U.S. 291), the U.S. Supreme Court ruled that when a parent goes to due process and prevails, the IDEA does not allow the parent to be reimbursed for the cost of an expert witness. The majority of the Court acknowledged that when Congress enacted the IDEA it indicated that cost could include reimbursement for expert witnesses and their fees, but the Court found that the IDEA does not clearly allow such reimbursement. This means then that even if you win your case in due process, you will not be reimbursed for the cost of having an independent evaluator testify.

Preparing Witness Questions

Write out a list of questions for each witness. The following is a general outline:

- Ask the witness to identify him- or herself—for example, "Please state your name, occupation, and place of employment."
- Ask about the witness's experience, education, training, and specific expertise in the area of dispute—you can refer the witness to the résumé or written articles that you included in your exhibits.
- Establish the witness's knowledge of your child—for example:
  - *"Have you met my son, Philip Lavelle?"*
  - *"Please tell us when, for how long, and for what purpose."*
  - *"Did you also observe him in school?"*
  - *"Please tell us when that was and for how long."*
- Ask questions to elicit your witness's opinion about the issues in dispute, for example:

- *"You stated that you tested Philip. What tests did you administer?"*
- *"What were the results?"*
- *"What do those results mean?"*
- *"What conclusions did you draw regarding Philip's reading difficulties?"*
- *"How severe are his difficulties?"*
- *"In your professional opinion, what is the appropriate way to help Philip improve his reading?"*
- *"Do you have any specific recommendations regarding Philip's reading needs?"*
- *"What is your professional opinion regarding Philip's prognosis as a successful reader if he is not provided the help you recommend?"*

> **TIP**
>
> **Keys to preparing your witnesses.** As a general rule, witnesses must be able to clearly state what your child needs and why, the consequences if those needs are met, and the detriment to your child if they are not.

Preparing Your Witnesses

Before the hearing, meet with your witnesses and go over your questions. Their answers may lead to new questions you'll want to ask or trigger a new strategy or approach. Explain that after you're done asking questions, the school district representative will cross-examine the witness by asking additional questions.

Some witnesses, particularly any school employees who agree to testify for your child, may be unwilling to meet during school hours. You may have to arrange to meet them at their homes. Others may not want to meet at all. What should you do about witnesses who can help your case but won't talk to you ahead of time? If you can't discuss the case before the hearing, you won't know exactly how the witness will testify. Taking this kind of risk may backfire. One strategy is to leave the person off your witness list and hope the district calls him or her so you can cross-examine. Of course, if the witness is the only person who can testify about a certain element of your case, then this may not be wise.

Another strategy is to include the person on your witness list, but don't ask him or her to testify during your presentation. Then, either cross-examine if the school calls the witness, or use him or her as a rebuttal witness to counter something said by a school district witness.

Just before the hearing date, get back in touch with your witnesses to tell them:

- the date, time, and location of the hearing
- what time you need them to arrive to be ready to testify—be sure to let them know that they might not be called on time if an earlier witness took longer than expected or the hearing officer breaks early, and
- how long you expect their testimony to take.

Preparing Yourself as a Witness

You will most likely be a witness at the hearing. You have valuable information about your child's history, previous programs, and needs, as well as your worries, your frustrations, and what teachers have said to you about your child.

Your testimony should cover only matters that you know firsthand. Although you can testify about the evaluation done on your child and what the evaluator told you, the evaluator is in a better position to give this testimony. In general, your testimony should cover the areas in which you are the expert, particularly if no one else will testify on the issue.

You can present your testimony in one of two ways: You can respond to questions (just like you will be asking questions of your witnesses) asked by your spouse, a relative, or close friend, or you can make a statement covering all issues of importance. You can either read your statement or give it from notes. After you're done answering questions or making your statement, the school district representative will cross-examine you.

Your testimony should be clear, specific, and objective. Break down your points into the following areas, using your mediation statement as a guideline:

- a general description of your child, including age, strengths, and weaknesses (your child profile, discussed in Chapter 10, can help here)

- your child's disability and the effects of that disability
- any secondary difficulties due to the disability—such as emotional problems
- your child's educational history—that is, the current program and class, and previous placements
- the particular issues in dispute and your desired resolution
- your observations at class visits, meetings with teachers and other professionals, and the IEP meeting (for example, "On February 12, 20xx, I visited the second-grade class at Tower School and I observed ….")
- statements others have made to you that support your point of view, including your reaction to those statements—for instance, "On November 3, 20xx, Mr. Mastin of the school district told me there was no room for my child in the second-grade class at Tower School; I confirmed this conversation in a letter, my Exhibit F, to which Mr. Mastin did not respond."
- your child's specific educational needs and the consequences if they are not met—for example, "Given the assessment by Dr. Pollack, I believe a placement in a program other than the second-grade class at Tower School will have serious emotional and cognitive consequences for my child."

Your Child as a Witness

As mentioned above, there may be situations in which you want to call your child as a witness. For example, if your child is in high school, is deaf, and wants an interpreter, then her testimony about the isolation she feels without access to classroom communication may be powerful. When she testifies, however, the other side may try to trick her. You have to be absolutely sure your child is prepared to testify, understands what the other side may ask, and whether the pluses from her testimony will be outweighed by the negatives. You may want to consult with experts, such as your pediatrician or another adult your child trusts, to make sure that testifying (and particularly undergoing cross-examination) would not be harmful to your child.

Prepare Questions for School Witnesses

Preparing questions for school witnesses is more difficult than preparing for your own witnesses because you don't know exactly what they'll say. Still, you can probably guess what many witnesses will say, because you heard their opinions at the IEP meeting.

Start by reviewing your files, the transcript or notes of the IEP meeting, and the school district's exhibits (you'll get them five days before the hearing). Then make a list of questions to strengthen your case or at least undermine what the school district's witnesses might say.

> EXAMPLE: Your child's teacher said something very important to you when you visited your child's class. You sent a letter confirming what was said ("Thanks for talking to me today. I was glad to hear that you agreed Jake should remain in a regular class with the help of an aide"). The teacher never objected to your confirming letter, but you now believe she will say the opposite at the hearing. Be ready to point out the discrepancy—for instance, "Ms. Jenkins, you testified this morning that you feel Jake should be placed in a special education class. Do you recall when we met on October 15, and you told me that Jake was doing well in the regular class but needed an aide to keep up? You don't recall that meeting? Please look at Exhibit B, my November 1 letter to you."

Exchange Witness Lists and Evidence

Remember, you should submit a list of your witnesses and must submit copies of written exhibits at least five days before the hearing begins. (20 U.S.C. § 1415(f)(2).) Once you have your exhibits (organized in binders) and your list of witnesses, make two copies. Keep the originals for yourself, send one copy to the hearing officer, and send the other copy to the school district representative. To have proof that the others received the items at least five days before the hearing, send them certified mail, return receipt requested.

Rules of Evidence

You may have heard of something called the "rules of evidence." These formal rules, which are very specific and sometimes quite arcane, are used in courts to guide judges in deciding what evidence can be included and what must be excluded. These rules don't have to be followed at due process hearings, but the hearing officer can use them as appropriate.

For example, some rules relate to hearsay evidence—information that a witness did not hear or receive directly. "I saw Jack hit Frank" is not hearsay; "Jack told me that Frank hit Bill" is hearsay evidence and can be excluded at a due process hearing.

Don't worry too much about formal rules of evidence. If the other side objects to a question you ask because it violates a rule of evidence, ask the hearing officer to explain the rule, and then rephrase your question.

The Due Process Hearing

The hearing normally proceeds as follows:

1. The hearing officer gives an overview of the hearing process. The hearing officer will usually identify and confirm the witness list and the exhibits that you and the school district submitted.
2. The hearing officer turns on the tape recorder, and the formal hearing begins.
3. The parties introduce themselves on tape.
4. You make your opening statement.
5. The school district makes its opening statement.
6. You question (direct examine) your witnesses.
7. The school representative questions (cross-examines) your witnesses.
8. You ask more questions of your witnesses (redirect) if you want, the school representative cross-examines again (called recross), and so on.
9. The school district calls its witnesses with the same pattern of direct examination, cross-examination, redirect, and recross.

10. You call (or call back) witnesses after the school finishes, if you want. These are called rebuttal witnesses and are used to clarify or contradict testimony raised by the other side. The school district has the same right.

11. You give a closing statement, if you want.

12. The school district gives a closing statement, if it wants.

13. The hearing officer adjourns the hearing.

14. You and the school district submit written briefs discussing the facts presented at the hearing and any applicable law (see "Posthearing Briefs," below).

15. The hearing officer issues a written decision.

Keeping Track During the Hearing

You want to have an ongoing record of the testimony during the hearing, because you may need to refer back to previous testimony. For example, say the district calls a witness who testifies for 45 minutes on various issues. When you cross-examine this witness, you want to refer back to a specific statement he made that contradicted other testimony or ask him to clarify something he said. You need to be able to refer to earlier statements.

Taking notes is the logical way to keep track; however, it will be difficult for you to do so while also conducting the hearing. Instead, have someone else take notes for you, recording statements of each witness, while you also take notes on key statements. (You can do this on paper or a laptop computer.) If you had a notetaker at the IEP meeting, consider using the same person, who is probably very familiar with the issues by now. You can tape the hearing, but you won't have time to review taped testimony while the hearing is going on. Also, it is more difficult to try to find an exact statement on a tape than to simply refer to written notes.

How do you use the notes? During your cross-examination, you say something like, "Mr. Adams, you testified that, let me see [look at your notes], and I quote, 'I don't think James needs an aide in class.' Is that correct?" If he concurs, then point out evidence that contradicts him, such as "In her testimony yesterday, Dr. Markham stated that you told her on April 29, 20xx, that James needed an aide. Which statement should we believe?"

Make an Opening Statement

You can use the opening statement you prepared for mediation as a starting point, but you will need to change it for a hearing. At mediation, you can say anything; your aim is to reach a compromise. At a hearing, however, your aim is to prove your case. Your opening statement, therefore, should emphasize what you want for your child and how that is supported by evidence. This doesn't mean you shouldn't include items for which your evidence is weak, but it does mean you should carefully think about what you're requesting—and how likely you are to get it. The hearing officer will consider not only your evidence, but your credibility. If you ask for something unsupported by any evidence, your credibility may be affected.

Be sure to include these details in your opening statement:

- basic facts about your child, including age, disability, and current educational program
- a clear statement of your child's needs and the dispute that brought you to the hearing, and
- a brief statement that what you want is supported by evidence, such as "Cheryl needs a full-time aide, as we will clearly show with evidence, including the testimony of several different professionals and Exhibits B, D, and M."

Opening statements can be any length, but five to 15 minutes is typical. If you can, don't read a verbatim statement—instead, use notes to guide you in making your points. If you're very nervous, however, it's okay to read a statement. It is important to express your feelings and bring the human element into the hearing. Be careful not to ramble in an unfocused way or attack school district representatives on a personal level, but don't hesitate to make a strong, clear statement of what your child needs.

Questioning Your Witnesses

After opening statements, your witnesses will testify. Think carefully about the order in which you want to present their testimony. You are telling a story, and you need to present the details of the story in an order that will make sense to someone who has little or no prior knowledge of the situation. It's often best to begin with someone (possibly you) who can give general background information about your child. Next, you might want a witness who can present the evaluation data, such as your independent evaluator.

After that, you want to go to the core of the dispute and make your case. For example, you and the school district disagree on placement and a related service. During the past year, your child was in a regular class, with no assistance. You want your child to stay in that class with an aide; the school district has offered placement in a special day class. Your first witness can give the details of the regular class. The second can talk about why your child needs that class. The third can describe the services offered by the aide. The fourth can explain why your child needs that aide.

Of course, you may have to modify the presentation and go out of order if a witness is available only on a certain day or at a certain time. Or, you may choose a different order to maximize impact. In some instances, the witness who will give the most dramatic and effective testimony should go last, so the hearing officer is left with that impression. Or that person might go first, to set a tone for the rest of the hearing. Only you can decide which strategy will be most effective in your situation.

Questioning Reluctant Witnesses

Question reluctant witnesses with care. First, ask the hearing officer to note that the witness is not cooperative. To ensure the person's attendance at the hearing, you should have issued a subpoena. At the hearing, ask something like "Mr. Perez, are you testifying voluntarily?" The response will be something like "No. As you know, I was subpoenaed by you."

Another possibility is to begin your questioning with a statement such as "This witness, Mr. Hobson, the fourth-grade teacher, would not talk to me prior to the hearing. I am calling him as a hostile witness."

Further Suggestions on Questioning Witnesses

No matter how much you prepare, you won't be able to anticipate exactly how the questioning will go. Be ready to depart from your planned questions. For example, a witness might answer in a way slightly different from what you expected, requiring you to ask follow-up questions. Or the witness may say the opposite of what you expect.

Here are some tips to help you question witnesses:

- Ask for a brief break if you need to gather yourself or consider new questions.
- Keep track of your questions. If you veer off on a line of questioning you had not planned, mark where you are on your list of questions so you can come back to it later.
- Don't ask a question to which you don't know the answer, particularly of a school witness.
- Don't overwhelm the hearing officer with a ton of facts. Parents often try to get everything into the record at the hearing. Know the difference between important facts and minutiae.
- Know when to stop. Stop asking questions when something powerful has been stated. Further questioning will only dilute the impact.
- Don't badger a witness. Ask questions in a firm way, and repeat them if necessary but don't become hostile, belligerent, or belittling.
- Don't play lawyer. You'll do fine with your own style and language.

How to Use Your Exhibits

Have your exhibits available so you can use them when you question witnesses. For example, "Tell me, Dr. Whitland, you said Monroe does not need counseling. Would you please look at Exhibit B, page 4? You reported last year that Monroe had severe emotional difficulties that were interfering with his education. Aren't severe emotional difficulties usually addressed in some kind of psychological therapy?"

Closing Statements

After all the evidence has been presented and all witnesses have testified, the hearing officer will ask if you want to make closing arguments or submit a written brief.

A closing statement, like the opening statement, is a powerful and precise summary of your arguments, but now you can refer to useful testimony from the hearing itself as proof of what you want. For example, you might say, "Every witness called by us agreed that Michele needs four sessions of speech therapy each week; not one of the school district's witnesses contradicted that. This is fully consistent with Dr. Hanover's written report, Exhibit L." Your closing statement might also note that the recommended education is consistent with the IDEA, and point out what may happen to your child if the hearing officer rules against you.

Posthearing Briefs

If you agree to submit briefs, the parties, with the help of the hearing officer, will set a short time frame (usually no more than ten days) to submit the briefs. The purpose of the briefs is to highlight the evidence that supports your case and bring any supportive law or cases to the attention of the hearing officer.

To develop your brief, first review your notes, your memory, and the evidence. The written brief should precisely point out the evidence that supports your case and the evidence that contradicts the school district's point of view. If there are legal issues, you should review the IDEA and any court cases that support your analysis of the law. (See Chapter 14 for advice on legal research.)

It may be quite daunting to think about writing this brief after all the work you've already done, particularly the legal part. If you don't want to hire a lawyer, I strongly recommend that you contact one of the many nonprofit organizations that can help children with disabilities. While they may not be able to represent you at the hearing, they may be able to provide you advice about the brief and even what regulations and cases might apply (if you let them know the legal issues).

Hearing Decision and Appeals

After the hearing, you're entitled to a written decision, including findings of fact. The hearing officer must have "substantive grounds" for the decision, which must include a finding of whether the child received a free appropriate public education (FAPE). (20 U.S.C. § 1415(f)(3)(E).) Many courts have found that a school district's violation of IDEA procedures constitutes a denial of FAPE.

Both you and the school district have the right to appeal the decision to state or federal court, theoretically all the way to the U.S. Supreme Court. If you lose, several factors will help you decide whether or not to appeal:

- **Strength of your case.** You should already have considered this as part of your decision to pursue due process. For an appeal, you must look at your situation with a more critical eye. Many reviewing courts will defer to the administrative decision and won't want to rehear the evidence anew. Even if the court takes a fresh look at the evidence, remember that a neutral third party has already ruled against you, which suggests that your case has some problems.

- **Costs of an appeal.** There are various costs involved in appealing a hearing decision to court, including filing fees, fees for serving papers on the school district, witness fees, and other trial costs (such as copying exhibits). There's one more cost: potential attorney fees. While nonattorneys can represent themselves in court, I strongly recommend hiring an attorney for the appeal. At the very least, have an attorney who specializes in the IDEA review your case and advise you of your chances on appeal.

- **Time.** If you or the school district want to appeal the due process hearing decision, you must do so within 90 days after the decision is issued (not the date you actually receive it), unless your state law establishes a different time limit for such appeals. (20 U.S.C. § 1415(i)(2)(B).) Contact your state department of education or a parental support group to find out about your state's timelines. (See Appendix B on this book's Companion Page on Nolo.com for contact information. See Chapter 16 for the link.)

Filing a Complaint

A s mentioned in Chapter 12, informal negotiation and due process are typically used to resolve factual disputes between you and the school district. But what if your concern isn't over a program, service, or other factual matter—that is, who is right and who is wrong? What if you believe that the school district has violated a legal requirement under the IDEA? You can use the IDEA complaint process. You can find the regulations regarding complaints at 34 C.F.R. §§ 300.151–153.

When to File a Complaint

The IDEA statutes and regulations set out the school district's legal obligations. Excerpts of key sections of the IDEA are contained in Appendix A on this book's Companion Page on Nolo.com. (See Chapter 16 for the link.)

Here are some common school district actions (or inactions) that are legal violations of the IDEA:

- failing to provide a child's records
- failing to do evaluations
- failing to meet evaluation and IEP timelines
- failing to hold an IEP meeting, either an annual IEP meeting or an IEP meeting you request because you want to change your child's IEP
- failing to allow parents to effectively represent their child in the IEP meeting—for example, by limiting who can attend or by intimidating the parents
- failing to follow required procedures before suspending or expelling a special education student
- failing to discuss all elements in an IEP meeting—goals, placement, related services, transition plans
- failing to implement an agreed-to IEP—for example, if your child's IEP calls for three sessions of speech therapy each week and the school district provides only one session, and
- failing to give notice before changing a child's IEP. Your district cannot change your child's IEP without giving you notice of that change and holding an IEP meeting.

"Complaint" or "Due Process Complaint"?

They might sound alike, but there are important differences between a "due process complaint" (see Chapter 12) and a "complaint" as discussed in this chapter. To clarify:

File a *due process complaint* when you have a factual dispute about your child's IEP. For example, you want your child placed in program A and the school district offers program B, your child needs three weekly sessions of physical therapy and the district offers none, or you want your child mainstreamed and the district offers placement in a special day class.

On the other hand, when you believe the district has violated a legal duty—by not complying with one of the many requirements under the IDEA—then file a *compliance complaint* as described in this chapter.

A story about a recent case of mine shows the sometimes-uncertain line between compliance complaints and due process complaints. My client had an IEP that all parties agreed to. The IEP called for the student's placement in a program outside the district and for the district to provide related services at the outside placement. This was fine until the second year, when the outside program refused to allow the student to stay unless the sending school district continued to pay for the related services. The school district refused, and the outside program kicked my client out. There was no dispute over the need for the placement or the related service that made that placement possible, but only who would pay, the sending district or the outside district.

I knew if I filed a compliance complaint, it would take weeks, if not months and, meanwhile, my client would be without his program. I also knew that a due process filing is supposed to involve a factual disagreement, which was not present here. Still, I decided to file for due process, which allowed me to then file a "stay put" motion, asking the hearing officer to order the student back to his program pending the hearing. The hearing officer so ordered, and my client was returned to the outside district, with the sending district paying for the services. Ultimately, the case was resolved successfully.

You should file your complaint within a year after the violation occurs. You should also send a copy of your complaint to the school district. To be safe, send this copy—and the complaint you file with a state or federal agency—by certified mail, return receipt requested.

Collective Complaints: There's Strength in Numbers

If your school district is violating the law in a way that affects a group of children, consider filing a complaint together. A complaint filed by more than one family can be more effective. Your state department of education has a legal duty under the IDEA to monitor all school districts to make sure they are following the law—and to take any necessary steps to force a recalcitrant district to shape up. States are usually more sensitive to what may be a pattern of IDEA violations rather than a one-time incident. If you are able to show that many children are being hurt by the district's failure to follow the law, your state department of education may be quicker to step in and take action. And it's much less costly for a group of parents to hire one attorney to draft and submit a complaint than for each family to hire its own lawyer. See Chapter 15 for a more detailed discussion about the value of parent groups.

Where to File a Complaint

The common violations of the IDEA we have listed are not the only grounds for a complaint. If you believe your school district has violated the IDEA or any state special education law, contact your state department of education (or a locally designated agency) or the U.S. Department of Education, Office for Civil Rights (OCR). Contact information for both can be found through the U.S. Department of Education website at www.ed.gov.

You can file a complaint with either the state or federal education agency. Both handle violations of the IDEA, state law, or Section 504 of the Rehabilitation Act of 1973.

RELATED TOPIC

See Chapter 7 for a brief description of Section 504, which prohibits schools from denying access to children with disabilities.

State departments of education are primarily geared toward investigating IDEA violations, but they will also look into complaints regarding Section 504. In contrast, the federal OCR is primarily concerned with Section 504 or discrimination violations, but will also investigate IDEA complaints.

Before deciding where to file a complaint, contact your state department of education and the regional office of the OCR and ask the following questions:

- What kinds of complaints do they investigate?
- What is the deadline for filing a complaint? Section 504 complaints must be filed within 180 days of the last alleged act of discrimination against your child. IDEA complaints must be filed within the time established in your state statute of limitations (discussed in Chapter 12).
- How do they handle complaints? In some states, an IDEA or Section 504 complaint is investigated initially by the school district. If you have a choice, opt for an investigator who is not associated with your school district.
- What are their timelines for investigating complaints?
- What remedies are available, such as reimbursement for attorney fees or the cost of related services?

Notifying the U.S. Department of Education, Office of Special Education and Rehabilitative Services

In addition to filing a complaint, you can notify the U.S. Department of Education, Office of Special Education and Rehabilitative Services, Office of Special Education Programs (OSEP). OSEP will neither investigate the problem nor issue a decision. But OSEP has overall responsibility for monitoring how states implement the IDEA and might consider your comments when conducting its annual review of the programs in your state. You can find OSEP's contact information at www.ed.gov.

What to Include in a Complaint

Your state department of education may have a complaint form for you to use. OCR has one, but you aren't required to use it. (OCR's complaint form is available online at www.ed.gov/about/offices/list/ocr/complaintintro.html.)

Whether you use a form or simply write a letter, include the following information:

- Your name and address (a telephone number where you may be reached during business hours is helpful, but not required).
- Your child's name, the school he or she attends, and the name of the school district.
- As precise a description as possible of the violation, including the date, time, and location. If you cite more than one violation or you have very broad concerns, be as specific as possible, describing each violation separately. Include a statement that "the school district violated Part B of the IDEA."
- The applicable section of the IDEA or any state law, if you know it. Key sections of the IDEA are cited throughout this book, and Appendix A on this book's Companion Page on Nolo.com includes excerpts of the IDEA. (See Chapter 16 for the link.) Contact your state department of education for state special education laws and regulations.
- The remedy you want, including reimbursement for costs incurred due to the district's violations.
- You must sign the letter. (34 C.F.R. § 300.153(b).)

A sample complaint letter is shown below.

Sample Complaint Letter

February 5, 20xx

John Harrington, Director
Compliance Unit
Special Education Division
Department of Education
721 Capitol Mall
Sacramento, CA 95814

Dear Mr. Harrington:

I am formally requesting that you investigate legal violations by the Valley Unified School District, 458 4th Street, Visalia, California. I am making this request pursuant to the IDEA and state law, which gives me the right to file a complaint if I believe the school district has violated the IDEA.

The facts in this matter are as follows:

I requested an IEP meeting on October 14, 20xx, just after my child was determined eligible for special education. The school district did not contact me to schedule an IEP meeting until February 2, 20xx, at which time I was told that the meeting would be March 5, 20xx. By doing this, the school violated Part B of the IDEA, which provides that an IEP will be held within 30 days of a determination that a child needs special education and related services. I request that an IEP meeting be held within 15 days of the conclusion of your investigation. I also request reimbursement for the cost I incurred to hire a private physical therapist because of the school district's failure to address my child's needs.

Please contact me to confirm receipt of this request, set up times for me to meet with your investigator, and establish timelines for completing the investigation.

Sincerely,

Becky Masteron
Becky Masteron
6004 Green St.
Visalia, CA 95800

What Happens When You File a Complaint

After you file your complaint, the investigating agency will most likely:

- meet with you to discuss the case
- give you an opportunity to provide additional written or oral information
- review evidence and records
- meet with the school district
- give the school district an opportunity to present its side of the story, and then
- issue a decision.

The IDEA requires that the state issue its decision within 60 days after the complaint is filed. This requirement can be extended if there are "exceptional circumstances" or if the parties go to mediation to resolve the complaint. (34 C.F.R. § 300.152.)

If the agency finds that the district violated the IDEA, the agency will make recommendations that the school district must follow to comply with the law. The decision can be appealed to the U.S. Secretary of Education.

Due Process and Complaints

You can simultaneously go through due process and file a complaint alleging a legal violation. If the district is found to have violated the law, you would certainly want the due process hearing officer to know. Indeed, if timing permits, you may want to file your complaint first so you can submit the decision as an exhibit at the due process hearing. Note, however, that the portion of your complaint alleging a factual dispute can be set aside to be resolved through due process. (34 C.F.R. § 300.152(c).)

Finally, the line between a factual due process complaint (discussed in Chapter 12) and a legal complaint (discussed in this chapter) may not always be clear. For example, in your child's current IEP, the district may have agreed to continue providing a specific related service that it provided last year, but it stated in the most recent IEP meeting that your child now needs less of that service. In this case, you might file a due process complaint because you have a factual dispute—for the current year, the parties cannot agree on the related service. But you might also file a legal complaint if the district stops providing the related service altogether. When it is not absolutely clear whether you should file a due process complaint or a legal complaint, do both.

Lawyers and Legal Research

L awyers (also called attorneys) can play an important role in special education. While the purpose of this book is to guide you through the IEP process without an attorney, there may be times when you might need to hire or at least consult one.

This chapter covers:

- how an attorney can help with the IEP and other special education procedures
- what to consider when using an attorney in special education
- finding an effective attorney
- how attorneys are paid
- resolving problems with your attorney, and
- doing your own legal research.

How a Lawyer Can Help

Generally speaking, a lawyer can help you in one of two ways. A lawyer can provide advice and assistance as needed throughout the IEP process while you do most of the work, or a lawyer can be directly involved as your formal representative.

Here are some of the specific tasks a lawyer can help you with:

- securing your child's school files
- requesting an evaluation or an IEP meeting
- preparing for the IEP eligibility meeting
- preparing for the IEP program meeting—including drafting goals, your child's profile, and program and service descriptions; reviewing supportive evidence and materials; suggesting who should attend and what material will be most effective; and providing pointers about the IEP meeting
- attending an IEP meeting (remember to notify your school district before the meeting if your lawyer will attend)
- reviewing evaluations and IEP forms before you sign them
- researching a specific legal issue that applies to your situation
- helping you informally resolve a dispute with the school district
- assessing the strength of your case, if you're considering filing a complaint or pursuing due process

- preparing for and attending mediation and the due process hearing
- writing a posthearing brief
- preparing a complaint for you to file with the appropriate educational agency, and
- representing you in court.

You may choose to have a lawyer do everything from beginning to end in the IEP process or handle only certain tasks. For example, you might want to attend the IEP meeting yourself, but have a lawyer review the IEP document before you sign it.

Do You Need a Lawyer?

Because lawyers can be expensive—and because hiring a lawyer definitely makes the IEP process more adversarial—you'll want to think carefully before bringing one. Here are some factors to consider:

- **Complexity of the case.** The more complicated your case is, the more likely it is that you could benefit from some legal advice. A dispute involving complicated placement and service issues, for example, might require the special knowledge and experience of an attorney.
- **Strength of your case.** If you really don't know whether you have a good case against the school district, consider talking to a lawyer. A good attorney should tell you how strong your case looks and, therefore, whether or not your situation justifies hiring him or her.
- **Your time and energy.** If you work full time, are a single parent, or have a difficult schedule, you may want someone else to take charge. On the other hand, if you have the time and energy to represent yourself and your child, hiring an attorney may not be necessary.
- **Your budget.** Attorneys aren't cheap. Can you afford the help? Are you entitled to reimbursement for your legal costs? (See "How Attorneys Are Paid," below.)
- **Your self-confidence.** The purpose of this book is not only to help you advocate for your child, but also to give you the confidence to be an effective advocate. Still, you may prefer to hire a lawyer rather than wage the fight on your own.

- **Who represents the school district.** If the school district has an attorney, you may want the same protection and leverage.
- **Your relationship with the district.** Hiring an attorney may change your relationship with the school district. When you involve attorneys, the atmosphere becomes more formal and potentially combative. School personnel will likely be more guarded and may view you as a troublemaker or squeaky wheel. Of course, if you are at the point where you may need an attorney, your relationship with the school district has already changed. Your child's welfare is more important than a cordial relationship with the school district.

Nonprofit Legal Clinics

There are nonprofit organizations that provide legal assistance in special education, disability rights, or what is generally called "public interest law." Your school district should have a list of disability-specific or special education nonprofit legal clinics in your area. Also see the organizations listed in Appendix B on this book's Companion Page on Nolo.com (see Chapter 16 for the link).

There are advantages and disadvantages to using a nonprofit legal clinic rather than a private attorney. Advantages to using a nonprofit include:

- the attorneys have likely worked in special education and have handled many cases
- nonprofits often do not charge for their services or have significantly reduced rates, and
- nonprofits, particularly disability-focused offices, have special knowledge and often a strong passion about the issues.

But there are disadvantages to using a nonprofit:

- demand is often greater than supply; you may have to wait some time for an appointment, even just to have someone assess your case, and
- nonprofit organizations often have limited resources—some focus on either precedent-setting cases (unusual disputes) or cases that will have an impact on a large number of children—and may not handle individual cases.

Finding an Attorney

Special education attorneys are not as numerous as personal injury or business lawyers. It is also unlikely that attorneys working in more standard areas of law—such as wills and estates, criminal law, family matters, or corporation law—will know anything about special education law.

You may be tempted to hire the attorney who did your will, your sister-in-law who just graduated from law school, or the attorney whose ad in the phone book promises the lowest rates. But special education law is highly specialized. Hiring an attorney who does not know the law or have experience in special education will significantly increase your chance of failure, and could ultimately cost you more rather than less. When you pay an attorney, you are paying for all the time spent on your case, including time spent doing research. You don't want to pay an attorney for on-the-job training.

Compile a List of Potential Attorneys

To find the right lawyer, compile a list of potential candidates. Here's how:
- Ask other parents in the school district.
- Ask your pediatrician or other health care professionals.
- Ask school district personnel—the district is required to maintain a list of attorneys and other advocacy resources for parents.
- Contact your state's special education advisory commission and ask for referrals. The IDEA requires each state to have a special education commission, composed of educators and parents, which advises the state about special education. The commissioners should have plenty of special education contacts.
- Contact your state department of education and ask for referrals.
- Contact a nearby Parent Training and Information (PTI) Center (see Appendix B on this book's Companion Page on Nolo.com. See Chapter 16 for the link.)
- Contact a local disability rights advocacy organization (see Appendix B on this book's Companion Page on Nolo.com. See Chapter 16 for the link.)

- Contact a low-cost or free legal clinic, such as legal aid—while most offices focus on common civil issues (such as domestic disputes or evictions), some offices do special education work for low-income people.
- Use your personal network—friends, colleagues, neighbors, or coworkers who know special education lawyers or who know lawyers who can recommend good special education lawyers.

How Not to Find a Special Education Lawyer

There are several bad ways to find a special education lawyer. Avoid these traps for the unwary:

- **Heavily advertised legal clinics.** While they may offer low flat rates for routine services such as drafting a will, most make their money on personal injury cases. I am not aware of any such clinics offering special education help.
- **Referral panels set up by local bar associations.** Bar association panels usually do minimal screening before qualifying lawyers as experts in certain areas. While you might get a good referral from these panels, it is highly unlikely that you'll find a special education lawyer listed.
- **Private referral services.** When it comes to services that advertise on TV and billboards, forget it. It is highly unlikely they offer any special education help.

Call the Attorneys on Your List

Once you have a list of recommended attorneys, you can either narrow it down to one or two individuals who were enthusiastically recommended or make initial contact with everyone on your list.

Try to have a brief phone conversation or ask for a short meeting. Some attorneys will chat with you briefly over the phone to determine the nature of your case and whether or not you need an attorney. Other attorneys may have you speak with an assistant, complete a form describing your case, or make an appointment to come in and talk about the case. Before making an appointment, find out the following information:

- the attorney's fee
- how the attorney will review the case and decide whether or not you should proceed
- how much the initial review costs, and
- whether you can talk briefly to decide if it's worth sending in a retainer. (If your case is complicated, this might not be an option —you can't expect an attorney to listen to an hour-long explanation of your child's situation during an initial screening call.)

Meet With the Best Candidates

Make an appointment with those candidates who seem like the best prospects. Naturally, if there is a fee for the initial intake, you may want to see only a few attorneys. Be sure to ask what records the attorney needs to evaluate your case.

When you meet with an attorney, you should ask about your specific case, of course. You also want to ask about the attorney's:

- years of experience
- specific special education experience
- experience with your particular legal issue (such as a due process hearing)
- knowledge of special education law and the IEP process
- experience with your school district
- general style—is the attorney confrontational or cooperative (for example, does he or she like mediation or think it's a waste of time?)
- references, and
- fees.

Pay attention to the answers. Does the attorney clearly answer your questions about fees, experience, and your specific legal issues? Does the attorney objectively assess your chances in due process? If he or she makes you uncomfortable, think carefully about whether the lawyer's expertise and success rate is worth putting up with a difficult style.

Will the attorney provide the type of help you want? Is the attorney willing to advise you now, but hold off on full participation unless and until you need it? If the attorney wants to take over the case but you want only a consultant, you have the wrong attorney.

Your Responsibility in Working With an Attorney

Your attorney should be responsive and courteous, and keep you informed. But the client-attorney relationship is a two-way street. Keep the following in mind:

- Vague questions are likely to receive vague responses; be clear and specific when you discuss matters or ask questions.
- No matter how good an attorney is, the quality of the case—that is, the strength of the evidence—is the key to success. Your attorney cannot transform a bad case into a good one.
- You have some of the responsibility for controlling your legal bill. Be especially aware of time. If you talk to your lawyer for 30 minutes, you will be billed for 30 minutes, even if you feel you were "just chatting."
- You cannot call up an attorney, chat for five minutes, and have your problem resolved. I frequently receive phone calls that go something like this:

   "Hello. I have a question about special education. Do you know special education law?"

   "Yes."

   "My daughter has an IEP on Thursday. She is learning disabled, and I want her placed in a private school. The school district has offered a special day class. What do you recommend?"

   If I tried to answer that question, I would be doing a disservice to myself and the caller. And the caller is being unfair. Many lawyers will try to answer simple questions over the phone from first-time callers—such as, "Can you tell me if a school has to do an evaluation of a child before the child enters special education?"—but most questions are more complicated than that. It is unfair to assume that an attorney can either provide a simple answer to a complex question or provide free advice.

Will the attorney be accessible? This is important—the most common complaint is that attorneys don't return phone calls, respond to faxes or email, or make themselves available when a client calls. Discuss the attorney's response time. While no attorney should be expected to respond instantly, you shouldn't have to wait more than a day or two, except in rare circumstances.

Ask for a Case Evaluation

A good attorney will evaluate the evidence before giving you any advice. After reviewing your case materials, a good attorney should be able to:

- tell you the strength of your case
- explain the process
- evaluate your documents and potential witnesses
- tell you if additional supportive material is needed
- estimate the cost of hiring an attorney for due process or beyond
- estimate how long your case may take
- provide insights into school district personnel, particularly if the attorney has worked with the district before, and
- provide a cost-benefit analysis of hiring the attorney to represent you versus using the attorney as an adviser only.

A Word on an Attorney's Style

Some attorneys are pleasant, patient, and good listeners. Others are unpleasant, impatient, and bad listeners. Although you may want the former, you may get the latter. Whatever the style of your attorney, make it clear that you know the attorney is busy, but you expect the attorney to treat you courteously, explain matters, keep you fully posted about what is happening, and include you as an active partner in the process. An effective professional relationship must be based on mutual respect.

Furthermore, the attorney should contact you regarding any decision to be made, whether scheduling a meeting, deciding on tactics, reviewing a key issue, or considering a possible resolution of the dispute.

If at any time you don't understand what your attorney has said, requested, or planned, ask for clarification. If the answer isn't clear, ask again. Although you hired the attorney for professional expertise and knowledge—and therefore have relinquished a certain amount of control—it does not mean you should be kept in the dark.

How Attorneys Are Paid

How you pay your lawyer depends on the type of legal services you need and the amount of legal work involved. Once you choose a lawyer, ask for a written agreement explaining how fees and costs will be billed and paid. In some states, a written agreement is required by law; even if it isn't, always ask for one. A good attorney will provide you with a written contract (whether you ask or not). Be sure to tell the lawyer how much you are able (and willing) to spend—if you and the lawyer agree on a cap or limit on legal fees, that should also go into your fee agreement.

As your case progresses, you'll want to make sure you receive a bill or statement at least once a month. A lawyer's time adds up quickly. If your lawyer will be delegating some of the work to a less experienced associate, paralegal, or secretary, the delegated work should be billed at a lower hourly rate. Make sure this is stated in your written fee agreement.

Lawyers' Billing Methods

Lawyers charge for their services in three different ways:

Hourly rate. Most special education attorneys charge by the hour. In most parts of the U.S., you can secure competent representation for $200 to $400 or more an hour. Many clients prefer an hourly rate to a flat fee (discussed next) because you pay only for the actual time the lawyer spends on your case. Comparison shopping among lawyers can help you avoid overpaying, but only if you compare lawyers with similar expertise. A highly experienced special education attorney (who has a higher hourly rate) may be cheaper in the long run than a general practitioner (at a lower rate). The special education attorney won't have to research routine questions and should be able to evaluate your case quickly.

Legal Time
How much time your attorney will spend on your case depends on the nature of your dispute. The following can serve as a general guideline for the amount of time required for common legal tasks:
• initial review of your records and interview with you.........2–3 hours
• help you with the IEP process—developing a blueprint, contacting evaluators and school personnel, drafting goals and objectives ....3–5 hours
• attend the IEP meeting...2–4 hours (per meeting)
• prepare for and attend mediation session............................. 3–8 hours
• prepare for and attend hearing.. 10–35 hours

Flat rate. A flat rate is a single fee that will cover all the work the lawyer agrees to do—for example, the amount the attorney will charge you to prepare for and attend the IEP meeting, or prepare for and conduct the fair hearing. You are obligated to pay the flat fee no matter how many hours the lawyer spends on your case, assuming the lawyer does the work. A flat fee can be quite economical if the fee is reasonable and you anticipate a lot of work. On the other hand, if the case is resolved early in the process, you may end up paying much more than you would have paid in hourly fees. Most special education attorneys charge by the hour and may be unwilling to work for a flat fee.

Contingency fee. Contingency fee arrangements are rarely used in special education cases. A contingency fee is a percentage of whatever money the party wins; if you don't win anything, the attorney doesn't earn anything. Because almost all successful special education cases require the school district to provide a program or service rather than pay an award of money, don't expect a special education attorney to work on contingency.

Legal Costs

In addition to the fees they charge for their time, lawyers bill for a variety of items. These costs can add up quickly and may include charges for:

- photocopies
- faxes
- postage
- overnight mail
- messenger services
- expert witness fees
- court filing fees
- long-distance phone calls
- process servers
- work by investigators
- work by legal assistants or paralegals
- deposition transcripts
- online legal research, and
- travel.

Some lawyers absorb the cost of photocopies, faxes, and local phone calls as normal office overhead, but that's not always the case. When working out the fee arrangement, ask for a list of costs you'll be expected to pay. If the lawyer seems intent on nickel-and-diming you or hitting you with a $3-per-page fax charge, you should talk about it. While this may not reflect the attorney's skills or ability to win a case, it may raise red flags about how he or she does business.

Reimbursement for Legal Fees and Costs

If you hire an attorney *and* you prevail at mediation or the hearing, you are entitled to be reimbursed by the school district for your attorneys' fees and other due process costs. (20 U.S.C. § 1415(i)(3).)

But your right to reimbursement can be limited. First, you are not entitled to reimbursement for the fees you paid an attorney to attend the IEP meeting, unless the meeting was required as part of due process. This might happen if the due process hearing officer orders a second IEP meeting to discuss matters that were improperly omitted in the first meeting.

Second, you are not entitled to reimbursement if the school district makes a settlement offer ten days before the due process hearing, you reject the offer, *and* the hearing officer finds that what you actually won in due process is no better than the school district's settlement offer. If the hearing officer finds that you were substantially justified in rejecting the settlement offer, however, you are entitled to full reimbursement. What constitutes "substantially justified" is not defined in the IDEA.

Third, the hearing officer can reduce the amount of attorneys' fees to which you are entitled if the officer finds that any of the following are true:

- you unreasonably protracted the final resolution of the controversy
- the attorneys' fees unreasonably exceed hourly rates that others in the community charge for similar services
- the time and services provided by the attorney were excessive, or
- the attorney failed to provide certain information to the district required by law. (20 U.S.C. § 1415(i).)

You should carefully discuss these reimbursement issues with your attorney before you evaluate any settlement offers or decide to request a fair hearing.

CAUTION
You may have to pay the school district's attorneys' fees. The 2004 amendments to the IDEA add provisions that make parents liable for the school district's attorneys' fees, in certain limited situations. See Chapter 12 for more information.

Reducing Legal Fees

There are several ways to control legal fees.

Be organized. Especially when you are paying by the hour, it's important to gather important documents, write a short chronology of events, and explain a problem concisely to your lawyer. Keep a copy of everything you give to your lawyer.

Be prepared before you meet your lawyer. Whenever possible, put your questions in writing and mail, fax, or deliver them to your lawyer before all meetings or phone conversations. Early preparation also helps focus the meeting so there is less chance of digressing (at your expense) into unrelated topics.

Carefully review lawyer bills. Like everyone else, lawyers make mistakes. For example, 0.1 of an hour (six minutes) may be transposed into 1.0 (one hour) when the data is entered into the billing system. That's $200 instead of $20 if your lawyer charges $200 per hour. Don't hesitate to question your bill. You have the right to a clear explanation of costs.

Ask your lawyer what work you can do. There are some things you can do to save time. For example, you could go through the school's record and highlight key statements. Or you could talk with important witnesses to find out their attitudes about key issues in the case. Some attorneys may be comfortable with your doing substantial work; others will not be. Be sure to discuss this ahead of time.

Resolving Problems With a Lawyer

If you see a problem emerging with your lawyer, don't just sit back and fume. Call or write your lawyer. Whatever it is that rankles—a too high bill, a missed deadline, or a strategic move you don't understand—have an honest discussion about your feelings.

If you can't frankly discuss these matters with your lawyer or you are unsatisfied with the outcome of any discussion, it's time to consider finding another lawyer. If you don't, you may waste money on unnecessary legal fees and risk having matters turn out badly.

Here are some tips on resolving specific problems:

- If you have a dispute over fees, the local bar association may be able to mediate it for you.
- If a lawyer has violated legal ethics—for example, had a conflict of interest, overbilled you, or didn't represent you professionally— the state agency that licenses lawyers may discipline the lawyer.

- Where a major mistake has been made—for example, a lawyer missed the fair hearing deadline for submitting the witness list and exhibits—you might even consider suing for malpractice. Many lawyers carry malpractice insurance.

Remember, while there will be times when you question your attorney's tactics, you have hired someone because of his or her expertise and experience. Before confronting the attorney, ask yourself whether the attorney misfired or you are overreacting.

If you decide to change lawyers, be sure to end the first professional relationship before you start a new one. If you don't, you could find yourself being billed by two lawyers at the same time. Also, be sure all important legal documents are returned to you. Tell your new lawyer what your old one has done to date and pass on the file.

Your Rights as a Client

As a client, you have the right to expect the following:
- courteous treatment by your lawyer and the lawyer's staff members
- an itemized statement of services rendered and a full explanation, in advance, of billing practices
- charges for agreed-upon fees and nothing more
- prompt responses to phone calls and letters
- confidential legal conferences, free from unwarranted interruptions
- up-to-date information on the status of your case
- diligent and competent legal representation, and
- clear answers to all questions.

A final word on attorneys: We live in a time when public attitudes about attorneys are negative, to some degree rightfully so. There are, of course, many conscientious attorneys, particularly in the special education field, where you will actually find a high percentage of compassionate, able, and decent professionals.

Doing Your Own Legal Research

Using this book is a good way to educate yourself about the laws that affect your rights as a parent of a special education child. Chapter 2 has already provided you with much of the key legal language of the IDEA. But because the laws and court decisions of 50 states are involved, no one book can give you all the information you need.

There's a lot you can do on your own, once you understand a few basics about law libraries, statute books, court opinions, and the general reference books that lawyers use. Some basic legal research skills can help you determine how strong your case is and the best and most effective way to go forward. Whether the issue is private school placement, the type or amount of a related service, an evaluation question, or an eligibility issue, the IDEA and judicial decisions can help you judge the strength of your case.

EXAMPLES:

- You want your child in a private school that has an identical program to the one available in your school district. Legal research should lead you to the conclusion that your position isn't a winning one. The law is clear—there is no right to a private school in this situation.
- Your daughter is deaf and you want her to have an American Sign Language (ASL) interpreter in her mainstreamed class. You do some research and find that the IDEA does not require a specific language or methodology in the class. You realize that you will have to prove that your child cannot benefit from her education without ASL.
- You want your child who has some autistic behaviors to be mainstreamed with an aide. You visit a law library and discover that in the case of *Sacramento City Unified School Dist., Bd. of Educ. v. Rachel H.*, 4 F.3d 1398 (9th Cir., 1994), the court established guidelines for determining when a child is entitled to be mainstreamed, including an analysis of:

- the academic and nonacademic benefits to the child
- the effect of the placement on the teacher and other students, and
- the cost of the aides and services needed to mainstream.

The materials you can research include the following:

- IDEA statutes and regulations (excerpts are in Appendix A on this book's Companion Page on Nolo.com. See Chapter 16 for the link).
- state statutes
- court cases interpreting the IDEA and other relevant statutes
- explanatory documents, such as the U.S. Department of Education policy guidelines and correspondence (these documents do not have the authority of a statute or court case, but they reflect the Department's analysis of the law)
- hearing decisions (available through your state department of education and the *Individuals with Disabilities Education Law Reporter*, discussed below)—although these are binding only on the parties to that specific hearing, they may be of value to you in showing how hearing officers make decisions in your state, and
- law review and other articles about the IDEA and special education issues.

CAUTION

Get the right IDEA. When doing your own research, be sure that you have the latest version of the IDEA (the 2004 reauthorization) and the most recent regulations (issued in 2006). Key sections of both are in Appendix A on this book's Companion Page on Nolo.com (see Chapter 16 for the link).

Individuals with Disabilities Education Act (IDEA): Where to Find It

Like all federal laws, the IDEA is found in a multivolume series of books called the United States Code (U.S.C.), which is available in most libraries and online. The U.S.C. consists of separate numbered titles, each covering a specific subject matter. The IDEA is found in Title 20, beginning with Section 1400. Appendix A on this book's Companion Page on Nolo.com includes a copy of key sections of the IDEA statute. (See Chapter 16 for the link.)

You can find annotated versions of the U.S.C., which include not only the text of the IDEA, but also summaries of cases that interpret the IDEA and a reference to where each case can be found. Annotated codes also list articles that discuss the IDEA. Annotated codes have comprehensive indexes by topic, and are kept up to date with paperback supplements (called pocket parts) found inside the back cover of each volume or in a separate paperback volume. Supplements include changes to the IDEA and recent cases.

Your school district is required to provide you with copies of federal law—that is, the statutes and regulations of the IDEA. Your school district, however, is not required to inform you of any changes to the IDEA made by Congress or of any legal decisions on the IDEA. One source of up-to-date information, including policy guidelines on the IDEA, is the U.S. Department of Education (www.ed.gov). But that's not the only source.

Special newsletters provide extensive detail about most fields of law. Special education has one such publication called the *Individuals with Disabilities Education Law Reporter* (IDELR), published by LRP Publications (contact information is in Appendix B on this book's Companion Page on Nolo.com, see Chapter 16 for the link). IDELR issues a bimonthly highlights newsletter, along with IDEA court rulings, hearing decisions, Department of Education policy statements, and other publications. IDELR has a subject index, making it easy to locate the specific cases you want to review. At a current cost of over $1,000 per year, IDELR is aimed at special education lawyers and school districts.

Some law libraries subscribe to IDELR—call the nearest law libraries and ask. Some school districts also subscribe. If this fails, contact a local nonprofit special education or disability organization in your area and ask if they receive IDELR.

State Statutes

As noted in Chapter 2, each state has passed a law that parallels the IDEA. States are allowed to develop laws that provide students with greater rights than those provided in the IDEA. You should take a look at your state's special education laws, which are available in many public libraries and all law libraries.

Many states also make their statutes available online (see "Online Legal Research," below). In some states, statutes are organized by subject matter, with each title, chapter, or code covering a particular legal area—for example, the vehicle code or the corporations code. Most states have some kind of education code. In some states, statutes are simply numbered sequentially without regard to subject matter, meaning you'll have to use the index to find what you need. State codes are like the federal U.S.C., with annotated volumes, indexes, and pocket parts.

Some states have their own regulations implementing special education laws; check your state department of education for information about these regulations.

RELATED TOPIC
You can find the contact information for your state on the U.S. Department of Education website (www.ed.gov).

Court Decisions

When Congress passes a law, it cannot address every possible situation or clarify what each section of the law means. It is the job of a court— federal or state—to interpret the applicable laws and apply them to particular facts. The court will often explain, clarify, and even expand or limit what actually appears in a statute. These court decisions are often referred to as "case law."

Court decisions are published in state or federal reporters. Each decision has a name and a citation, indicating the volume, name, and page of the reporter in which it appears, the court that issued the decision, and the year of the decision. With the citation, you can locate the printed decision.

> EXAMPLE: The first special education case to reach the U.S. Supreme Court was *Board of Education of the Hendrick Hudson School District v. Rowley.* It concerned a deaf child who needed a sign language interpreter in her regular classroom. The U.S. Supreme Court said she didn't need one because she was passing from grade to grade (even though not having an interpreter caused her to miss 40% of classroom communication).
>
> The case was first decided by a federal trial court: The case citation is 483 F.Supp. 536 (S.D. N.Y. 1980). This means that the case can be found in volume 483 of a reporter called the Federal Supplement, starting at page 536. The court that issued the decision was the federal court for the Southern District of New York. The case was decided in 1980.
>
> That decision was appealed, and the case citation of the appeal court's decision is 632 F.2d 945 (2d Cir. 1980). This means that the decision can be found in Volume 632 of the Federal Reporter (2d Series), starting at page 945. The court that ruled on the appeal was the Second Circuit Court of Appeals. The appeal was decided in 1980.
>
> The citation of the U.S. Supreme Court decision is 102 S.Ct 3034 (1982). The decision can be found in volume 102 of the Supreme Court Reporter, starting at page 3034. The Court decided the case in 1982.

Most cases involving a federal law such as the IDEA are decided by the federal courts. The IDEA also gives you or the school district the option of appealing the due process decision to a state court, however. Each state has a unique reporting system, but decisions are usually found in regional reporters. For example, in the case of *State v. Bruno*, 673 A.2d 1117 (Conn. 1996), the decision was published in volume 673 of the regional law reporter called the Atlantic Second Series and begins on page 1117. The case comes from the state of Connecticut and was decided in 1996.

Finding Cases on Special Education

Every decision that a court issues is specific to the facts of that case. Even though a case addresses the same underlying legal concepts as yours, it might be very different, factually, from your child's situation. A court case decides whether IDEA procedures and rules were followed in the context of one particular factual situation, for one particular child.

Every once in a while, a court will issue a broader decision that applies more generally. For example, in a famous case in 1986, a federal court ruled that IQ tests were not valid for determining whether African-American students have learning disabilities. (*Larry P. v. Riles*, 793 F.2d 969 (9th Cir. 1984).) It is very unusual, however, for a court to make this kind of blanket ruling.

You can find cases that interpret every aspect of the IDEA, including evaluation, educational methodology, eligibility, placement, services, suspension, and expulsion. One great way to find cases is through IDELR, mentioned above. IDELR has a set of books called *Topical Index/Current Decisions*. Each book covers cases reprinted in particular volumes of IDELR. The topics are arranged alphabetically. You can use the index to look up topics that apply to your situation.

IDELR reprints not only court decisions, but also decisions made by hearing officers (usually referred to as SEA, or state educational agency, decisions) and the federal Office of Civil Rights (which investigates Section 504 complaints). IDELR also includes IDEA policy analyses by the U.S. Department of Education, Office of Special Education Programs (OSEP). These materials can be of real value to your child, because they indicate how these departments and agencies interpret the IDEA's legal requirements.

RESOURCE

Further reading on legal research. *Legal Research: How to Find & Understand the Law,* by the Editors of Nolo (Nolo), gives easy-to-use, step-by-step instructions that will help you find legal information.

When you research cases, be sure the case you find has not been overturned or replaced by a more recent court decision. You can do this with a set of books known as *Shepard's*. A friendly law librarian might have the time and patience to guide you, but if not, Nolo's book *Legal Research* has an easy-to-follow explanation of how to use the *Shepard's* system to expand and update your research.

When you find a court decision, there will be a short synopsis of the decision at the beginning. This synopsis not only will help you determine whether the case is relevant to your situation, but also will tell you what the court decided. After the case synopsis, there will be a list of numbered items, each item followed by a short summary. The numbers (1, 2, 3, and so on) refer to the location in the written decision where that legal issue is discussed.

Keep in mind that your situation may or may not relate exactly to a particular court decision. It will depend on how similar the facts are and whether your situation and the legal decision involve the same sections of the IDEA. The more alike the facts and pertinent parts of the IDEA, the more you can use the decision to your advantage. But the existence of a case that supports your position does not mean that the school district has to apply or even abide by that decision. It is certainly a very persuasive precedent, but it is just an example of how one court has ruled in a similar situation.

If the decision was reached by the U.S. Supreme Court, the federal court of appeals covering your state, your federal district court, or your state supreme court, the case represents the law in your area. Decisions in other federal circuits can be useful as long as there is not a different legal standard in your circuit.

If you find a case that is similar to yours and the decision is a good one, think about writing to your school district, explaining why you believe you'll prevail in due process.

Letter Encouraging School Board Settlement

Date: April 20, 20xx

To: Howard Yankolon, Superintendent
Eugene School District
15578 South Main
Eugene, OR 97412

Re: Clara Centler, student in Westside School, fifth grade

I appreciated your efforts at the April 14, 20xx, IEP meeting; as you know, we are in disagreement about Clara's need for a one-on-one aide so she can be mainstreamed.

I have requested a due process hearing. I have also done some research on this matter and determined that the facts and the law in the U.S. Supreme Court's decision in *Sacramento City Unified School Dist., Bd. of Educ. v. Rachel H.* are almost identical to our dispute. I strongly believe that with the Supreme Court's direction in that case, it would be a real waste of time and district money to go to due process.

I am therefore requesting that you consider this and meet with me to discuss a possible settlement of our differences.

Sincerely,

Stuart Centler

Stuart Centler
78 Pine Ave.
Eugene, OR 97412
Phones: 555-5543 (home); 555-0933 (work)

CAUTION

Do legal research with care. Analyzing case law and the meaning and reach of legal statutes can be complicated. Make sure you know what you're talking about before you cite the law. While you can learn a good deal, becoming expert at legal research requires care, time, and training. Proceed carefully, and use what you learn with caution.

Key Court Decisions About Special Education and the IDEA

In *Board of Education of the Hendrick Hudson School District v. Rowley*, 458 U.S. 176 (1982), the U.S. Supreme Court ruled that a deaf child was not entitled to a sign language interpreter in order to "benefit from special education" because the IDEA did not promise any particular result and the child's education without the interpreter was "reasonably calculated" to provide educational benefits. In this case, Amy Rowley was in kindergarten and, according to the Court, was able to understand enough to pass to the next grade.

The *Rowley* decision set the stage for the next 30+ years, establishing what many considered a vague and low standard of what a school district had to provide a child with disabilities. While subsequent courts tried to give the special education community a better sense of what "appropriate" and "educational benefit" meant, there was no clear-cut rule. Courts used phrases like the IEP should "[lead to] significant learning and meaningful benefit" or "more than negligible benefit"; "[result in] measurable and adequate gains in classroom"; and "[provide] some benefit."

While some of these phrases clearly created a higher standard than established by the *Rowley* Court, the terms were still hard to pinpoint in terms of detail. It is difficult to be very specific about "reasonably calculated" and "meaningful."

Finally, in 2017, the Supreme Court took up the *Rowley* standard in *Endrew F. v. Douglas County School District Re-1*, 137 S. Ct. 988 (2017). The Court ruled that an IEP must be "reasonably calculated to enable appropriate progress in light of the child's circumstances." This standard is still full of vague and fluid language, but it did establish that there must be appropriate "progress" (not just some benefit) that is consistent with the child's unique circumstances. *Endrew F.* involved a child with autism, but the ruling applies to all children with a disability under the IDEA; thus, this new and stronger standard applies to your child.

In *School Committee of Town of Burlington, Mass. v. Department of Educ., Mass.* 471 U.S. 359 (1985), a family who unilaterally places a child in a private school does not give up the right to be reimbursed by the school district if a court ultimately determines that that private placement is appropriate; a family should not have to choose between placing a child and the possibility of not receiving reimbursement solely because of that initial choice.

In *Honig v. Doe*, 484 U.S. 305 (1988), the Court found that the "stay put" requirement (to keep children in their current placement during court proceedings) was a valid part of the IDEA and prevented schools from unilaterally changing a child's program.

In *Florence County School District Four v. Carter*, 510 U.S. 7 (1993), the Court held that a parent may be provided reimbursement for placement in a private program even if the program does not meet specific standards of the state educational agency.

In *Cedar Rapids v. Garret*, 526 U.S. 66 (1999), the Court found that nursing services are "related services" that may be required under the IDEA to "assist a child with a disability to benefit from especial education."

In *Schaffer v. Weast*, 546 U.S. 49 (2005), a child with a learning disability sought school district payment for a private school placement. The Court in this case affirmed lower decisions that the student had not proven his case. The Court held that the burden of proof in any due process complaint is on the party who files the complaint. So, if you file a complaint against your school district, you have the burden of proving that what the district is providing is not appropriate and that the IEP goals, placement, and services you want for your child are appropriate.

In *Deal v. Hamilton County Board of Education*, 392 F.3d 840 (6th Cir. 2008), the court found that a significant procedural violation by a school district may be evidence of a denial of a free appropriate public education (FAPE); in this case, the court found that the fact that the district had predetermined a child's IEP before the IEP meeting was a significant violation of the law.

In *Forest Grove Sch. District v. T.A.*, 557 U.S. 230 (2009), the U.S. Supreme Court ruled that a child with a learning disability who was not served appropriately by his school district was entitled to be placed in a private program placed by the school district.

In *T.K. v. New York City Dep't of Educ.*, 779 F. Supp. 2d 289 (E.D.N.Y. 2011), the court recognized that students who suffer from a learning disability are at a greater risk for bullying than their non-disabled peers and that IEPs should take this into account.

In *E.M. v. Pajaro Valley Unified Sch. Dist. Office of Admin. Hearings*, 758 F.3d 1162 (9th Cir. 2014), the court held that under the IDEA, a student, including a student with learning disabilities, could qualify under two different IDEA categories of disability.

Online Legal Research

Every day, a growing number of basic legal resources are available online. If you are comfortable using the Internet, you may find doing research online easier than using books. Online documents often have links that let you jump from one topic to another, and you can access many different documents without ever leaving your chair. If you don't have Internet access at home, check with your local public library to see if it offers free Internet access.

The sources below provide access to a variety of legal information:

- **www.nolo.com.** Nolo's Internet site contains helpful articles, information about new legislation, and a legal research page you can use to find state and federal statutes.
- **www.law.cornell.edu.** This site is maintained by Cornell Law School. You can find the text of the U.S. Code, federal court decisions, and some state court decisions. You can also search for material by topic.
- **www.govinfo.gov.** This site provides the entire Code of Federal Regulations.
- **www.statelocalgov.net.** This comprehensive site provides links to state and local government websites. Look here to find a link to your state's department of education, your county government's website, and perhaps even a website for your city or town.

In addition, Appendix B on this book's Companion Page on Nolo.com includes a section entitled "Legal Resources on Special Education." (See Chapter 16 for the link.) These resources include websites that offer a wealth of legal and practical materials on special education.

Parent Organizations

The first word in the IDEA is "Individuals." Special education law and philosophy are based on the individual child, which makes it difficult to approach special education from a collective or group perspective. Each IEP is different. That is why this book focuses on strategies and procedures for parents acting alone.

There are, however, situations in which a group of parents working together can have a tremendous impact on a school district and the programs available for children with disabilities. When a group of parents approaches a school to recommend changes, the school is more likely to take notice. A parent group can also serve as an invaluable resource for information and support as you navigate the special education process.

Join a Parent Organization

There are many ways to find an existing parent group. You can start by getting in touch with the local PTA. In addition, most school districts have a parent advisory committee (sometimes called community advisory committees, or CACs) specifically formed for special education matters. If you haven't already done so, contact your school district to find out about that committee. It is likely composed of special education professionals and other parents. If you can't find information on a local group, try the state level. Appendix B on this book's Companion Page on Nolo.com contains a state-by-state list of Parent Training and Information Centers (PTIs). (See Chapter 16 for the link.) PTIs are parent-to-parent organizations that can provide advice, training, and even advocacy help.

A parent organization can help you in several ways:

- There is strength in numbers. School districts often pay more attention to four parents versus two, and ten parents versus five.
- A parent group can provide you with all kinds of important information about the school administrator, staff, existing classes, the local IEP process, and outside support professionals, such as independent evaluators, private service providers, private schools, and attorneys.

- A parent group can suggest successful educational strategies or methodologies geared to your child, and even give you sophisticated information about the IDEA and its legal mandates.
- A parent group can provide the emotional support you will need to navigate the special education process and reinforce the important feeling that you are not alone.

CAUTION

Community advisory committees may include school district representatives. School personnel regularly attend meetings of these committees, so parents may find it difficult to speak frankly. This is not to say that you shouldn't trust or include school personnel, but you should recognize that there may be times when the presence of school personnel inhibits honest discussion of certain issues. If this is the only organization in your area, consider forming an independent parent organization.

Form a Parent Organization

If your community doesn't have a parent organization, the existing group is too tied to or influenced by the school district, or the existing group doesn't meet your needs, you can organize a new group. How do you begin?

First, consider how wide or narrow you want your focus to be. If your numbers can support such a group, you may want to form an organization of parents whose children have similar disabling conditions. You don't need a lot of people. A handful of parents can be quite effective. There is certainly nothing wrong with forming a cross-disability group, and the parents in your area may prefer it. The strength that comes from a large group can often offset the challenges that come with a diversity of concerns.

Sometimes a few simple phone calls will lead to very useful recommendations. Here's how to get started and prepare for your first meeting:

- Invite all possible parents who fit within your chosen scope.
- Ask them for agenda ideas, focusing on common issues and concerns.

- Ask them for the names of other parents to invite.
- Ask your child's teacher or pediatrician to mention the meeting to other parents who might be interested.
- Ask the PTA and your school district to announce the meeting or to include information on it in any mailings.
- Place an announcement in your local newspaper.
- Contact local disability organizations. They may be able to connect you with other parent support groups in your state. They may also be able to advise you if you encounter problems.

At your first meeting, you can decide how formal you want to be and what issues you want to focus on. If you take the formal route, you'll need to select a name, elect officers, decide whether to charge dues (and if so, how much), collect those dues, and establish regular meetings.

No matter how formal or informal you are, you need to spend some time discussing your purpose and what you hope to accomplish. Do you simply want to establish better ties with the school administration? Do you want to address specific concerns, such as the quality of a particular class, intimidation by school personnel during the IEP process, or certain procedures that you find unfair? Once you decide which issues you want to tackle, you can figure out how to formally contact the district and raise your concerns.

At later meetings, consider inviting guests, such as representatives of the school district or a local special education attorney. The attorney may charge for his or her time. Your dues or an additional contribution from each family can cover the cost. Also, consider developing a newsletter (online is easiest) to maintain communication with other parents in your area.

A successful group will develop important contacts with the district, represent a collective strength that can affect district decision making, and provide a way to express specific concerns directly and powerfully.

Get Involved With the School District

Whether you work alone or with a group, there are many ways to improve your child's educational program through direct involvement with the school district. Volunteer at school or in the administrative office, run for school board, or assist in school fundraisers. Generally, this kind of activity gets you involved, opens doors, and allows you to meet the people in charge. This often can foster a good relationship with school personnel, making it easier for you to pick up the phone and call about—and resolve—a problem.

The same advice goes for your parent group. You should meet with the district on a somewhat regular basis, to find out how you can help the school. Build a relationship between your group and the school. Ultimately, you and the school district really do have the same goal: to help your child grow into an effective, productive, and happy adult.

How to Use the Companion
Page on Nolo.com

This book has a "companion" webpage, which you can find at **www.nolo.com/back-of-book/IEP.html**

There you can download, for free, some invaluable resources, including forms, letters, and checklists to help you through every stage of the IEP process; a sample filled-out IEP form; key special education laws and regulations; information for advocacy, parent, and disability organizations; and a comprehensive explanation of the severe discrepancy model, introduced in Chapter 7. These resources are contained in five appendixes, as follows:

Appendix A: Special Education Law and Regulations

Appendix B: Support Groups, Advocacy Organizations, and Other Resources

Appendix C: The Severe Discrepancy Model

Appendix D: Sample IEP Form

Appendix E: Forms

Using the Forms From the Companion Page

Go to the Companion Page at **www.nolo.com/back-of-book/IEP.html** and click the icon "Download Forms."

To use the form files, your computer must have specific software programs installed. Here is a list of types of files provided by this book, as well as the software programs you'll need to access them:

- **RTF.** You can open, edit, print, and save these form files with most word processing programs such as Microsoft *Word*, Windows *WordPad*, and recent versions of *WordPerfect*.
- **PDF.** You can view these files with Adobe *Reader*, free software from www.adobe.com. Government PDFs are sometimes fillable using your computer, but most PDFs are designed to be printed out and completed by hand.

Editing RTFs

Here are some general instructions about editing RTF forms in your word processing program. Refer to the book's instructions and sample agreements for help about what should go in each blank.

- **Underlines.** Underlines indicate where to enter information. After filling in the needed text, delete the underline. In most word processing programs you can do this by highlighting the underlined portion and typing ctrl-u.

- **Bracketed and italicized text.** Bracketed and italicized text indicates instructions. Be sure to remove all instructional text before you finalize your document.

- **Optional text.** Optional text gives you the choice to include or exclude text. Delete any optional text you don't want to use. Renumber numbered items, if necessary.

- **Alternative text.** Alternative text gives you the choice between two or more text options. Delete those options you don't want to use. Renumber numbered items, if necessary.

- **Signature lines.** Signature lines should appear on a page with at least some text from the document itself. Every word processing program uses different commands to open, format, save, and print documents, so refer to your software's help documents for help using your program. Nolo cannot provide technical support for questions about how to use your computer or your software.

CAUTION

In accordance with U.S. copyright laws, the forms provided by this book are for your personal use only.

List of Forms

The following forms come in Rich Text Format (RTF) and Adobe Acrobat (PDF).

Form Title	RTF File Name	PDF File Name
Request for Information on Special Education	SpecialEdInfo.rtf	SpecialEdInfo.pdf
Request to Begin Special Education Process and Evaluation	BeginProcess.rtf	BeginProcess.pdf
Request for Child's School File	FileRequest.rtf	FileRequest.pdf
Request to Amend Child's School File	Amendfile.rtf	Amendfile.pdf
Special Education Contacts	Contacts.rtf	Contacts.pdf
IEP Journal	IEPJournal.rtf	IEPJournal.pdf
Monthly IEP Calendar	IEPCalendar.rtf	IEPCalendar.pdf
IEP Blueprint	IEPBlueprint.rtf	IEPBlueprint.pdf
Letter Requesting Evaluation Report	Evaluation.rtf	Evaluation.pdf
Request for Joint IEP Eligibility/Program Meeting	MeetingRequest.rtf	MeetingRequest.pdf
Progress Chart	Chart.rtf	Chart.pdf
Program Visitation Request Letter	VisitRequest.rtf	VisitRequest.pdf
Class Visitation Checklist	Checklist.rtf	Checklist.pdf
Goals Chart	Goals.rtf	Goals.pdf
IEP Material Organizer Form	Organizer.rtf	Organizer.pdf
IEP Meeting Participants	Participants.rtf	Participants.pdf
IEP Meeting Attendance Objection Letter	Objection.rtf	Objection.pdf
IEP Preparation Checklist	PrepChecklist.rtf	PrepChecklist.pdf
Letter Confirming Informal Negotiation Results	Negotiation.rtf	Negotiation.pdf
Letter Requesting Due Process	DueProcess.rtf	DueProcess.pdf

Index

⚖️ NOLO   *Save 15%* off your next order

Register your Nolo purchase, and we'll send you a
coupon for 15% off your next Nolo.com order!

Nolo.com/customer-support/productregistration

On Nolo.com you'll also find:

Books & Software

Nolo publishes hundreds of great books and software programs for consumers and
business owners. Order a copy, or download an ebook version instantly, at Nolo.com.

Online Forms

You can quickly and easily make a will or living trust, form an LLC or corporation,
apply for a provisional patent, or make hundreds of other forms—online.

Free Legal Information

Thousands of articles answer common questions about everyday legal issues,
including wills, bankruptcy, small business formation, divorce, patents,
employment, and much more.

Plain-English Legal Dictionary

Stumped by jargon? Look it up in America's most up-to-date source for
definitions of legal terms, free at Nolo.com.

Lawyer Directory

Nolo's consumer-friendly lawyer directory provides in-depth profiles of lawyers all
over America. You'll find information you need to choose the right lawyer.

IEP10